A Program *to* End Hunger

HUNGER 2000

Tenth Annual Report on the State of World Hunger

Bread for the World
INSTITUTE

1100 Wayne Avenue, Suite 1000
Silver Spring, Maryland 20910
USA

Printed on recyclable paper with soy inks

Bread for the World Institute

President
David Beckmann

President Emeritus
Arthur Simon

Director
Richard A. Hoehn

Editor
James V. Riker

Co-Editor
Elena McCollim

Design
Dennis & Sackett Design, Inc.

© 2000 by Bread for the World Institute
1100 Wayne Avenue, Suite 1000
Silver Spring, MD 20910-5603 USA
Telephone: (301) 608-2400   Fax: (301) 608-2401
E-mail: institute@bread.org
Web site: www.bread.org

Printer: HBP, Hagerstown, MD

Cover Photo: The World Bank

Manufactured in the United States of America
First edition published January 2000
ISBN 1-884361-08-0

Table of Contents

Acknowledgments

We are deeply grateful for the valuable insights provided by sponsors, cosponsors and colleagues at two consultations related to this report and in response to drafts. Those who provided comments include: Teresa Amott, Bucknell University; Christopher Barrett, Cornell University; Gezahegne Bekele, General Accounting Office; Kay Bengston, ELCA; Rebecca Blank, White House Council on Economic Advisors; Jim Bowman, Lutheran World Relief; Lynn Brantley, Capital Area Community Food Bank; J. Larry Brown, Center on Hunger and Poverty, Tufts University; Lynn Brown, World Bank; Heather Bullock, Aide to Senator Ted Kennedy; Frederick Buttel, University of Wisconsin-Madison; Robert Cassani, International Fund for Agricultural Development; Edward Chesky, Economic Consultant; Marc J. Cohen, International Food Policy Research Institute; John T. Cook, Boston University School of Medicine; Jim DeVries, Heifer Project International; Deborah DeYoung, Aide to Congressman Tony Hall; Peter Eisinger, Wayne State University; Andy Fisher, Community Food Security Coalition; Rafael Flores, UN/ACC/Sub-Committee on Nutrition and IFPRI; Rueben Gist, Capital Area Community Food Bank; Robert Greenstein, Center on Budget and Policy Priorities; Lawrence Haddad, IFPRI; Douglas Hicks, University of Richmond; Mary Ann Keeffe, USDA; Susan Lambert, IFAD; Ann Lui, Save the Children; Bahman Mansuri, IFAD; John Mason, Tulane University; Peter Matlon, United Nations Development Programme; Bruno Mauprivez, International Monetary Fund; Nora McKeon, Food and Agriculture Organization; Martin McLaughlin, Center of Concern; Joseph Mettimano, UNICEF; Derek Miller, RESULTS; Kimberly Miller, Aide to Congressman Tony Hall; Dan Misleh, United States Catholic Conference; Bruce Moore, The Popular Coalition to Eradicate Hunger and Poverty; Doug O'Brien, Second Harvest; Walter Owensby, Presbyterian Church USA; Rajul Pandya-Lorch, IFPRI; Robert Patterson, FAO; Per Pinstrup-Andersen, IFPRI; Janet Poppendieck, Hunter College, CUNY; Kim Posich, RESULTS; Don Reeves, Consultant; Curt Reintsma, USAID; William Rivera, University of Maryland; Donald Rogers, Catholic Relief Services; Mark Rosegrant, IFPRI; Dorie Seavey, Center on Hunger and Poverty, Tufts University; Thomas Shortley, World Food Programme; (former) Senator Paul Simon, University of Illinois-Carbondale; Lisa Smith, IFPRI; Jean Stokan, SHARE Foundation; J. Dirck Stryker, Associates for International Resources and Development; Yassin Wehelie, FAO; Jim Weill, Food Research and Advocacy Center; Vera Weill-Hallé, IFAD; Dennis Weller, USAID; Bruce White, National Council for Agricultural Education; Maurice Williams, Overseas Development Council; Lisa Wright, Church World Service; Pat Young, World Food Day; Elizabeth Yu, Mennonite Central Committee; Margaret Ziegler, Congressional Hunger Center.

We appreciate the assistance of the following people and institutions in obtaining data: Robert Cassani, IFAD; Lisa Greenwood, USDA; Loganaden Naiken, FAO; Robert G. Patterson, FAO; Mark Rosegrant, IFPRI.

The following Bread for the World members and Bread for the World/Bread for the World Institute board members and staff provided comments and assistance: Patricia Ayres, Marie Bledsoe, Robert Cahill, Kay Dowhower, Tim Ek, Kay Furlani, Janet Green, Rebekah Jordan, Marilyn Marks, David Miner, Carlos Navarro, Sister Jane Remson, Barbara Rockow, Felipe C. Salinas, Arthur Simon, J. William Stanton, Paul B. Thompson, Michelle Tooley, Betty Voskuill, William Simpson Whitaker, Father Clarence Williams; Ray Almeida, Kimberly Burge, Mai Bull, Niloufer De Silva, Lynette Engelhardt-Stott, Sara Grusky, Donna Hodge, Barbara Howell, Diane Hunt, Andrea Jeyaveeran, Michael Kuchinsky, Margaret Cohen Lipton, Karin Lyttkens-Blake, Henri Maingi, Kristy Manuliak, Jim McDonald, Shohreh Peterson, Susan K. Park, Beverly Phillips, Lynnise Phillips, Kathy Pomroy, Michael Rubinstein, Katherine Simmons, Carole Southam, David Suley, Kim Wade, Don Walter, Don Williams, Lynora Williams, Dolly Youssef.

Rachel Rudy prepared the statistical tables.

Themes of Annual Reports on the State of World Hunger

Bread for the World Institute

Hunger 1990: A Report on the State of World Hunger

Hunger 1992: Ideas that Work

Hunger 1993: Uprooted People

Hunger 1994: Transforming the Politics of Hunger

Hunger 1995: Causes of Hunger

Hunger 1996: Countries in Crisis

Hunger 1997: What Governments Can Do

Hunger 1998: Hunger in a Global Economy

Hunger 1999: The Changing Politics of Hunger

Foreword

The message of *A Program to End Hunger* feels to me like a word from God. When the prophet Isaiah received a word from God, it felt like a coal in his mouth – a burning word that must be spoken.

This report affirms that we could end the kind of widespread hunger we now take for granted. There are fewer hungry people in the developing countries now than 25 years ago, and this progress could be accelerated. The United States is the only industrial country that still puts up with widespread hunger within its borders.

The cost of assuring that virtually everyone in the United States has enough to eat is affordable. The cost to the United States of helping to end the severe hunger and deprivation that afflicts hundreds of millions of people in developing countries would be shockingly small.

Hunger causes great suffering and loss – weakened babies who die from measles or diarrhea, school children whose minds and bodies will never reach their full potential, men and women who lack energy and drive. Widespread hunger hurts everyone by breeding disease, sapping the strength and creativity of workers, and spawning violence.

Hunger, poverty, racism, addiction, violence, environmental stress and many other social problems are knotted together. Each problem makes the others worse. But hunger is one that we can actually solve – one string that can be pulled out of the knot!

Churches, charities, businesses, state and local government, the governments of other nations, and hungry people themselves all have roles to play in ending hunger. But we need to get our government to do its part. Churches and charities cannot do it all.

The U.S. government has a leadership role to play in ending hunger, both domestically and worldwide. The report gets specific about one set of U.S. policies that could lead to the end of hunger. But we get specific mainly to show that ending hunger is indeed within our reach. There are various ways the U.S. government could help overcome hunger.

Will the United States and other nations seize this wonderful opportunity? That depends mainly on whether individuals – people like you and me – decide to dedicate some of our time, resources and citizen influence to the cause of justice for hungry people.

Few of us feel up to the job of turning the course of history. Isaiah felt entirely inadequate to see the vision he was given. But the angel who touched the coal to Isaiah's lips assured him that God would use him, despite his shortcomings, to deliver a world-shaking message to his neighbors and nation.

Please join Bread for the World or, in other ways, help to achieve the changes in culture and politics that could end hunger in our time.

David Beckmann
President, Bread for the World and
Bread for the World Institute

Introduction

By Richard A. Hoehn

The day that hunger is eradicated from the earth, there will be the greatest spiritual explosion the world has ever known. Humanity cannot imagine the joy that will burst into the world on the day of that great revolution.

Federico García Lorca, Spanish poet
and dramatist, 1898-1936.

© Roshani Kothari

W orld hunger can be ended. The United States could cut in half the number of its people who are hungry or food insecure in just a few years for an additional $5 billion a year ($18 a person) invested in nutrition programs; and do its part to cut world hunger in half by 2015 for just $1 billion more.

The total, $6 billion, is less than one third of one percent of the federal budget. People in the U.S. spend five times as much on dieting.

The World Food Summit proposed that world undernutrition be reduced 50 percent by 2015. The total cost would be $60 billion over 15 years or $4 billion per year in increased spending. If the United States would put up the first $1 billion (roughly what Americans spend on snowmobiles, or $4 per person, per year) other developed nations would come up with the rest.

In addition to funds, hungry people need policy changes to help them earn a living and have a voice in political decision making. Citizen participation in open, accountable and transparent institutions is, arguably, the most powerful vehicle for social change. "There is broad recognition that fighting poverty often means changing the balance of power in society."[1]

The level of effort required to end widespread hunger is relatively small. When Y2K popped into view, the U.S. government saw it as an emergency and spent more than $8 billion; U.S. corporations spent $50 billion, and the world spent more than $500 billion.

The benefits of ending hunger are so huge that any rational person has to wonder why we have not done it already. Death, especially infant mortality, and disease rates would fall. Children would

Hunger is one problem we can actually solve. But we need to get our government to do its part. Churches and charities cannot do it all.

— David Beckmann, President, Bread for the World and BFW Institute

be healthier, happier and more able to learn. Productivity would rise as workers no longer had to work on empty stomachs. People would no longer lose their sight due to vitamin A deficiency. No more horrific pictures of babies with distended bellies, protruding ribs and flies crawling on their faces. It would even save money that we now spend on health, violence, and other problems that stem partly from hunger.

A spirit of progressive social change has breathed through the 20th century, sometimes with hurricane force, sometimes a still small voice, but mostly in our day-to-day deeds – contributing money to a cause, doing a good job on the job, taking care of our families, volunteering in the community, participating in the political arena.

This, the most violent century in human history, has also been a time of immense progress. Nuclear bombs were dropped on Japanese civilians, but widespread nuclear war was avoided in the half century that followed. A hundred years ago New Zealand was the only country in which women had the right to vote. Today, formal suffrage exists in all but a handful of countries. Some African Americans who rode at the back of the bus fifty years ago in the United States now own buses and are members of Congress.

Strategies to End Hunger

	Livelihood	Social Investment	Empowerment
United States	Jobs with livable incomes	Nutrition, education and health care	Campaign finance reform and grassroots organizing
Developed countries and international agencies	Debt cancellation for poorest countries	Poverty-focused aid	Democratic global institutions
Developing countries	Economic growth that creates jobs and assets for poor people	Poverty and gender-focused policies	Participatory governance

As a century of tragic wrongs closes, respect for human rights is the strongest it has ever been. Repressive regimes even feel compelled to say they protect human rights; words that, over time, are used by the public to hold their oppressors accountable.

The percentage of the world's people who are hungry has declined in the 20th century. In the worst famines of the century: an estimated 5.5 million people died in the Ukraine in 1932-33; 3 million people in Bengal in 1943; and 23 to 30 million people in the Chinese famines of 1958-61.[2] More recently, an estimated 270,000 to 1 million North Koreans died of starvation between 1995 and 1998.[3] Imagine famine, then a world without famine.

The world's population leaped from 1.26 billion to 6 billion in the 20th century and yet economic growth, social programs and the spread of democracy have led to a decline in the number of people who starve. "Virtually no one was seen to die of 'starvation' per se in Bosnia or Kosovo, for example, nor for that matter inside Rwanda in 1994."[4]

Famine is in-your-face hunger. Undernutrition – a lack of calories and/or essential vitamins, minerals or proteins – is less visible, and thus harder to document. By last count (1995-97),

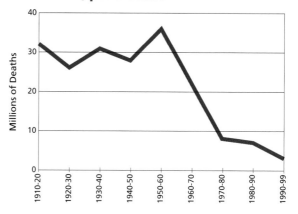

Figure 1. Net Global Starvation Deaths, in Millions, per Decade

Source: Steven Hansch, "How Many People Die of Starvation in Humanitarian Emergencies," Center for Policy Analysis on Refugee Issues, Refugee Policy Group, June 1995. Data compiled by the author from information gathered from journals and government publications.

791 million people in the developing world suffered from this silent killer.

An estimated 17 percent (8,549,000 people) of all deaths in the world in 1990 were due to malnutrition, unsafe water and sanitation.[5] If that 17 percent were applied to the years since 1950 (when the situation was even worse), more than 418,000,000 people have died of hunger and poor sanitation in the past 50 years; nearly 3 times the number of people who have died in all wars of the past 100 years.

The failure to end hunger has been the 20th century's greatest moral blindspot. The promise that now, for the first time in human history hunger could be ended relatively easily and quickly, is good news for a new century.

Although people are hungry because they are poor and political systems do not function properly; because of wars or because people belong to oppressed ethnic and racial groups, we do not have to end all these problems to end hunger. Ending hunger is an achievable semi-final to social justice.

The United Nations Development Programme calculates that the basic human needs of all people could be met by investing $40 billion per year (see p. 22). This large agenda includes education, basic health care and nutrition, reproductive health and family planning and clean water supply and sanitation for all. It would take much less to end the most extreme deprivation – hunger.

The famine of 1932-33 was the most terrible and destructive that the Ukrainian people have experienced. The peasants ate dogs, horses, rotten potatoes, the bark of trees, grass – anything they could find. Incidents of cannibalism were not uncommon. The people were like wild beasts, ready to devour one another. And no matter what they did, they went on dying, dying, dying.

They died singly and in families. They died everywhere – in the yards, on street-cars and on trains. There was no one to bury these victims of the Stalinist famine....

I was thirteen years old then, and I shall never forget what I saw. One memory especially stands out: a baby lying at his mother's breast, trying to wake her.

A man is capable of forgetting a great deal, but these terrible scenes of starvation will be forgotten by no one who saw them.

– Fedor Belov, *The History of a Soviet Collective Farm*, NY: Praeger, 1955, pp. 12-13.

> As a Maryknoll missioner in the Philippines was being robbed, the villager apologized, "Please forgive me. This is our work. We are very poor!"
> – Thomas Marti, M.M., "Missioner Tales," *Maryknoll*, March 1999, 6.

Seeing the end of hunger will be like seeing the finish line in a long-distance race. While you are running, you get more and more exhausted. You wonder why you ever signed up for the race and you think about the more pleasant things you could be doing. But then you see the finish line and you get a final burst of energy that enables you to pick up speed and make a strong finish.

If we accept the World Food Summit goal and reduce hunger 50 percent by 2015, the momentum achieved will be so exciting that the world will be energized to end hunger – plausibly, by 2030. The United States could end hunger and food insecurity within its own borders much more quickly. Once a decision is made, the job could be done within five years.

By "ending hunger," we do not mean that no person will ever go hungry. Even in the United States, addictions and other destructive behavior might still lead to occasional hunger. Worldwide, tyranny and war would still provoke outbreaks of hunger. But routine, mass hunger would be a thing of the past.

Major social change is possible. The proportion of hungry people in the developing world has dropped from one-third to less than one-fifth since 1970. The absolute number has also declined in spite of there being 2 billion more people to feed.

Think of the momentum achieved in environmental issues. Thirty years ago, if you were an environmentalist, you might be called a "flake." Today the environmental movement is mainstream, backed by hundreds of millions of people

A World Without Hunger

Winners of our student poetry contest, Anna (age 7) and Sarah Deitz (age 9) attend elementary school in Dayton, Ohio.

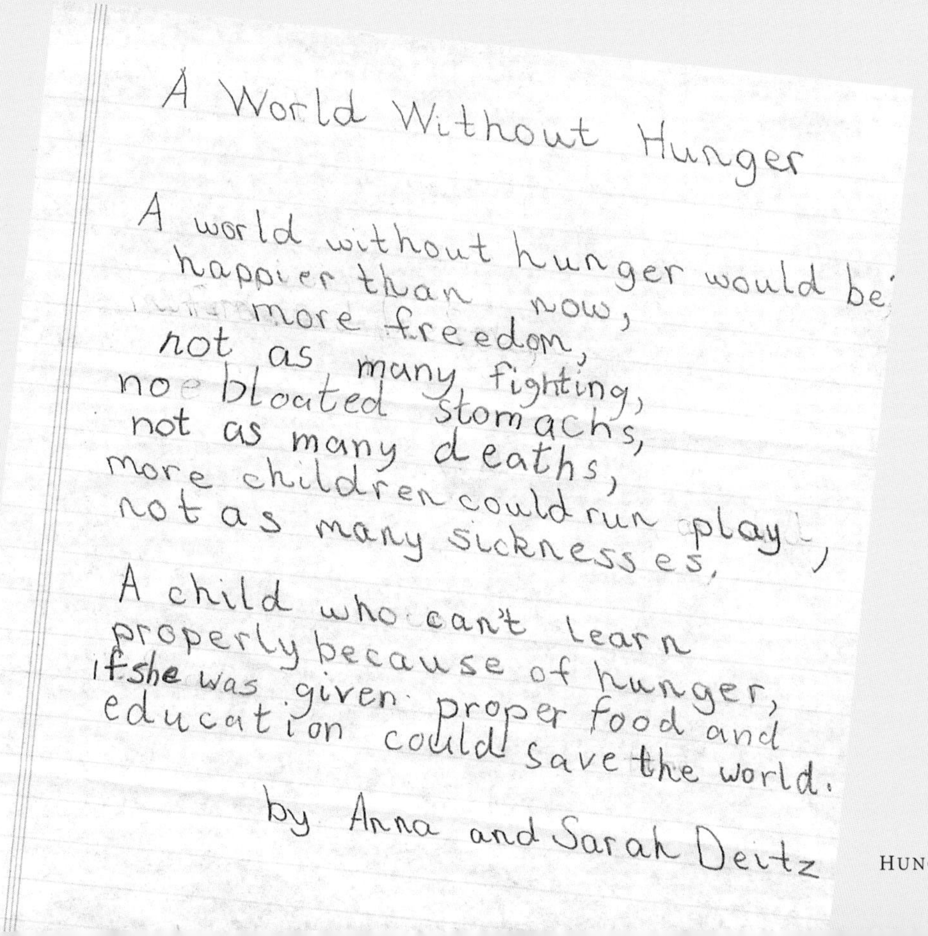

A World Without Hunger

A world without hunger would be:
happier than now,
more freedom,
not as many fighting,
no bloated stomachs,
not as many deaths,
more children could run play,
not as many sicknesses,

A child who can't learn
properly because of hunger,
if she was given proper food and
education could save the world.

by Anna and Sarah Deitz

© Earl Dotter

Americorps members gain construction skills.

Chapter 1 details the extent of world hunger and progress made toward ending hunger. It outlines a feasible program for ending hunger through combined livelihood, social investment and empowerment strategies; and estimates the cost of cutting hunger in half by 2015.

Chapter 2 focuses on hunger in the United States and argues that an additional $5 billion a year for Food Stamps and other nutrition programs would cut hunger and food insecurity in half. Chapter 2 also outlines a more ambitious program to address the longer-term structural causes of hunger. Full employment and grassroots organizing are critical empowerment strategies.

Full funding for Food Stamps would do the most to take the immediate bite out of hunger. Food Stamps are not welfare, but a social investment in the nation's future. Low-income families who receive food stamps are better able to provide good nutrition for today's children, tomorrow's workforce; better able to supplement low-paying jobs precisely so families need not rely on welfare.

Chapter 3 uses a wide-angle lens to review what developed countries and international agencies can do. Relief from unpayable debt and using the funds that are freed up for poverty reduction is the first and most pressing step, but trade rules also have deep and lasting effects. While trade can

around the globe, and therefore their governments. Visionary ideas can become reality and reshape the world. The vision of ending hunger is such an idea.

Fifty nations have given women the right to vote in the past 50 years. Change is possible. Big change. Now is the time to think about ending hunger. We can see the light at the end of the tunnel, and it illumines the smiling face of a healthy child.

The first chapter of *A Program to End Hunger* says that undernutrition can indeed be cut 50 percent by 2015. We are, obviously, using different standards for "ending hunger" in the developing world and in the United States. In the developing world we are talking about reducing undernutrition – lack of sufficient calories and nutrients to meet the basic physical requirements for active and healthy lives. When we speak of ending hunger and food insecurity in the U.S., we are talking about eliminating undernutrition and also making sure that people are not forced by poverty to skip meals for a day or two toward the end of the month.

A Fair Share: Working to End Hunger

Bread for the World's nationwide campaign in 2000, *A Fair Share*, will help end hunger in the United States, especially for working families, by pushing for improvements in the Food Stamp Program and an increase in the minimum wage. About 1,000 churches across the country will hold "Offerings of Letters" and invite their members to write Congress on these priority hunger issues. Volunteer leaders will engage their churches, campuses and community groups, work with local media or meet personally with members of Congress. The campaign is expected to mobilize 100,000 letters to Congress in 2000.

For more information, call Bread for the World at 1-800-82BREAD or visit the web site: **www.bread.org**.

Jubilee 2000 supporters form a human chain around the U.S. Treasury on the occasion of the 1999 G-7 Summit.

open up huge economic opportunities, labor, environmental and food security rights must be protected so that the system does not benefit rich people at the expense of poor people.

The chapter also argues for poverty-focused aid and more democratic global institutions. Nongovernmental organizations play a vital role in helping the World Bank and the International Monetary Fund to be more transparent, accountable and participatory.

"In the year 2000, four-fifths of the people in the world will be living in the developing countries, most with improving conditions. But the number in absolute poverty and despair will still be growing," i.e., unless we all do something about it.[6] Chapter 4 argues that developing countries themselves have a huge responsibility to respond to their peoples' problems. Governments and the private sector need to promote economic growth, human rights, and civic participation; reduce gross income inequalities within their own borders; and invest in programs that empower vulnerable citizens. Governments need to invest in poverty and gender-focused programs and policies, since research has long shown that programs for women have the greatest payoff for long-term development.

The world currently produces enough food to feed everyone. This is a tremendous, little recognized achievement. Scientists, extension agents and farmers have successfully collaborated to increase food supplies. Senator Richard Lugar (R-IN) observes that his family farm now produces three times as much as when his father tilled the land.

While short-term shortages arise here or there and while millions of poor farmers are unable to produce sufficient food to care for their families, the overall supply of food is adequate to feed the world. But, under pressure of environmental or other changes, today's surpluses could become tomorrow's shortages. A sustainable agricultural base is the absolute *sine qua non* for feeding the world.

Chapters 5 and 6 lay out action priorities for institutions and for individuals. While charities, religious organizations and businesses have major roles and responsibilities toward solving hunger, the big bump has to come from governments and intergovernmental institutions; and among them particularly the United States because of its enormous wealth and power in global affairs. "To whom much is given, shall much be required."

Chapter 5 outlines feasible changes that could transform U.S. politics regarding hunger. It calls for a broad campaign to get the United States to move toward ending hunger. Chapter 6 is about what individuals can do. The needed change must begin with us as individuals one by one, taking steps to move our nation and world toward ending hunger.

A Program to End Hunger: Hunger 2000 has been an ambitious undertaking. So many complex interrelated factors; so many unknown variables. Will global warming wipe out large portions of agricultural land? Will we, the body politic, be so numbed by affluenza, that we fail to press our governments, both developed and developing, to be responsible toward needy people? Will "death by chocolate" be more important than death by hunger?

Hunger is a window, a lens, through which to view the past century and the end of hunger a banner to raise over the next. Food, along with air and water, is the most basic requirement for human survival. If you have any power at all, you will feed yourself and your family. Parents may forgo food so their children might eat. Families may forgo nutrition to preserve long-term assets. But, in the final and most desperate situation, food is the last thing people give up and hungry people are the poorest, the most powerless people on the face of the earth.

The world should not stomach another century in which malnutrition-related causes contribute to half of child deaths in the developing world.

García Lorca describes the end of hunger as a time in which there will be a "spiritual explosion." Mahatma Gandhi said, "If God came to India, He would have to come as a loaf of bread." And the biblical book of Revelation describes a time of heavenly perfection when "They shall hunger no more, neither thirst any more . . . and God will wipe away every tear from their eyes." Ending hunger is a spiritual task and the spirit of the human community will sparkle on the day hunger

Which one of us will look the hungry child in the face and say "Sorry, the vision of ending hunger is too great, the reach too far," that "your hunger cannot be cured?"

— DEBORAH LEFF, PRESIDENT AND CEO OF AMERICA'S SECOND HARVEST, ADDRESS TO THE SECOND HARVEST NATIONAL CONFERENCE, SEPTEMBER 26, 1999.

The FDR Memorial occupies seven open-air acres of land near the Tidal Basin; the designer created four architectural "rooms" that represent each of the four terms of Franklin Delano Roosevelt's presidency. In the section dedicated to the second term, 1937-40, one of the sculptures depicts a breadline – five bronze figures of men with overcoat collars turned up, eyes and hat brims turned down, shoulders bent, as they line up against the brick wall of a soup kitchen waiting for the door to open.

I've noticed since the FDR Memorial opened a couple of years ago that when tour buses unload platoons of school kids to visit the memorial, the youngsters invariably move towards the breadline and insert themselves between the bronze figures and pose for their souvenir snapshots. I'm struck by an irony that the children would not have the health, wealth, education, economic security, and long life expectancy that they take for granted had not government in the form of Social Security and other legislative initiatives, stepped in to do something during the Great Depression to combat poverty and protect the elderly, the disabled, and the survivors of breadwinners who lost their lives.

The inscription above the breadline sculpture reads: "I see one-third of the nation ill-housed, ill-clad, ill-nourished." And these additional words of President Roosevelt are carved on stone nearby: "The test of our progress is not whether we add more to the abundance of those who have too much; it is whether we provide enough for those who have too little."

– Father William J. Byron, S.J. in Woodstock Theological Center. Excerpted from: "Social Security Reform and Catholic Social Teaching," *Woodstock Report*, June 1999, No. 58, Georgetown University, Washington, DC. Fr. Byron, a founder of Bread for the World, has also served as chairman of its board.

ends. Humanity's new day comes not with the turn of a calendar page, whether century or millennium. It comes when love for the neighbor gets translated into the end of hunger.

We are ready for that day. We want it so badly we can, well, taste it. We can do this. We really can make this happen, along with other people, each doing their part.

John van Hengel is credited with starting the first food bank in the world in Phoenix, Arizona about 30 years ago. Today America's Second Harvest network of food banks distributes one billion pounds of donated food and grocery items to needy families annually.

Bread for the World grassroots members Pat Pelham, Elaine Van Cleave, Roger McCullough and Bobby Cardwell brought letters from Our Lady of Sorrows Catholic Church and spoke so persuasively with Rep. Spencer Bachus (R-AL) in March, 1999 that he agreed to be an original cosponsor of the Debt Relief for Poverty Reduction Act. Bachus has played a critical role in winning debt relief for the poorest countries and reforms to direct the benefits to hungry and poor people in those countries.

Carlos Ochoa of the International Potato Center in Peru scours the mountainsides and jungles of Latin America to find and preserve nature's edible tubers and then helps farmers in similar climate and soil areas to grow these species as a local food crop.[7] The sum is greater than the parts. Efforts like these are changing the face of hunger.

© Celia Escudero-Espadas

James P. Grant was the Executive Director of UNICEF from 1980 to 1995. Former U.N. Secretary-General Boutros Boutros-Ghali said of him, "Very few men or women ever had the opportunity to do as much good in the world as James Grant; and very few have grasped that opportunity with such complete and dedicated commitment." Jim Grant's favorite passage is said to be from George Bernard Shaw:

> This is the true joy of life, the being used for a purpose recognized by yourself as a mighty one. I am of the opinion that my life belongs to the whole community and as long as I live in it, it is my privilege to do for it whatever I can. Life is no brief candle to me. It is a sort of a splendid torch which I have got hold of for the moment, and I want to make it burn as brightly as possible before handing it on to future generations.[8]

Lift high the torch that announces the end of hunger. Celebrate the new century with a commitment to end hunger…soon!…and by working together as part of a world community of conscience.

Imagine the joy that will burst into the world on the day hunger is ended.

DR. RICHARD A. HOEHN is director of Bread for the World Institute. E-mail: rhoehn@bread.org.

Humanity's new day comes… when *love* for the **neighbor** gets translated into the *end* of **hunger**.

Who Is My Neighbor?

By Angel Mortel

When Chad and I first arrived in our neighborhood – *Jardim Guaraní* – I felt nervous in a strange place. We stopped the car before our newly rented house and started unloading boxes and suitcases. Neighbors sat in front of their houses chatting. I could feel all eyes on our every move. They had to be wondering, Who are these strange-looking people? Their watching increased my anxiety tenfold.

Just as I opened the car door to pull out a suitcase, I was startled by a little voice saying *"oi"* (hi) behind me. I whipped around in a panic and greeted by three smiling faces, I said hello. One asked if we were moving in and I said yes. He said, "Oh, so you're our neighbors!" and gave a huge grin. I introduced myself and learned their names: Francisco, Jorge and Pablo. We chatted a little and they went on their way. As they turned to go, Francisco said *"bem-vindo!"* (welcome). The warmth in his voice made me feel welcome.

Little did I know these kids would continue to touch and even pain my heart at times. After that first day, our little neighbors continued to visit. They were often barefoot and dirty. They live several doors down in a tiny house with a front yard filled with garbage and no running water or electricity.

Fifteen kids and one adult are said to live there – two families, Francisco's and Pablo's. Francisco and Pablo are cousins and Pablo's mother takes care him and two siblings. Francisco's mother is in jail and his father wants nothing to do with the kids. Most of Francisco's brothers and sisters are living with different aunts until their mother gets out of jail.

The kids would come by, chat a little and then ask for something to eat. The first time, I was taken aback. It had not occurred to me that such polite, joyful and energetic kids might be hungry. I gave each a piece of fruit. Soon they were coming every day, sometimes three times a day and five kids at a time. Neither Chad nor I have known what to do. So, we just continue handing out food.

Late one night Chad and I were at a bus station an hour's ride from home. In the distance I saw a young boy, barefoot and dirty, begging from people awaiting the buses. I thought, "How sad that such a little boy, maybe eight years old, is out this late at night begging." He suddenly ran toward me and shouted gleefully "Angélica!" I was startled but in an instant recognized Pablo. I asked him what he was doing out so late, alone and far from home. He said he was "working" – he had to bring home some change to help out his mother.

Another night, Chad and I had just gone to bed when I heard my name called at our front gate and recognized Francisco's voice. The kids had come by a few times late at night and been scolded for doing so. We ignored his calls, but he persisted. Finally, he stopped and we assumed he had gone home.

Then, on our bedroom wall, I saw the shadow of a little body walking on the roof of our garage up toward our window. We heard a tap and I cried, "Francisco!" Chad flew out of bed, angry. Francisco, slightly scared, said he was sorry, but he wanted to borrow electricity from us. He had electrical wire in his hand.

Francisco explained he wanted to climb our electrical pole and tap into our line (something many people do here). He said there was no electricity in his house and his family needed it desperately. Chad and I agreed it was just too dangerous and ordered him down. But I could not get the disappointment in his face out of my mind for days.

With the means available today, poverty, hunger and disease can no longer be regarded as either normal or inevitable.

– Pope John Paul II, Address to the Food and Agriculture Organization of the United Nations, November 18, 1999.

© Ricardo Funari

In my encounters with my little neighbors, I feel sadness, joy, confusion. I feel sad when I see them barefoot, dirty and hungry, and when the other neighbors tell them to go away. But I feel great joy when I see them playing in the street, when they sing me songs, when they stop by to chat, when they run up for a hug, when they ask how to say words in English. I feel God so present in them: their strength, perseverance, love, ability to survive, frailty and innocence. It gives me great joy just to see them alive and smiling!

At the same time, I cannot disregard my intense confusion about how to interact with them. Should I heed our other neighbors' warnings? Will they take advantage of me? Will I get involved in something dangerous? Or should I put my total trust in God and "love (my) neighbor as (I) love (myself)?"

Although I still struggle, I think Jesus pretty clearly gives the answer in the parable of the Good Samaritan. At the end, Jesus asks, "In your opinion, which one of these three acted like a neighbor toward the man attacked by robbers?" The lawyer answers, "The one who was kind to him." Jesus replies, "You go, then, and do the same."

ANGEL MORTEL and her husband, CHAD RIBORDY, are Maryknoll Missionaries in São Paulo, Brazil. E-mail: sejup1@ax.apc.org. This piece is from their newsletter, *A Vida é Assim* (That's Life), September, 1999. Angel was previously a staff member at Bread for the World.

CHAPTER 1

World Hunger Can Be Ended

BY JAMES V. RIKER AND ELENA MCCOLLIM

It is unacceptable that even one person in the world go hungry, no matter within which border that person lives. Borders don't exist when there is hunger. And we are all morally diminished as citizens of this planet if that happens during our lifetime. We have sufficient resources, and we have the intelligence and technology to create abundance. We need to have the will to share it equitably.[1]

Christine Vladimiroff, prioress of the Benedictine Sisters of Erie, chair of Bread for the World's board of directors, and co-chair of the U.S. Food Security Advisory Committee.

World Bank

World hunger can be ended. We have already made significant progress. Thirty years ago there were 959,000,000 undernourished people in the developing world. Today there are 791,400,000 people in spite of a 2 billion rise in population (see Figure 1.1).[2]

It is feasible to reduce the number of undernourished people worldwide 50 percent by 2015. The cost would be an additional $4 billion per year, of which $1 billion would come from the United States.

This global effort requires policy changes and private initiatives to help hungry people earn a living and have a voice in public life. Once the 2015 target is achieved, we can build on this momentum to bring hunger to an end perhaps by 2030.

Although the specific strategies differ by region, country and community, the goal is universal – assuring that every person has access to enough safe, nutritious and culturally acceptable food to sustain an active and healthy life (see Table 1.1). The chief strategies are: improve livelihoods, invest in health and education and empower poor people to participate in decisions that affect their lives.

A Program to End Hunger: Hunger 2000 presents a politically feasible and economically affordable plan for overcoming widespread under-nutrition worldwide in the early 21st century.

© Ricardo Funari

Figure 1.1: Number of Undernourished People, Developing World, 1969-1997

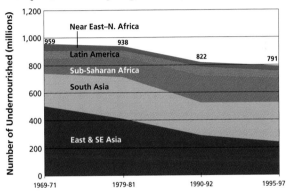

Source: FAO estimates, October 1999.

Table 1.1: Key Hunger Terms

Key Terms	Definition
Hunger	A condition in which people do not get enough food to provide the nutrients (carbohydrates, fats, proteins, vitamins, minerals and water) for active and healthy lives.
Malnutrition	A condition resulting from inadequate consumption (undernutrition) or excessive consumption (overnutrition) of a nutrient that can impair physical and mental health, and cause or be the consequence of infectious diseases.
Undernutrition	A condition resulting from inadequate consumption of calories, protein and nutrients to meet the basic physical requirements for an active and healthy life.
Food Insecurity	A condition resulting from inadequate consumption and access to sufficient nutritious food to sustain an active and healthy life.
Food Security	Assured access for every person to enough nutritious food to sustain an active and healthy life. It includes: food availability (adequate food supply); food access (people can get it) and appropriate food utilization (their bodies can absorb essential nutrients).

Facing page: Senegalese women harvest maize.

Hunger in the Developing World

Undernourishment has declined steeply in East and Southeast Asia over the past 25 years (see Figure 1.2). The Asian and Pacific region, however, still accounts for nearly two-thirds of all undernourished people in the developing world.[3] Throughout Asia, an estimated 525 million undernourished people still struggle to meet their basic nutritional needs and are, as a result, vulnerable to disease and untimely death.

Food security in the developing world varies by region according to levels of food availability, access and utilization. People in the Near East, North Africa and Latin America have the most food security, and people in South Asia and Sub-Saharan Africa the least (see Table 1.2).

The absolutely worst conditions continue to be in Africa. One out of every three people in Sub-Saharan Africa is undernourished. High government debt burdens, inadequate funding for health and education, pervasive poverty, poor agricultural productivity on fragile lands, weak government institutions and the AIDS pandemic all are causes.

The largest number of people who suffer nutritional deficiencies live in South Asia, where poverty, discrimination against women, unsafe water and poor sanitation contribute to poor health. Over 50 percent of children under the age of 5 are stunted (i.e., low height based on age) and/or underweight (i.e., low weight based on age) due to insufficient food consumption and poor health conditions.[4]

The Asian financial crisis of 1998 and 1999 suddenly increased the number of people in absolute poverty (incomes below one dollar per day) from 1.3 billion to 1.5 billion people.

Countries in Transition

Many countries of the former Soviet Union, Central Asia and Eastern Europe undergoing the transition from centrally-planned to market-based economies have experienced economic hardship and rising levels of undernutrition during the 1990s – 22 million undernourished

Figure 1.2: Percentage of Population Undernourished, Developing World, 1979-1997

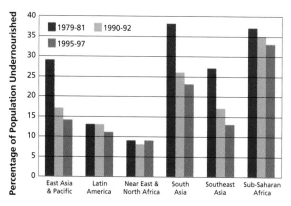

Source: FAO, October 1999.

Table 1.2: Food Security by Developing World Region

Developing World Region	Food Availability Calories per day per person[a]		Food Access Percent of population undernourished[b]		Food Utilization Percent of children under 5 underweight[c]	
East and Southeast Asia	Moderate	2,669	Moderate	14	Low	21
Latin America	High	2,798	Moderate	11	Moderate	10
Near East and North Africa	Very High	2,990	Moderate	9	Moderate	17
South Asia	Moderate	2,448	Low	23	Very Low	51
Sub-Saharan Africa	Low	2,182	Very Low	33	Low	33

Sources: (a) FAO, "FAOSTAT Database," Rome: FAO; (b, c) FAO, The State of Food Insecurity in the World, 1999, Rome: FAO, 1999, Tables 1-2. Calorie availability data from 1997, undernourished from 1995-1997 and underweight from 1987-1998.

people in Russia and other Commonwealth of Independent States (CIS), and 4 million in Eastern Europe. The percentage of children under age 5 who suffer from moderate and severe underweight, wasting and stunting has also increased (see Table 1.3). Poverty has skyrocketed to 29 percent in Uzbekistan, 50 percent in Kazakhstan, and 76 percent in Krygystan.[5]

The region needs broad-based economic growth through improved agricultural practices, investment in health and nutrition and better education for women. Economic and social progress also depends on developing democratic institutions.

Strategies That Work

East and Southeast Asian countries' sound economic policies and social progress have reduced hunger. Many of these governments invested heavily in health, education and nutrition. Green Revolution agricultural technologies improved food production, nutrition and economic prosperity throughout much of the region.

From 1981 to 1992, the countries of East and Southeast Asia reduced the number of undernourished people at the average rate of 12.4 million people per year (see Figure 1.3), with approximately 34,000 people per day moving out of hunger. Yet, these remarkable gains were made vulnerable by authoritarian government,

Figure 1.3: Change in the Number of Undernourished People Annually, Developing World, 1971-1997

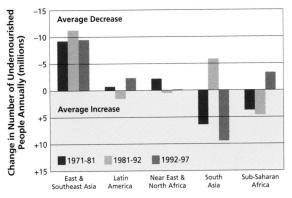

Source: Bread for the World Institute estimate, 1999.

Table 1.3: Children under 5 in Countries in Transition Who Suffer from Moderate and Severe Underweight, Wasting and Stunting

	Percent Underweight	Percent Wasting	Percent Stunting
Eastern Europe			
Azerbaijan	10	3	22
Croatia	1	1	1
Czech Republic	1	2	2
Hungary	2	2	3
Romania	6	3	8
Serbia (former Yugoslavia)	2	2	7
CIS Countries			
Kazakhstan	8	3	16
Russian Federation	3	4	13
Tajikistan	n.a.	n.a.	30
Uzbekistan	19	12	31

Sources: UNICEF, *The State of the World's Children 1999*, New York: UNICEF, December 1998, 99-101. All data is from 1990-1997.

The Politics of Food Security in Kosovo

By Don Walter

In March 1998, Serb forces, under the direction of Slobodan Milosevic, began a year-long, scorched earth campaign, systematically destroying food-making, gleaning and storage capacity in Kosovo. The goal was to starve ethnic Kosovar Albanians into submission or force them to leave. Snipers fired on farmers planting and harvesting their crops. Storage facilities were destroyed and humanitarian food aid workers were harassed, detained and even killed. Since mid-1998, the Serbian military had severely "restricted the importation of basic items into Kosovo, including wheat, rice, cooking oil, sugar, salt, meat, milk, livestock, heating fuel and gasoline.... [And] killed livestock, dropping their carcasses into wells to contaminate the water."[1]

By June 1999, these acts, coupled with outright violence and killing, created more than 850,000 refugees, most of whom had fled to neighboring Albania, Montenegro and Macedonia.[2] Once the peace accords were signed, 740,000 refugees returned to Kosovo by the end of July. While the dislocation lasted only a few months, the aftershocks will be felt years to come.

Even in peacetime, Kosovo does not produce enough to feed its people. Hindered by a cold climate with a short growing season and rocky landscape, only a limited amount can be grown. Before the conflict started, Kosovo was importing 200,000 metric tons of wheat annually.[3] Little was harvested in 1998. The U.N. estimates that only about 173,000 of 494,000 acres of arable land were planted in Kosovo during 1998-1999.[4] Wheat harvests for 1999 are a paltry 113,000 tons, compared to the normal pre-war level of about 300,000 tons.[5] Kosovo's farmers have limited means to produce food because the Serbian military confiscated or destroyed large numbers of farming tools and machinery in the province.

The farming sector was not the sole target of Serb aggression. A European Union study of 1,383 villages found damage to 120,000 homes, with 78,000 severely damaged or destroyed.[6] This means that 300,000 to 400,000 people do not have habitable dwellings. Serbian scorched earth policies and NATO bombing destroyed hundreds of bridges, roads, train tracks, TV and radio stations, power plants, hospitals and businesses. Land mines, unexploded ordnance and booby traps present even more problems.

The peace accords reached in June 1999 allowed refugees to return. Repatriating nearly 1 million displaced people and establishing a minimal level of food security in Kosovo will demand an enormous amount of energy, resources and time. "What is clear is that this is going to be one of the most overwhelming challenges we've ever faced," said Paula Ghedini, a spokesperson for the U.N. High Commission on Refugees (UNHCR).[7]

The United Nations World Food Programme estimates that relief and reconstruction efforts will be necessary in the region for at least the next three years. The cost of maintaining peace and rebuilding is estimated between $2-3 billion annually.[8] On June 9, 1999 the U.N. appealed to the international community for an additional $473 million in emergency aid for Kosovo, bringing the total to more than $740 million.[9] Despite promises, international aid from donor nations has been slow to arrive.

The situation in Kosovo is indeed bleak. Did it have to reach this point? In March 1998, the Food and Agricultural Organization of the United Nations (FAO) issued Special Alert No. 281, warning of the dangers of violence in the region, highlighting the possible food security implications. Violence in the area, according to the report, could impair or destroy the agricultural and food-processing industries in the province causing long-term problems. "Any further disruption in agriculture, given the high underlying unemployment and dependency on agriculture, will aggravate the already difficult food supply situation in the province.... There is urgent need for appropriate contingency planning."[10] Likewise, the World Food Programme warned of an impending crisis in June 1998. Despite these warnings the international community did not immediately act.

The most important lesson learned from the Kosovo crisis is that the international community needs to pay more attention to food security early-warning systems. Unfortunately, what happened

© David Brauchli/Newsmakers

in Kosovo is happening in other parts of the world virtually unnoticed by the international community. In Africa, refugee crises exist in the Democratic Republic of Congo and the Sudan. In Angola, a country torn by civil war for the last 30 years, 1.7 million are homeless and 200 people die each day of malnutrition-related diseases. Catherine Bertini, executive director of the U.N. World Food Programme, says: "It is vitally important that this tragedy receive the same priority that the members of this [U.N.] Council so recently gave to making the progress in Kosovo."[11]

Despite difficult circumstances, international relief agencies have effectively responded to the complex political and humanitarian crisis in Kosovo. The World Food Programme and other agencies have provided essential food aid to over 1.3 million people, constituting 80 percent of Kosovo's population.[12] Their timely actions have ensured that peoples' critical food, health and security needs were addressed and that the process of peace-building can take root.

DON WALTER, a Mickey Leland Hunger Fellow with the Congressional Hunger Center, served a policy placement with Bread for the World Institute in 1999. E-mail: donwalter@yahoo.com.

[1] Bill Frelick, "Genocide by Mass Starvation," *Los Angeles Times*, April 25, 1999.

[2] United Nations High Commission for Refugees, June 1999.

[3] FAO/GIEWS, *Special Alert No. 291*, April 9, 1999, at: www.fao.org/giews/.

[4] *New York Times*, June 9, 1999.

[5] FAO/GIEWS, *Special Report*, July 28, 1999 and August 30, 1999, at: www.fao.org/giews/.

[6] Steven Erlanger, "Kosovo Now Losing war Against Winter," *New York Times*, August 8, 1999, 1, 4.

[7] *New York Times*, June 9, 1999.

[8] Kurt Schork, "U.N. Broods on Danger, Difficulty of Kosovo Return," *Reuters*, June 9, 1999.

[9] *New York Times*, June 9, 1999.

[10] FAO/GIEWS, *Special Alert No. 281*, March 17, 1998, at: www.fao.org/giews/.

[11] Evelyn Leopold, "U.N. Council Told to Pressure Angolans into Peace," *Reuters*, August 23, 1999.

[12] FAO/GIEWS, Special Report, August 30, 1999, at: www.fao.org/giews/.

Women farmers winnowing wheat in Myanmar.

*The outcome of the war on hunger,
by the year 2000 and beyond, will be
determined not by forces beyond human
control, but by decisions and actions
well within the capability of nations
and people working individually
and together.*

— REPORT OF THE PRESIDENTIAL COMMISSION
ON WORLD HUNGER, 1980.

cronyism and corruption, which contributed to
Asia's financial crisis in 1997-1998. The crisis
pushed an estimated 200 million additional people into poverty, temporarily reversing a decade's
worth of progress against hunger. In Indonesia
and elsewhere food riots and popular protests for
political reforms underscore the need for transparent, participatory government institutions.

An effective strategy to reduce hunger
needs to be tailored to each country's specific
circumstances. It needs to draw on the efforts and
insights of civil society agencies, international
organizations, and private business – not just
government alone.[6] Effective community mobilization is crucial to ensure that household food
security initiatives benefit poor and hungry people. Strategies will evolve over time, depending
on what works best in practice. But the following
section outlines a general approach that is drawn
from the experience of many countries in
recent decades.

Strategies to End Hunger

Three sets of strategies are crucial to ending
hunger in the developing world. Each of these is
discussed in greater detail in the chapters that
follow.

Livelihood strategies assure people access to an
adequate income and other resources to meet
basic nutritional needs. Broad-based economic
growth creates jobs, improves incomes and builds
assets for poor and hungry people.

However, sound economic growth and sustainable development will not occur in the poorest
countries unless their debt burden is reduced.
Debt cancellation that channels savings into
reducing hunger and poverty in the 41 poorest
countries will make a much needed contribution
to improving the lives of over 700 million people
in the developing world. The debt burden faced by
many poor countries severely limits the resources
available to pursue sound development that
enhances the livelihood opportunities for poor
and hungry people (see pp. 57-62).

The private sector is central to livelihood
strategies. Most income-earning opportunities are
and will continue to be in the private sector.
Developing country governments can help by
adopting policies that promote broad-based
economic growth. These include investment in
rural development and microenterprise, and in
some cases land reform, as well as sound macroeconomic management and policies that provide
the right signals for productive economic growth.

Social investment strategies, such as education
and health care, help people provide for their own
basic needs and contribute to the larger society.
Developed countries and international agencies
should provide poverty-focused and results-
oriented aid that supports social investment and
promotes income-earning opportunities.
Poverty-focused aid can transform people's ability
to ensure their food security in normal times.
Developing countries can improve women's education and legal status, and invest in nutrition,
education, sanitation, and child survival and
health care programs.

Empowerment strategies strengthen poor and
hungry peoples' ability to influence decisions that
affect their lives. Developed countries and international agencies can reform the international
economic institutions – the World Bank, the

A mural in South Africa urges voter participation.

International Monetary Fund and the World Trade Organization – to be more democratic, and to take the needs of poor people seriously. Making global institutions more transparent, accountable and participatory will help foster democratic governance at the national and local levels.

Developing countries can promote civic participation of hungry and poor people, especially women, and build effective governance and social institutions. "The global challenge remains how, in the next five years, to build up a critical constituency in each developing country which would actively champion the…cause of eliminating hunger among at least half of its victims."[7]

Previous efforts to overcome major diseases worldwide have had remarkable success. Governments, international agencies and a cadre of health-care workers and volunteers worked together to eradicate smallpox, which was killing tens and hundreds of millions of people. Smallpox was banished in 1980 and polio is expected to be by 2005.[8] While a heavy element in these campaigns was a technical solution – vaccines – they also required political commitment, action by the private sector and by grassroots individuals and organizations around the globe. So, too, will ending hunger.

I hope we will start the new millennium with a new resolve: to give every person in the world – through trade and technology, through investments in education and health care – the chance to be part of a widely shared prosperity, in which peoples' potential can be developed more fully…. For me it is a personal priority of the highest order.

– PRESIDENT BILL CLINTON[9]

The Cost of Ending Hunger

At the 1996 World Food Summit, the nations of the world agreed to the goal of cutting undernutrition in half by the year 2015. The Food and Agriculture Organization (FAO) estimates that an additional $6 billion per year to current official development assistance (ODA) would be required to meet the 1996 World Food Summit goal.[10] The FAO estimate assumed a strategy that would depend very heavily on agriculture and food aid.

An independent study commissioned by the U.S. Agency for International Development (USAID) concludes that less than half that amount, only $2.6 billion per year, is required to meet the World Food Summit goal. The U.S. share would be $685 million per year.[11] This study assumes that the resources would go into the types of projects that have had the biggest impact on reducing hunger in different regions. The single biggest investment would be in agriculture, but investments in basic health and education, safe water and governance can sometimes do more to reduce hunger. The study extrapolated its global cost estimate from the actual effects of USAID-funded projects.

The USAID study did not include the cost to the United States of debt reduction for the poorest countries, which would be about $250 million annually for four years. Because of that omission and to steer clear of over-optimism, we conclude that the cost to the United States of cutting undernutrition in the developing world in half would be about $1 billion a year. That is $1 billion for focused and effective hunger-reducing investments. The global cost of halving undernutrition

The Critical Role of U.S. Leadership

By Rep. Tony P. Hall

Unprecedented cuts in U.S. foreign aid are weakening our ability to spread peace and democracy, and to fight hunger and poverty. In the 51 years since the successful Marshall Plan, there has been a wealth of good news from developing countries.

Worldwide, one person in five knows the pangs of persistent hunger today – compared with one in three 25 years ago. Since 1960, developing countries' citizens have added 20 years to their expected lifespan, increased their literacy rate by a third, cut their infant mortality by more than half and nearly doubled the number of children enrolled in grade school.

We know that hunger can be ended. In recent decades, the proportion of the world's population that is hungry has dropped by 50 percent and the absolute number has fallen by 17 percent. But an astounding 791 million people in the developing world – and an additional 31 million people in our own bountiful country – still face hunger as a regular fact of life. These numbers are especially appalling because we have the know-how and the resources to end this scourge.

What is lacking – and what the 1996 World Food Summit hoped to produce – is a renewed political commitment to put hunger at the top of the policy agenda. While the *U.S. Action Plan on Food Security* sets laudable goals, it is up against daunting trends due to declining foreign aid and waning leadership. It is going to take top-level political muscle to turn this tide and make the plan's vision a reality.

Our investment in development aid gets proven results, and our ability to design and implement effective projects has matured. Equally important, developing countries have created a climate where aid can have a long-term impact – policies such as opening trade, securing private property rights and adopting sound fiscal policies. These are essential for long-term success in fighting poverty, and in the poor countries where these practices are in effect, two dollars in private investment follows every dollar spent on aid.

Ironically, as a World Bank report recently said, "just as aid is poised to become its most effective, the volume of aid is declining and is at its lowest level ever." And our lost opportunities are compounded by the signal America's foreign aid budget

cuts send to other nations. Where U.S. dollars once helped to leverage other nations' investments, those nations now are following our lead toward inappropriately low levels of development aid.

While the U.S. has seen increases in foreign aid in the past two years, they do not come close to restoring our leadership. And they are undercut – both morally and in real financial terms – by our continuing failure to pay our arrears in United Nations dues.

Nor have the increases been matched by a restoration of our food aid, which provides a foundation for our other development initiatives. Our Food for Peace program now feeds 40 million fewer people than just a decade ago. And our contributions to the World Food Programme also have plummeted, in effect cutting 48 million people off from emergency aid the United Nations is struggling to give famine victims and others in desperate need of food.

These declines in aid are not warranted by progress in developing nations, where needs remain acute. The world's poorest countries will need 80 percent more food within the next ten years than they have now. Today, 1.3 million people lack clean water and 1.5 million people have no housing whatsoever. As ever, children are hardest hit. Each year 500,000 children's deaths during childbirth could be prevented if their mothers were to take prenatal precautions that they now cannot afford or understand.

Our food aid and foreign aid help the poorest countries somewhat – but the greatest impact of our leadership and investment may be in leveraging the commitments of Europe, Japan and others who could do more to help.

The reason to help the poor is written in the faces of the many people I have seen in my visits to developing countries. But it is equally clear in the faces of Americans. We should not deceive ourselves into thinking that we can create a gated community for ourselves, one that keeps away the sickness and evil that poverty breeds. Instead, we should invest in proven strategies to fight disease, alleviate poverty and eradicate hunger.

First, if we are serious about reasserting our leadership in helping developing nations' progress, we have to do right by the organizations that

United Nations General Assembly.

prove their effectiveness every day in poor nations. These are organizations that pioneered some of the most successful approaches to easing suffering and increasing opportunity; organizations that make sure those approaches really work; organizations like the United Nations Development Programme, UNICEF, the World Food Programme and the International Fund for Agricultural Development.

By overwhelming margins, Americans care deeply about humanitarian work, peace and the United Nations. The evidence shows that Americans – by a 3-to-1 margin – say we should pay our dues and – by a 4-to-1 margin – say we should strengthen the United Nations. They are ill-served by Members of Congress who would have our nation – history's most powerful and prosperous – shrink from the challenge of helping the world solve its problems.

Second, there are key areas where U.S. leadership can make a difference in fighting poverty and hunger. For example, it is time to respond further to the growing calls for debt relief. A sound debt relief initiative is needed that diverts payments on old debt to funds that could be invested in carefully targeted development initiatives.

Many churches and charities across our country are banding together to build support for relief to countries that are crippled by debt. Debt's chains block countries from making investments that could help their people help themselves. In Sub-Saharan Africa, nations are making payments of $12 billion each year on old debt – six times the amount it would take to school *all* African children.

Despite some impressive gains by some countries, sub-Saharan Africa is the only place in the world where malnutrition has gotten worse since 1970. One in three young children suffers from malnutrition. One child in five still dies before age five. And half of Africa's children are not immunized against polio, tetanus and measles.

The United States took a significant step in the right direction in 1998 by passing and enacting into law the *Africa: Seeds of Hope Act* (now Public Law 105-385). This measure was designed to better focus existing aid programs that benefit rural producers who represent a majority of Africans, yet have the lowest incomes and suffer from the worst food shortages in the world.

The *Africa: Seeds of Hope Act* is a small but important step in helping to unleash Africa's vast potential to feed itself, to thrive and to prosper. Without a strong and vibrant agricultural sector, that will not happen. By focusing resources on farmers, the measure works to ensure the long-term political stability and economic growth of the world's most famine-prone region. Congress should closely follow its implementation, but its next responsibilities include payment of arrears to the United Nations, passage of debt relief legislation and a reversal in the decline of our foreign aid budget.

This is an era of unprecedented opportunity for the United States, as the most powerful nation on earth, to eradicate hunger in our own great country, and help shape a more food secure future for all. This is a moral imperative closely tied to our deepest values, and it is also in our own economic and security interests. I urge the Administration and the Congress to give the fight against hunger the priority it should have as we enter the new millennium and the attention needed to make the dream of ending hunger a reality. I am confident that we can restore America's leadership in aiding developing nations in ending hunger.

Representative TONY P. HALL (D-OH), the only member of Congress to attend the 1996 World Food Summit, serves on Bread for the World's board of directors and is founder and co-chair of the Congressional Hunger Center. Web site: **www.house.gov/tonyhall**.

Children are weighed and measured for undernutrition in Burkina Faso.

If we channeled just $40 billion each year away from armies into anti-poverty programs, in 10 years all of the world's population would enjoy basic social services – education, health care and nutrition, potable water and sanitation. Another $40 billion over 10 years would provide each person on this planet with an income level above the poverty line for their country.

– OSCAR ARIAS, RECIPIENT OF THE NOBEL PEACE PRIZE[13]

by 2015, by our estimate, would be about $4 billion a year.

The United States issued its Food Security Action Plan for reducing hunger worldwide in March 1999.[12] Many government agencies and a diverse array of agricultural, anti-hunger, university and business groups were able to agree on lines of action (not unlike those recommended in this report) that would dramatically reduce hunger. But despite the USAID consultant study, the U.S. government committed no additional money and launched no new initiatives.

The resources required to eradicate hunger and meet basic human needs, while significant, are affordable. The United Nations Development Programme (UNDP) has estimated that providing primary health care, basic nutrition, education, clean water and sanitation for all people would cost an additional $40 billion a year (see Table 1.4).

The Costs of Not Ending Hunger

The human misery that comes from hunger, disease and undernutrition goes beyond quantification. The World Bank has calculated that "the worldwide loss of productivity caused by four types of malnutrition – nutritional stunting and wasting, iodine deficiency disorders and deficiencies of iron and vitamin A – amounted to almost 46 million years of productive, disability-free life."[14] If each year of lost productivity were valued at just $350, which is roughly the per capita income level at which families escape undernutrition, the lost productivity due to

hunger could be estimated at $16 billion a year. In other words, a global investment of roughly $4 billion a year to cut hunger in half could increase the productivity of people who now go hungry by $16 billion a year.

Another World Bank study estimates that if micro-nutrient deficiencies cost South Asian countries the equivalent of over 5 percent of Gross National Product in productivity, then in 1995 Bangladesh and India alone lost $18 billion in economic output.[15] Yet a third World Bank study estimates that undernutrition in India alone costs

Table 1.4: Cost of Meeting Basic Human Needs for All

Priority	Additional Resources Required (U.S. $ Billion per year)
Basic Education for All	$ 6
Basic Health Care and Nutrition for All	$ 13
Reproductive Health for Women	$ 12
Clean Water Supply and Sanitation for All	$ 9
Total	$ 40 billion

Source: United Nations Development Programme, *Human Development Report 1998,* New York: Oxford University Press, 37.

$10 billion a year in lost productivity and illness.[16] Clearly, the global cost of overcoming hunger is only a fraction of the cost of allowing hunger to persist.

Scenarios for Reducing Hunger

What program for reducing hunger worldwide is politically and economically feasible, over what period of time? At the World Food Summit of 1996, leaders from 186 countries officially agreed to the goal of cutting the number of undernourished people 50 percent by the year 2015. We believe that goal is still achievable if there is concerted and sustained action by all sectors of society in both the developed and developing world.

However, we will not achieve the Summit goal unless more is done by all. The U.S. General Accounting Office (GAO) concludes that the current level of effort by developed and developing countries is inadequate to meet the Summit's goal.[17] Nearly 60,000 people a day need to be moved out of hunger to meet this goal. With an estimated 791 million people chronically undernourished in 1997, food security must become a higher priority for nations, businesses and individuals.

Experts vary on whether undernutrition will increase or decrease in the early 21st century. A

© Celia Escudero-Espadas.

USAID study projects that the number of undernourished will increase to about 915 million people by 2015, unless systematic efforts are taken to combat undernutrition in the developing world.[18] However, the Food and Agriculture Organization of the United Nations (FAO), based on the current rate of progress, projects that the number of undernourished will be reduced to 638 million people by 2015, yet far short of the goal of 400 million people set at the 1996 World Food Summit.[19] The International Food Policy

Table 1.5: Number of Undernourished People by Developing World Region, 1970 to Mid-1990s

Region	Number of Undernourished People, 1969-1971 (in millions)	Number of Undernourished People, 1995-1997 (in millions)	Percent Change, (+/−) 1969-1997
East and Southeast Asia	506	241.6	−52.2
Latin America	55	53.4	−2.9
Near East and North Africa	51	32.9	−35.5
South Asia	238	283.9	+19.3
Sub-Saharan Africa	108	179.6	+66.3
All Developing Regions	**959**	**791.4**	**−17.5**

Sources: (a) FAO, "Information Note on Estimation of the Number of Undernourished," Committee on World Food Security, Rome, 2-5 June 1998; (b) FAO, *The State of Food Insecurity in the World, 1999*, Rome: FAO, 1999, Table 1.

Research Institute's (IFPRI) most optimistic projection is that the number of countries facing food insecurity will decline from 27 to 16 by 2010 (see Table 1.6). [20] But IFPRI also projects that by 2020 one in four children under the age of five – as many as 135 million children – will be chronically undernourished in the developing world, compared to one in every three children in 1995.[21] Child undernutrition is projected to decrease in all regions except Sub-Saharan Africa (see Table 1.7).[22]

These estimates, while using different assumptions, are prepared in good faith and with great rigor. *A Program to End Hunger: Hunger 2000* examines three scenarios for reducing hunger in half in the developing world (see Figure 1.4). Scenario 3 provides our reasonable extrapolation of what it would take to cut hunger in half if modest changes in funding and policies were enacted.

Scenario 1 projects the likely outcome of the status quo, which assumes no additional institutional effort or financial resources for reducing hunger worldwide than presently committed. The USDA projects that an estimated 1,083 million people may be undernourished by 2008.[23]

Table 1.6: Projections of Food Insecurity by Region in the Developing World, Mid-1990s to 2010

Region	Number of Countries Facing Food Insecurity (1990-1992)	Number of Countries Facing Food Insecurity (2010)
Asia	2	1
Latin America	3 (1 critical)	0
Sub-Saharan Africa	22 (6 critical)	15 (2 critical)
Total	27	16

Source: Per Pinstrup-Andersen, "Changing Approaches to Development Aid," *Global Governance*, 4(4), October-December 1998, 386.

Table 1.7: Projections of the Number and Percent of Undernourished Children by World Region, from 1995 to 2025

Country and World Region	Number of Undernourished Children, in 1,000s (1995)	Percent (1995)	Number of Undernourished Children (2020)	Percent (2020)	Number of Undernourished Children (2025)	Percent (2025)
China	18,030	17.40	9,965	10.86	5,573	6.46
Latin America	4,929	9.10	2,123	3.92	499	0.93
Near East and North Africa	5,634	13.20	4,239	8.89	2,235	4.70
South Asia	82,044	50.89	64,053	41.25	51,011	33.18
South East Asia	18,653	34.05	14,486	27.74	11,732	22.46
Sub-Saharan Africa	31,054	32.77	40,063	29.78	37,573	27.68
Total for the Developing World	160,344	31.36	134,929	25.19	108,623	20.52

Source: IMPACT Model Results, July 1999 version, personal communication, Mark W. Rosegrant, IFPRI.

As many as 1 billion people may be undernourished by the year 2025, unless accelerated efforts and additional resources are made to improve people's livelihoods, health and nutrition in the developing world.[24]

Scenario 2 projects the number of undernourished in the developing world will be 638 million people by 2015.[25] It is based on estimates by FAO that extrapolate the present rate of reducing the number of undernourished by an average of 8 million people a year. Bolder action and additional resources are required to meet the World Food Summit target. FAO concludes that the rate of reduction should average at least 20 million people a year in the developing world until 2015.

Scenario 3 is based on a study commissioned by USAID that projects as much as a 60 percent reduction in the number of undernourished people (an estimated 512 million people) by 2015 (See Table 1.8).[26] This accelerated level of effort in all five developing regions is technically feasible, and would require an additional $60 billion in resources over 15 years, or $4 billion per year.

Figure 1.4: Three Scenarios for Reducing Hunger

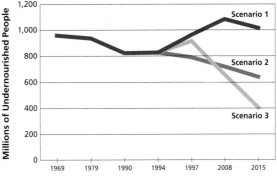

Sources: USDA, FAO, USAID.

It would move over 93,000 undernourished people out of hunger per day over this period. This level of effort represents an effective and affordable scenario that spells out the specific actions necessary to achieve the World Food Summit goal in the shortest time period and to build the momentum to end undernutrition before 2030.

Table 1.8: Scenario 3 – Estimated Impact of Actions on Reducing the Number of Undernourished People (in millions)

Type of Action	East and Southeast Asia	South Asia	Sub-Saharan Africa	Latin America	Rest of the World	Total Number of People	Total Cost (millions)
Political Stability	4	1	14	0	4	24	$ 513
Democratization	3	3	2	0	1	9	$ 1,710
Economic Openness and Reduced Food Tariffs	16	21	7	0	6	52	$ 1,997
Rural Roads	0	0	7	0	0	7	$ 1,172
Agricultural Research	0	137	27	0	0	162	$ 18,664
Safe Water	0	8	0	0	0	8	$ 1,885
Women's Education	10	121	21	0	0	151	$ 8,505
Targeted Income-Increasing Aid (Food Aid)	18	25	4	0	0	47	$ 8,889
Total Reduction in Number of Undernourished People	*51*	*316*	*80*	*14*	*50*	*512*	
Total Cost (millions)	*$4,041*	*$27,826*	*$10,886*	*$186*	*$396*		*$ 43,335*

Source: J. Dirck Stryker and Jeffrey C. Metzel, *Meeting the Food Summit Target: The United States Contribution – Global Strategy,* Agricultural Policy Analysis Project, Phase III, Research Report No. 1039, Prepared for the Office of Economic Growth and Agricultural Development, Global Bureau, U.S. Agency for International Development, Cambridge, MA: Associates for International Resources and Development, September 1998, 22.

© Roshani Kothari

Ending Hunger and Other Global Goals

The world food crisis of the early 1970s prompted experts and politicians together to address the challenge of ending hunger. Over the past twenty-five years, numerous international agency, government and nongovernmental representatives have issued official declarations and strategies for reducing and ending hunger in the United States and worldwide. At the World Food Conference of 1974, U.S. Secretary of State Henry Kissinger proclaimed that in 10 years no child should go to bed hungry.[27] Twenty-two years later at the 1996 World Food Summit, leaders from 186 nations officially committed themselves to reduce hunger in half by 2015. The statements and plans summarized in Table 1.9, in various ways, confirm that we possess the knowledge and resources to overcome the scourge of hunger. Despite these laudable efforts, none of these initiatives to date has garnered the necessary political leadership, broad-based constituency and financial resources to close the door on hunger. Now is the time for concerted global action.

In the 1990s, the nations of the world have met in a series of United Nations summits on global problems and agreed on common goals and action plans. These U.N. meetings have focused on important social and environmental concerns. The meetings signal growing recognition by governments worldwide that reforms are necessary in order to humanize the global economy.

Some of the global goals that have been adopted are shown in Table 1.10. These goals are clearly interrelated. Reducing child undernutrition or giving all children a chance to go to school are interlinked with reducing extreme poverty. A major conclusion of the Rio Summit on Environment and Development is that environmental protection depends on sustainable development among the world's poorest countries. Similarly, a major conclusion of the Cairo conference on Population and Development was that improving the skills and status of women (e.g., schooling for girls, and legal rights for women) is *the* most powerful way to reduce rapid population growth.

The international assistance agencies of the developed countries have together recognized the mutual interdependence among these global goals and are committed to focusing their aid programs to achieve them. The World Bank has formally adopted as its new mission statement "a world without poverty." At the 1999 annual meeting of the World Bank and International Monetary Fund (IMF), the Managing Director of the IMF passed out a summary of these global goals to all the finance ministers and central bank directors of member governments from the developed and developing world, urging them to meet these targets.

Educating girls is a powerful tool for fighting hunger and poverty.

© Celia Escudero-Espadas

Table 1.9: A Chronology of Major Statements for Ending Hunger

Year	Event or Forum	Main Goal and Objectives for Ending Hunger
1974	World Food Conference (Rome, Italy)	Called on all governments to accept the goal that in 10 years' time, no child would go to bed hungry, no family would fear for its next day's bread, and no human being's future and capacities would be stunted by malnutrition.
1979	World Conference on Agrarian Reform and Rural Development, FAO (Rome, Italy)	Encouraged governments to pursue agrarian reform and rural development activities in partnership with nongovernmental and farmers' organizations to improve agricultural food production.
1980	Report of the Presidential Commission on World Hunger (Washington, DC)	Recommended that the United States make the elimination of hunger the primary focus of its relationships with developing countries, beginning with the decade of the 1980s.
1989	The Bellagio Declaration: Overcoming Hunger in the 1990s (Bellagio, Italy)	Called for ending half the world's hunger before the year 2000, by: (1) Eliminating deaths from famine; (2) Ending hunger in half of the poorest households; (3) Cutting malnutrition in half for mothers and small children; and (4) Eradicating iodine and vitamin A deficiencies.
1990	The Medford Declaration to End Hunger in the United States (Medford, Massachusetts)	Called for virtually eliminating domestic hunger by 1995: (1) Use existing channels (i.e., public programs and voluntary food providers) to see that food is available to the hungry on an adequate and consistent basis; and (2) Promote adequate purchasing power and economic self-reliance of American households to achieve the goal of a hunger-free United States.
1992	World Declaration on Nutrition, International Conference on Nutrition, WHO/FAO (Rome, Italy)	Recognized that there is enough food for all people and that inequitable access is the main cause of hunger and malnutrition. Called for reducing severe and moderate malnutrition of children under 5 years old to half of 1990 levels.
1993	Conference on Overcoming Global Hunger, World Bank (Washington, DC)[1]	Recognized that defeating hunger requires the active participation and collaboration of national governments, international organizations, bilateral agencies, NGOs, community-based organizations and poor people's empowerment.

continues on next page

Table 1.9: A Chronology of Major Statements for Ending Hunger (continued)

Year	Event or Forum	Main Goal and Objectives for Ending Hunger
1994	The Salaya Statement on Ending Hunger (Salaya, Thailand)	Reaffirmed that ending hunger is a credible and achievable goal. (1) Increased funding needs to be redirected to addressing the needs of poor people, especially rural and urban households at risk of food insecurity; (2) Continued progress…can be achieved by improved communication, community organization and collaboration with local governments. Specific actions include empowering poor communities, education for women and providing safety nets for vulnerable populations.
1995	Conference on Hunger and Poverty, International Fund for Agricultural Development (IFAD) (Brussels, Belgium)	Recognized the important role of civil society, particularly grassroots organizations, in addressing the underlying causes of poverty and hunger. Created the Popular Coalition to Eradicate Hunger and Poverty to promote poor peoples' empowerment and access to productive resources; establish knowledge networks on lessons learned in the field; increase public awareness about effective policies to reduce hunger; and advance agrarian reform.
1995	2020 Vision Conference, International Food Policy Research Institute (IFPRI) (Washington, DC)	Developed a shared vision and strategy for action on how to meet future world food needs by 2020 while reducing poverty and protecting the environment. IFPRI is actively monitoring global trends and regional strategies for reducing food insecurity.
1996	Rome Declaration on World Food Security, World Food Summit (Rome, Italy)	Set the goal of reducing the number of malnourished people to half their present level no later than 2015. Priority is given to promoting food security and poverty eradication for present and future generations.
1999	U.S. Action Plan on Food Security (Washington, DC)	Highlighted policies that could dramatically reduce hunger in the U.S. and worldwide, but committed no new funds and promised no new initiatives to meet the World Food Summit goal of cutting hunger in half by 2015.

Source: Adapted from James V. Riker and Paul Nelson, "Political Strategies to End Hunger," In: *The Changing Politics of Hunger: Hunger 1999*, James V. Riker, ed., Silver Spring, MD: Bread for the World Institute, 1998, 91.

[1] Hans P. Binswanger and Pierre Landell-Mills, *The World Bank's Strategy for Reducing Poverty and Hunger: A Report to the Development Community*, Environmentally Sustainable Development Studies and Monograph Series No. 4, Washington, DC: World Bank, March 1995, 1.

Table 1.10: Global Goals

Forum	Goal	Timetable for Meeting the Goal
1990 World Summit for Children, New York	Reduce child malnutrition by 50 percent.	2000
	Achieve universal access to primary education.	2000
1992 World Summit on Environment and Development, Rio de Janeiro	Implement a national strategy for sustainable development in each country by 2005 in order to reverse the loss of key environmental resources at both the global and national levels.	2015
1994 World Summit on Population and Development, Cairo	Reduce the death rate for children under five in each developing country by two-thirds the 1990 level.	2015
	Reduce the rate of maternal mortality by three-fourths the 1990 level.	2015
	Assure access for all individuals of appropriate ages to reproductive health services through the primary health care system.	2015
1995 World Summit for Social Development, Copenhagen	Eliminate gender disparities in primary and secondary education.	2005
	Achieve universal primary education enrollment in all countries.	2015
	Reduce the proportion of people living in extreme poverty in developing countries by at least 50 percent.	2015
1996 World Food Summit, Rome	Reduce the number of undernourished people to half the 1996 level.	2015
World Health Organization, Geneva[1]	Reduce the prevalence of stunted children to less than 20 percent.	2020

[1] WHO, *Health for All in the 21st Century*, Geneva: WHO, EB101/88, 1998.

It only takes a modest level of funding from the world's nations to reduce hunger dramatically. For that reason – and because the pain and loss related to hunger are so intolerable – we argue that progress against hunger should be a leading goal – perhaps the leading goal – for international social progress. A recent poll finds that 4 out of 5 Americans say that poverty and hunger are the most important problems in the world today.[28] But we understand that progress against hunger and poverty, environmental degradation, unsustainable population growth, violence and tyranny are all interconnected and symbiotic.

The following general principles could advance progress against hunger and other social problems:

- *Synergy – Build effective partnerships that harness the collective energies flowing from a variety of actors at all levels to multiply the effects of actions against hunger.*

Ultimately, any success in ending hunger requires joint action by all sectors – government, the private sector, and civil society organizations (CSOs) such as non-profits and religious congregations – not just unilateral action.

An emphasis on synergy breaks with approaches that rely predominantly on zero-sum solutions and the distribution of existing resources rather than the creation of new ones. The more participants, the greater the support. Synergy leads to partnerships and collaboration around shared interests.

- *Peace and Stability – Ensure a peaceful and stable international order, global economy and global food system that enhances the security of poor and hungry people.*

War and conflict threaten people's security and livelihoods, too often leading to severe food crises: "In 1996 alone, armed conflicts, mostly civil wars, put at least 80 million people at risk of hunger and malnutrition."[29] Peace and stability are essential to reducing hunger and themselves depend on reducing hunger and poverty.[30] As former President Jimmy Carter argues, eradicating hunger is the first step to assuring peace:

"There can be no peace until people have enough to eat."[31] The increasing volatility characterizing the global economy has also led to social and political instability, of which the turmoil in Asia caused by volatile financial markets is only a recent example.

- *Sustainability – Promote an ecologically sound, regenerative and resilient global food system.*

Adherence to this principle counters the fragility experienced when people and systems try to cope with environmental degradation. To take one example, the devastation caused by Hurricane Mitch in Central America was accentuated by unsound farming and forestry practices in fragile environments, exposing the precariousness of life for people in the affected countries.[32] Civil society organizations in those countries are now responding by organizing reconstruction efforts along more sustainable and equitable lines.

- *Equity – Reduce inequality and promote equitable development and improved access to productive resources to enhance the livelihoods of hungry and poor people.*

Reducing inequality is desirable for moral reasons and for reasons of social stability. When people's access to assets, economic opportunity and social services is assured, individuals, families and societies experience a higher degree of well-being. There is a growing consensus that special attention should be focused on improving the livelihoods of poor people. As Michel Camdessus, Managing Director of the International Monetary Fund (IMF), argues: "The extent of poverty still present at the end of a century of affluence is intolerable. It is time to respond."[33]

- *Effective and Participatory Governance – Promote transparent and democratic practices, participation, and people's empowerment.*

Democratic practice, participation, and people's empowerment take many forms. "Both 'collaborative' (through civic cooperation) and 'adversarial' (through social criticism and political opposition) actions" have been necessary to bring about the progress that has already taken place, and both will be necessary to end hunger.[34]

© Ricardo Funari

- *Efficiency – Give priority to policies and practices that use human, economic and natural resources productively and in a resource-conserving manner.*

The synergies described above optimize resource allocation by tapping hitherto ignored possibilities. They rely on getting not only incentives and signals right but also relationships among the public, private, and voluntary-sector actors addressing hunger and poverty. We expect that actions to support one principle will reinforce the others. At the same time, we recognize that in certain situations these principles may suggest very different solutions and there will be trade-offs. The optimal solution is to strike a balance in favor of politically viable actions that will ultimately improve and enhance the lives of hungry and poor people that are appropriate to their circumstances.

Conclusions

Hunger remains a massive and grim reality in large parts of the world. But it is possible to eradicate hunger. Solutions include raising the earned incomes of hungry people, investing in human resources, and political empowerment. The cost would be modest, and progress against hunger would contribute to progress on other social problems. Global conferences and declarations have confirmed these conclusions.

In the following chapters, *A Program to End Hunger* examines the strategies and policies for ending hunger in the United States (Chapter 2), the role of developed countries and international agencies in supporting efforts worldwide (Chapter 3), and the vital role of the developing countries in ending hunger worldwide (Chapter 4). The critical missing dimension is to transform the politics of hunger to get the political commitment, leadership and resources from all sectors of society to act effectively (Chapter 5). Finally, Chapter 6 recommends ways that people – individually and collectively – can act in their roles as citizens, consumers, employers, workers, members of anti-hunger and faith-based organizations, and volunteers as part of a global movement seeking to create a world without hunger. The choice is yours!

DR. JAMES V. RIKER is senior researcher with Bread for the World Institute. E-mail: jriker@bread.org.
ELENA MCCOLLIM is a policy analyst with BFW Institute. E-mail: emccollim@bread.org.

CHAPTER 2

Ending Hunger in the United States

BY JAMES V. RIKER AND ELENA MCCOLLIM

The Food Stamp Program represents the pledge that hunger will not be tolerated in America. It is the tangible expression of the principle that everyone has a right to food for themselves and their families.

U.S. Department of Agriculture, www.usda.gov

I've Seen HUNGER in My Community,

A hungry child will Always CRY.

and It Looks Like This....

Alicia Dodson, 11, HALT Hunger Tampa Bay

The richest nation in history continues to permit 31 million people to be hungry or to risk hunger. That is mind-boggling and immoral. The human, moral, and political costs are incalculable.

The United States could cut domestic hunger and food insecurity in half by investing about $5 billion more in Food Stamps and other nutrition programs. Once the federal government decides to act, it would take only a year or two to cut U.S. hunger in half. This can be done, and it is the right thing to do.

The nutrition program improvements we recommend total $5 billion annually (see pp. 38-41). "The Costs of Ending U.S. Hunger" (see pp. 34-35) uses U.S. Census data to calculate what it would cost to provide sufficient food to nearly all hungry and food insecure families. The total cost would be about $7 billion. Despite the best efforts at precise targeting, the $5 billion expansion of the nutrition programs we are recommending would reach not only food-insecure households, other low-income households would also benefit. Nevertheless, it would surely reduce by at least half the number of hungry and food-insecure households in the United States.

A more comprehensive effort (outlined in pp. 41-55) could reduce poverty enough to end hunger and food insecurity in the United States.[1]

Livelihood strategies that emphasize jobs at a decent wage and income supports in a full-employment economy can provide people with the resources to meet their basic nutritional needs.

Social investments in nutrition, education and health have long-term benefits for all members of society; and

Empowerment of hungry and poor people is essential, so that they can influence the decisions (especially political) that affect their lives. If poor people had a strong voice in a responsive government, hunger would end quicker than a summer thundershower.

The Scandalous Status Quo

The U.S. Department of Agriculture uses U.S. Census data to assess the extent of food insecurity and hunger. When a family is described as "food insecure," it means at best that they are at risk of hunger and they adopt coping strategies ranging from lowering the quality of their diets, to skip-ping meals, to having the adults go a whole day without eating. When a household is classified as food insecure with hunger, even the children go without eating.

In mid-1998, U.S. unemployment was at a low 4.5 percent and inflation was 1.9 percent.[2] In spite of a global financial crisis that spread from Asia to Russia and Brazil, the U.S. economy remained strong in its eighth straight year of expansion. In 1998, 3.7 million U.S. households (3.6 percent) were, nonetheless, hungry and 10.5 million households (10.2 percent) were at risk of hunger.[3]

> The United States could cut domestic **hunger** and food insecurity in **half** by investing about $5 billion more in Food Stamps and other **nutrition** programs.

Thirty-one million people, including 12 million children, lived in those households which were at risk of hunger. Despite the booming economy, hunger and food insecurity persisted at about the level of 1995.[4]

While food insecurity declined between 1995 and 1997, it increased again in 1998. Nearly one in five children and more than one in ten adults live in a food-insecure (hungry or at risk of hunger) household.

The booming economy coincided with cutbacks in the very government programs that over the years have lifted millions of people out of poverty. The Food Stamp program is a prime example. During the period between the historic Field Foundation visit to Mississippi in 1967, which exposed deep hunger and poverty to a shocked nation, and the late 1970s, hunger declined dramatically. The expansion of the Food Stamp Program during this period made a big difference. Yet today this program – the most

The Cost of Ending Hunger

By John T. Cook

Ending Hunger Through Food Assistance

Over the past several decades, considerable emphasis has been placed on public and private food assistance programs as a means of reducing or preventing food insecurity and hunger. In recent years these two components of the national food assistance system have become more related, overlapping and integrated.[1] It is, however, still meaningful and useful to talk about public and private components separately, even though their separateness is becoming less clear.

Many people think of the national food assistance system as an "emergency" system. But this is being called into question. Emergencies, by definition, are temporary. Yet millions of food-insecure American households rely on the food assistance system for part of their food supply on an ongoing basis. The national food assistance system may be evolving toward a combination "emergency and maintenance" system, providing temporary assistance to some of its client base, and more long-term, or permanent food assistance to growing numbers of people.

A food assistance approach to eliminating food insecurity and hunger in the U.S. would use the public and private components of the overall hybrid national food assistance system to provide the food needed to eliminate food insecurity and hunger.

If we add estimates of the cost of the present system to the cost of the "food gap," the total cost of eliminating food insecurity and hunger in the short term is approximately $49.82 billion. However, **only about $6.9 billion of this amount is the "food gap," the cost of the additional amount of food needed yearly** above present expenditures.

This estimate of the total cost of eliminating food insecurity and hunger in the U.S. is quite low, especially when we compare it to the more comprehensive "income deficit" approach described below. The amount derived from that approach – which hinges on eliminating poverty as the way to eliminate hunger – is between $76.14 billion and $119.06 billion. The food assistance approach to ending food insecurity and hunger,

at $6.9 billion, is clearly a short-term emergency solution. It may bring all food-insecure households up to food security by closing their "food gap" temporarily, but it does not ensure that they stay food secure.

The "income deficit" approach is a longer-term solution that takes into account the entire range of families' basic needs. It relies on producing income levels necessary for families to achieve and maintain real economic independence.

The national food assistance system is a necessary component of the U.S. economic system, made necessary by the nature and structure of U.S. job markets and business priorities. It will remain an essential part of the American social welfare system indefinitely, and consequently it should be nurtured and supported as a way to end immediate hunger needs. However, greater emphasis is needed for the "income deficit" approach to eliminating food insecurity and hunger. Only through this kind of approach, and the institutional changes that it implies, will the U.S. ever truly succeed in eliminating food insecurity and hunger for its people for the long-term.

A Food Security Income-Deficit Approach

The "income deficit," sometimes referred to as the "poverty gap," is the amount of money needed to raise a poor household's income up to 100 percent of the poverty line. It is the difference in dollars between a household's income and its poverty threshold.

It is possible to calculate the average (for families of different sizes) amount of money representing 185 percent of poverty for food-insecure households. This is important because 96.3 percent of households at or above 185 percent of the poverty level are food secure. Closing this income gap would thus reduce overall food insecurity to about 3.7 percent, and hunger to about 1.2 percent by eliminating the "food security income-deficit." **The total cost of achieving this is between $76.14 billion and $119.06 billion** (the calculations and methodology are described in Appendix A, pp. 110-113).

A homeless person enjoys a Thanksgiving lunch in Los Angeles, California.

Summary and Conclusions

The two estimates of the cost of ending hunger summarized above can be viewed as the lower and upper limits of a continuum. The values between $7 billion and $119 billion represent different approaches between meeting short-term hunger needs, which leave people dependent on the largess of public opinion, and long-term self-sufficiency. The income deficit approach involves undertaking necessary human capital investments that yield large returns to society as a whole and all its members, rich and poor.

Food insecurity and hunger are not passive phenomena, but actively consume human resources that are urgently needed to support and improve the public good, and the health, productivity and vibrancy of our democratic social and economic institutions. Reducing and preventing food insecurity and hunger are not simply nice things to do, nor are they merely ethical imperatives. They represent absolutely necessary investments in our and our children's futures. Ending food insecurity and hunger are essential human capital investments in whose high returns we will all share. Similarly, failing to make these critical investments in our nation's human capital stock will harm us all, and prevent every citizen from achieving her or his fullest potential.

Every investment involves costs, and returns or benefits. Although a complete cost-benefit analysis is beyond the scope of this analysis, it is important to keep in mind the potential benefits that would result when considering and evaluating the range of costs presented above. Income is not a static phenomenon, but a flow. Income literally flows through families and back out into the community and economy in which they live. Eliminating the "food security income-deficit" by raising food-insecure households' incomes to 185 percent of poverty will not be a one-way flow, but a circular flow. The additional income involved would flow back into communities, states and the nation, in the form of expenditures on goods and services, taxes, savings and charitable donations. All people would benefit from these increased economic transactions, not just those making them.

In addition to the direct benefits from increased income and expenditures, a host of indirect benefits would result, many of which reduce the costs of treating and otherwise dealing with physiological and psychological problems caused or exacerbated by poverty, food insecurity, hunger and malnutrition. Reduced health care costs, lower special education costs and lower costs of crime, are just a few of the cost savings that would result from eliminating food insecurity and hunger. In addition, priceless benefits would accompany these cost savings by reducing the impairment of growth and cognitive development among our children. These benefits are both concrete and intangible. They will appear in the form of healthier, more productive citizens, and as greater levels of social coherence, satisfaction and happiness. More important, they will lead to higher expectations and greater hope for the future. These are our greatest national treasures and their value is without limit.

DR. JOHN T. COOK is assistant professor in the Department of Pediatrics at Boston University School of Medicine. E-mail: j.cook@bmc.org.

[1] Janet Poppendieck, *Sweet Charity? Emergency Food and the End of Entitlement*, New York: Viking, the Penguin Group, 1998.

Figure 2.1: Prevalence of Food Insecure Households in the United States, 1996-1998

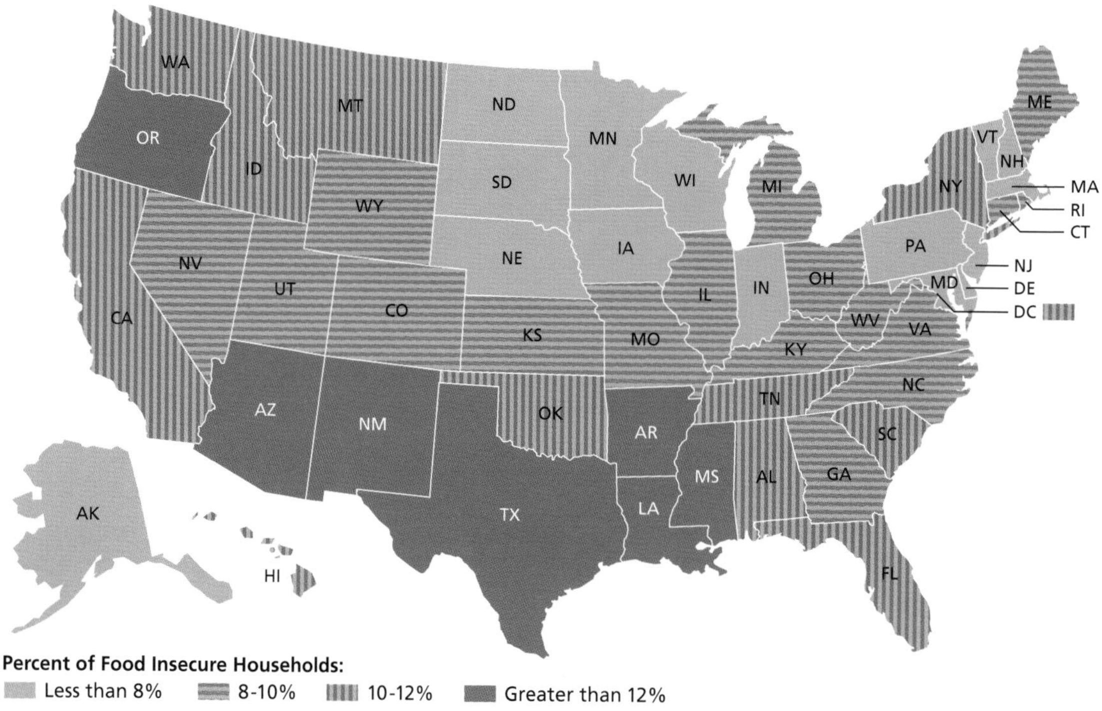

Percent of Food Insecure Households:
Less than 8%   8-10%   10-12%   Greater than 12%

Source: USDA, *Prevalence of Food Insecurity and Hunger by State, 1996-1998.* Report posted at: www.ers.usda.gov.

far-reaching of the federal nutrition programs – is in disarray. Nine million people have dropped off the Food Stamp Program in the last five years, and this may be the biggest single reason that hunger did not decline despite falling unemployment. Strengthening the Food Stamp program is the most obvious step the United States can take to reduce hunger.

Poverty...and Wealth

Not all poor people are hungry, but almost all hungry people are poor. The poverty rate dropped from 13.3 percent in 1997 to 12.7 percent in 1998, thanks to continued economic growth that finally began to reach low-income workers.[5] In 1998, unemployment dropped to its lowest level in 30 years, and it seems that this reduced poverty not only because more jobs were available but also because the tight labor market pushed wages up.[6]

Nonetheless, the poverty rate remained disturbingly high considering that unemployment was lower than in almost all the years of the 1970s, when the poverty rates were lower.[7] And while the child poverty rate dropped from 19.9 percent in

1997, it still remained alarmingly high at 18.9 percent in 1998.[8] Children comprise 39 percent of the poor population, but only about 26 percent of the total population.[9] And, the number of children living in extreme poverty – defined as less than one-half of the poverty line – had increased by 426,000 in 1997, to a total of 2.7 million children.[10] The Children's Defense Fund (CDF) ascribed this increase to the weakening of cash assistance and food stamps.[11]

The United States has one of the highest child poverty rates of any developed country. The child poverty rate in the United States is more than twice the average child poverty rate for other developed countries (see Figure 2.2). One obvious reason is that government transfers to poor children are, on average, more than twice as much in the other developed countries as in the United States.[12]

In 1995, the median African American household held wealth equal to $7,800, 12 percent of the $64,200 for White households.[13] African American families also have lower rates of home ownership than White families. However, the fastest growing rates of home ownership are found among African-Americans and Hispanics.

The income gap between rich and poor people is now at an all-time record.[14] The incomes of the wealthiest 2.7 million people are roughly equal to incomes of the poorest 100 million people.[15] If the minimum wage had grown at the same rate as the pay of CEOs since 1960, it would now be over $57 per hour.[16] Yet if disparities in income seem startling, inequalities in wealth are more so. While the top 1 percent of households controls 14.4 percent of all household income, that same 1 percent controls 38.5 percent of all wealth.[17] In the late 1990s, the share of income received by the bottom 80 percent of the U.S. population is at a record low, and deep inequality in resources leads to inequality in political influence. And, inequality in political influence is a main reason poor people remain poor.

This litany of numbers may blur the realities experienced in the lives of individual people – desperation, disease and early death. Even if we could put blinders on our moral scruples, a high rate of child poverty is bad for the whole society. The Children's Defense Fund estimates that for each year that 14.5 million children continue to live in poverty, their lifetime contribution to the U.S. economy declines by an estimated $130 billion because poor children tend to grow up to be less educated adults and less productive workers.[18] We can spend a little more now, or a lot more later.

Figure 2.2: Child Poverty Rates for Selected Countries, Mid-1990s

Percent of Child Poverty
(based on 50 percent of the child median)

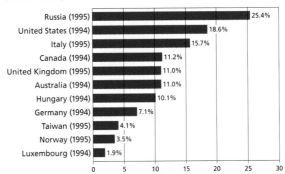

Source: Adapted from Bruce Bradbury and Marcus Jantti, "Child Poverty Across the Industrialized World: Evidence from the Luxembourg Income Study," Paper presented at the Conference on "Child Well-Being in Rich and Transition Countries: Are Children in Growing Danger of Social Exclusion?," September 30-October 2, 1999, Dommeldange, Luxembourg, Table 2.

Earnings Ratio: CEOs to Factory Workers

1980	42 to 1
1990	85 to 1
1998	419 to 1

– CEOs of major corporations

Source: *Business Week*, cited in "Executive Pay Watch," AFL-CIO, at: www.aflcio.org/paywatch/ceopay.htm. See also "The 1998 CFO Compensation Survey," *CFO Magazine* and Wm. M. Mercer Inc.

Table 2.1: Growing Gap in U.S. Income Distribution, 1977-1999

Household Income Group by Quintile	Share of All Income 1977	Share of All Income 1999	Average After-Tax Income (est.) 1977	Average After-Tax Income (est.) 1999	Percent Change in After-Tax Income (est.)
Lowest Quintile	5.7%	4.2%	$10,000	$8,800	−12.0%
Second Quintile	11.5%	9.7%	$22,100	$20,000	−9.5%
Third Quintile	16.4%	14.7%	$32,400	$31,400	−3.1%
Fourth Quintile	22.8%	21.3%	$42,600	$45,100	+5.9%
Highest Quintile	44.2%	50.4%	$74,000	$102,300	+38.2%

Source: Center on Budget and Policy Priorities, cited by David Cay Johnston, "Gap Between the Rich and Poor Substantially Wider," *New York Times*, September 5, 1999, 14.

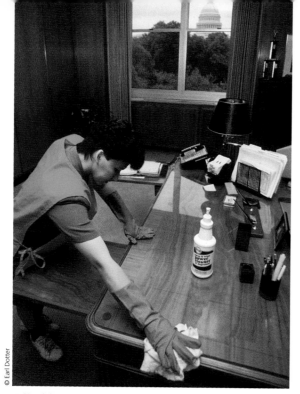

A livable wage is essential for justice.

The Legacy of Welfare Reform

The Personal Responsibility and Work Opportunity Reconciliation Act, passed in late 1996, promised to "end welfare as we know it." Aid to Families with Dependent Children (AFDC) was ended and a new program, Temporary Assistance for Needy Families (TANF), started. TANF replaced federal welfare funding with a lump-sum block grant to the states; required recipients to start work in two years or lose benefits; imposed a five-year lifetime limit on receipt of federal welfare benefits (but allowed states to set more stringent limits); and cut back other anti-poverty programs, including food stamps.

The welfare rolls plummeted from 12 million people in August 1996 to over 7 million people in March 1999. Some people feel good that they are now able to carry more of their own load. That is the good news. Whether and to what extent those leaving the rolls have found stable employment that keeps them above the poverty line ($16,660 for a family of four in 1998) is uncertain.

Many indicators suggest that the news is not as rosy as reported. NETWORK, a national Catholic social justice lobby, launched the Welfare Reform Watch Project to track the results of the reform. The study reveals that many people lack the support systems to facilitate the transition from TANF to work, such as child and health care. "The Politics of Welfare Reform" (pages 48-49) explores the difficulties they face. An Urban Institute study finds that most of those who have left welfare are working, but at low wages. One-third to one-half of them report serious struggles in feeding themselves and their families, and almost one-fifth report problems in paying rent.[19] A study by the Center on Budget and Policy Priorities further suggests that "state and national policies should provide economic supports for those who have left welfare for work but earn low wages and remain poor."[20]

Goals, Strategies and Policies

There are several ways of thinking about ending hunger in the United States. There is nothing mysterious or esoteric about what it would take. A first approach focuses on immediate strategies to close the "food gap." Expanding the national nutrition programs is a quick, direct solution. It should be put into effect.

We Know How: Nutrition Programs That Work

The national nutrition programs are an effective way to get food to families who need it. These include the Food Stamp Program, the Special Supplemental Nutrition Program for Women, Infants and Children (WIC), school feeding and several smaller programs.

Needed improvements in the national nutrition programs would cost about $5 billion annually, more than half the $7 billion grocery deficit that hungry and food-insecure families face. This $5 billion a year expansion of the national nutrition programs alone could reduce by at least half the number of hungry and food insecure families in the United States.

One survey of public opinion found that 60 percent of the U.S. public believe we need to spend more on food and nutrition programs. And yet, the recently announced *U.S. Action Plan on Food Security* provides no additional resources to reduce hunger in the United States or abroad.[21] More disturbing, the U.S. government's food and nutrition assistance has declined from 0.53 percent of Gross Domestic Product (GDP) in 1992 to 0.40 percent in 1999.[22]

Table 2.2: Proposed Federal Nutrition Agenda for the United States

Nutrition Assistance Program	Additional cost, $ million/year
Strengthening the Food Stamp Program (Includes):	
Restore benefits to vulnerable legal immigrants and raise the value of the car allowance	900
Eliminate cap on shelter allowance	100
Extend the time limit for 18—50 year olds	500
Re-index the standard deduction	400
Increase the benefit level by ten percent	2,400
Food Stamps subtotal	**4,300**
Special Supplemental Program for Women, Infants and Children (WIC)	
Fully fund WIC (make an entitlement)	500
Child (and adult care) nutrition programs	
Provide free universal school breakfast and strengthen CACFP	200
WIC, child and adult care nutrition subtotal	**700**
TOTAL	**5,000**

Bread for the World Institute estimates.

Food Stamps

The welfare reform act of 1996 was expected to "save" $57 billion. Of that amount, $30 billion was extracted from the Food Stamp Program by making many people ineligible and reducing benefits for the rest. The actual decline in spending on the Food Stamp Program has been even more drastic than what was expected. Due to welfare reform, many people do not know that still they qualify for food stamps. Some state and local governments have wrongly cut people who qualify from the Food Stamp Program. It would only cost about $7 billion to provide food to those households that are hungry or food insecure.

The U.S. Congress should strengthen the Food Stamp and other federal nutrition programs, and improve outreach so that these programs may serve all needy people. Food Stamps enables some low-income people to survive while working at low-paying jobs.[23] As "the first line of defense" against hunger, it is the most far-reaching of the federal nutrition assistance programs, benefiting

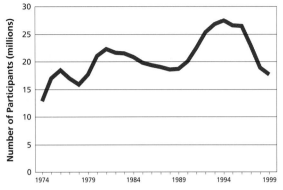

Figure 2.3: Food Stamp Participants, 1974-1999

Source: USDA, Food and Nutrition Service, Sept. 1999.

an average of 19.8 million people a month in 1998, although the numbers have subsequently declined (see Figure 2.3 above).[24] Food stamps help all eligible people to buy more food than they could otherwise and to enhance their nutrition. According to one study, food stamp shoppers eat 20 percent to 50 percent less junk food than non-recipients of any income level.[25] Not least, food stamps allow poor people the dignity of choosing their own food and eating it in their own homes – something often not possible in emergency feeding and charitable programs.[26] Also, the new electronic benefits transfer (EBT), a swipe card similar to a supermarket debit card, will further reduce misuse and non-food purchases. The new cards also give participants privacy and reduce stigma.

A family's monthly allocation of food stamps is based on an official Thrifty Food Plan. The Thrifty Food Plan formula has recently been updated, but is still inadequate to actually feed a family. Moreover, Congress decided in 1996 to phase in reduced monthly food stamp benefits. The average recipient's monthly food spending power will decrease by about 10 percent by 2002.[27] Congress should instead increase the value of the Thrifty Food Plan by 10 percent, especially for the poorest families. Congress should also restore food stamps to the 685,000 low-income legal immigrants in need of food who are still denied access to the Food Stamp Program.[28]

The value of the car that Food Stamp recipients may own also needs to be raised. The initial level of $4,500 was set in 1977 and has only increased $150 to $4,650 since that time. This represents an

USDA photo: 95C54623

Also, the standard deduction for food stamps should be indexed to inflation. This might cost an average of $400 million per year over a five-year period.

Increasing the value of the Thrifty Food Plan by 10 percent would cost about $2.4 billion a year. Adding this element to the other improvements to the Food Stamp Program – restoring benefits to vulnerable legal immigrants; raising the value of the car allowance; eliminating the cap on the shelter allowance; extending the time limits to 18 to 50-year olds; and indexing the standard deduction – results in a package that would cost about $4.3 billion a year (see Table 2.2, p. 39).

Other Nutrition Programs

The Special Supplemental Nutrition Program for Women, Infants and Children (WIC) is a highly effective and cost-efficient nutritional program with demonstrated health benefits. Providing prenatal nutrition and health care for pregnant women significantly reduces the risk of illness and fatal infections for infants.[30] An estimated 113,000 infants' lives have been saved due to the WIC program. Every dollar spent on WIC for pregnant women saves the federal government from $1.92 to $4.21 in Medicaid costs for newborns and their mothers.[31] WIC should be made an entitlement, with outreach to all eligible women, infants and children who currently do not receive any benefits. This might cost an additional $500 million annually.

increase of 3 percent, while used car prices have increased 170 percent.[29] Many of the working poor are denied food stamps for owning a car that exceeds this value, despite their need for a reliable car to get to work. Increasing the value of the car that recipients are allowed to own, plus restoring benefits to legal immigrants, would together cost about $900 million.

The limit on deductions allowed for shelter costs for families that participate in the Food Stamp Program should be eliminated. Presently, states must adjust food stamp benefits according to a family's housing and utility costs, often forcing them to make a choice among food, housing and heat. In 1996, 950,000 households, including 880,000 households with children, received lower food allowances because of caps on their high housing expenses. Housing expenses are not capped for elderly and disabled Food Stamp participants. Congress should remove the cap on the shelter deduction for families with children to receive increased food stamp benefits. This would cost about $100 million.

One of the changes brought about by welfare reform was the termination of food stamp benefits after 90 days for individuals aged 18 to 50 who are not raising minor children. Congress should change the rules back in order to allow these individuals to receive benefits for six months out of 12, instead of three out of 36, provided they are looking for a job but cannot find employment or a place in a work program. This change might cost about $500 million annually.

USDA photo: 95CN1241-6

Adequate nutrition is essential for children's learning.

Congress should continue to expand the School Breakfast Program, so that low-income children are assured adequate nutrition to benefit fully from their education. The National Advisory Committee of the Nutrition-Cognition Initiative has found that: "Inadequate nutrition is a major cause of impaired cognitive development [in children], and is associated with increased educational failure among impoverished children." Studies have shown that children who participated in the School Breakfast Program "have significantly higher standardized achievement test scores" than other eligible children who do not participate. [32] A demonstration project to test universal free breakfast has just been funded, and results may point to the need for funding a universal School Breakfast Program in the future. Right now, though, enacting a series of measures to improve the various child (and adult care) nutrition programs might cost about an additional $200 million per year.

Additional food assistance and outreach to senior citizens is also needed. As the number of senior citizens continues to grow in the 21st century, we must reaffirm our commitment as a society to meet their basic needs. Nearly two million elderly people in the United States face the difficult and untenable decision of "whether to pay their rent or buy food, or whether to pay for medicine or buy food. Those are choices no American should have to make."[33]

The cost of improvements in the above two areas – WIC, and child and adult care nutrition programs – would therefore be about $700 million per year. When added to the improvements to the Food Stamp Program recommended above, the entire package of policy prescriptions for meeting immediate food needs through the federal nutrition assistance programs comes to just over $5 billion a year (see Table 2.2, p. 39).

But if the short-term answer to hunger is so straightforward, why has it not happened before? Clearly, the missing ingredient is political will. Ending hunger requires leadership and action from all sectors of society, but especially government.[34] If Congress and the President would decide to expand the national nutrition programs, hunger would be cut in half within two years after the decision was implemented.

Ending Hunger As We Know It: A Comprehensive Approach

What is required to end hunger as we know it in the United States? These recommended federal nutrition program improvements should be part of a much larger, multi-faceted program to end hunger in America by reducing poverty. A comprehensive approach is required that promotes complementary strategies that allow workers to earn a livable income, invest in human resources, and make democracy work for everybody. This larger effort could be undertaken in various ways. Political liberals and conservatives might offer competing, but valid, approaches. The sections below sketch out one comprehensive approach in order to show that ending U.S. hunger is feasible and affordable.

Livelihood Strategies: Jobs at a Livable Income

U.S. workers used to be able to feed their families. But the wages of low-skilled people have lagged behind inflation for two decades. We need to reestablish an economy in which all full-time workers receive a livable income.

Government and business should take a leadership role in promoting opportunities for people to work. Government can create a favorable climate for business by avoiding unnecessary taxes and cumbersome regulations. One branch of the federal government, the quasi-independent Federal Reserve Board, can enact monetary policies that keep unemployment low:

> It now seems clear that the Federal Reserve Board's longstanding policy of tolerating high rates of unemployment as a means of combating inflation was a disaster for the working poor, creating a huge low-wage labor force for whom benefits are meager and insecurity and anxiety are a way of life. Only after years of steady national economic growth are real wages for this sector finally returning to the level of the 1970s.[35]

The federal government should also raise the minimum wage. A person working full-time at minimum wage earns only $10,700 per year, which is $5,960 below the 1998 poverty level for a family of four.[36] Studies indicate that a modest increase

The Scandal of Hunger in Washington, DC

The nation's capital is home to inequalities typical of developing countries. Washington is both extremely wealthy, boasting a per capita income second only to the state of Connecticut,[1] and devastatingly poor, allowing the persistence of the highest child poverty rate in the nation (40 percent).[2] Per capita, its residents hold more advanced degrees than any other municipality, but the public school system shows the lowest SAT scores and the highest high school drop out rate.[3] This is the capital of the free world.

In many ways, the problems that the District faces are a microcosm of the rest of the country, but they are further exacerbated by its unique political structure. There is no state government to oversee a strictly urban population and balance out the inequities of tax laws that benefit the 70 percent of District employees of Virginia, Maryland and West Virginia who carry their tax dollars back to the suburbs. The U.S. Congress approves the city's budget, while the federal government bureaucracy itself does not pay taxes to its ward. Citizens elect a non-voting delegate to the U.S. House of Representatives and a mayor whose power is limited.

The DC metro area is burgeoning from the economic boom, qualifying as one of the fastest growing regions in that nation. The caveat concerns where that growth is happening: it is concentrated in the eastern half of the city and suburbs.

A high poverty rate is costly to the city and the nation, and generates the same vicious cycle that traps individuals and families: as the tax base declines, the demand for social services to cope with high crime rates, drug problems and lack of adequate health care go up. The DC public school system, for example, spends almost $8,000 per student. Much of that money is not directly targeted to academics but goes for student health care, deteriorating buildings, metal detectors and other security measures. This is part of a system where 56 percent of eighth graders are reading below the average level.[4]

Myron Katz of the Brookings Institution comments that, "schools are not just instruction and textbooks, but, like neighborhoods, represent a series of reinforcing social networks that contribute to success or failure."[5] Across the Potomac River, Fairfax County spends approximately half of what the District spends per student and has one of the most successful school systems in the country. More actual dollars are being directly targeted to academics. Upwardly mobile people move to Fairfax County to benefit from better schools, thus further eroding the tax base, further lowering standards and continuing the cycle.

Many argue that the problem of hunger is understated because the poverty line is not appropriate to Washington's cost of living. The minimum wage in the city is one dollar higher than the

in the minimum wage does not change how many people employers hire. An estimated 11.8 million workers would benefit from a $1 increase in the minimum wage.[37] While a $1 increase would still not bring all of these workers up to the poverty line, it would be the first step on a long road to a decent wage.

Businesses can also ensure that full-time employees earn a decent wage – well above the national poverty levels – plus benefits, and that part-time employees are eligible for a proportionate benefits package (e.g., health insurance) that is affordable. But the current trend of businesses is to hire part-time rather than full-time employees, in order to avoid paying for benefits or giving people job security.

Figure 2.4: Hourly Wage for U.S. Workers

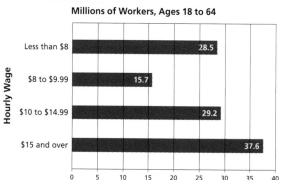

Millions of Workers, Ages 18 to 64

Hourly Wage	Millions
Less than $8	28.5
$8 to $9.99	15.7
$10 to $14.99	29.2
$15 and over	37.6

Sources: Economic Policy Institute and the Employment Policies Institute, cited in: Louis Uchitelle, "Minimum Wages, City by City," *New York Times*, November 19, 1999, C-1.

federal minimum, but that does not ensure that basic needs can be adequately met. For example, an employee earning $6.15 per hour, paying the lowest fair market rent for a two-bedroom apartment (as determined by the Department of Housing and Urban Development) is devoting 68 percent of her earnings to housing. Taking into account that 62 percent of families are headed by a single parent and only 9.9 percent of child support claims result in payment, little is left for food.[6]

The Capital Area Food Bank estimates that over 45,000 of the 109,000 children in Washington, DC are hungry or at risk of hunger.[7] Nearly 75 percent of all children qualify for the federally subsidized Free and Reduced-Price Lunch Program, yet less than half actually receive the benefits even though the programs are entitlements. Rueben Gist, Director of Advocacy at the Food Bank, says that is primarily because of ineffective outreach on the part of the federal government; families are not always aware they qualify.

The Summer Food Service Program is a further example of children paying the price of a poor administration. The DC Board of Education is one of the primary suppliers of meals in the Summer Program, but currently the program only operates when schools are in session, leaving a three week gap after the end of the summer session and the regular school year in which families are left to fend for themselves. Children and parents are fre-quently unaware that schools are not the only sites that provide these meals.

The reality that exists in Washington, DC is extreme. Most who come to view the monuments that celebrate the founding principles of this country do so without seeing that many within this city, and the rest of the country for that matter, live in a world in which these principles do not apply.

The eyes of the nation are upon the capital looking for leadership and answers to these difficult questions. It is not only the responsibility of those in the region to respond, it is a task for everyone. This city should serve as an example to the country and the world by overcoming the scandal of hunger.

[1] U.S. Department of Commerce, 1990 U.S. Census Data at: venus.census.gov/cdrom/lookup/932666249.

[2] Annie E. Casey Foundation, *Kids Count Data Book: 1999*, Baltimore, MD: Annie E. Casey Foundation, 1999.

[3] Ray Suarez, *The Old Neighborhood*, New York: The Free Press, 1999.

[4] *Kids Count*, 1999.

[5] Myron Orfield, *Washington Metropolitics: A Regional Agenda for Community and Stability*, Washington, DC: The Brookings Institution, 1999.

[6] Children's Defense Fund, *The State of America's Children Yearbook: 1999*, Washington, DC: Children's Defense Fund, 1999.

[7] D.C. Hunger Action, *In the Shadow of the Capitol: Childhood Hunger in Washington, DC*, undated.

The federal government should expand outreach to all eligible low-income people so that they benefit from the Earned Income Tax Credit (EITC). This program reduces or eliminates taxes for low-income working people and, in some cases of very low incomes, provides wage supplements. In 1998, EITC lifted 4.3 million people out of poverty.[38] In short, EITC makes work pay. The current level of EITC may be about right, but many poor workers do not know they qualify.

Public employment opportunities should be created for people who cannot find a private sector job. These jobs should not displace current workers. The Center on Budget and Policy Priorities calls for a new generation of community jobs programs. These should focus on chronic joblessness, rather than waiting until a recession; tie projects to needs in the community, such as the construction or rehabilitation of affordable housing; and help participants to quickly make the transition into unsubsidized jobs.[39]

Businesses can also make increased use of government incentives to hire previously disadvantaged workers. In April 1999, President Clinton announced that businesses participating in the nonprofit Welfare-to-Work Partnership have hired over 410,000 former welfare recipients.[40]

Accumulating productive assets is one way for low-income people to improve their livelihoods. Not only does building assets enable a family to climb out of poverty, it provides a financial cushion that protects families against hunger. The asset can consist of a savings account or a house. Therefore, government and civil society organizations should

Asset Development Strategies that Empower People

By Ray Boshara

Social worker Michael Sherraden has spent years talking to low-income families about their needs. He offers a simple but profound insight into the causes of, and solutions to, hunger: families need assets as well as income to improve their livelihoods. A savings account, a home, an education, perhaps a small business – assets are the foundation of the great American middle class. They are what provide people with stability, opportunity, hope and a stake in a community or nation. Asset building was the wisdom behind two of the U.S.'s most successful public policies: the Homestead Act and GI Bill.

Middle- and upper-income people have assets to help them through difficult times. Low-income people do not. Sherraden points out that, "Very few people manage to spend their way out of poverty."[1] It is like trying to borrow your way out of debt. The hole is too deep and you can't get out of it by digging deeper. Public policy can actually deny low-income people assets: if a family needs public assistance, they have to spend down their assets; if that family was already on public assistance, they could accumulate only limited assets. In a word, they were trapped.

Most disturbing, however, was that public policy – and tax policy, in particular – promote asset accumulation only for middle- and upper-income Americans through, for example, the home mortgage interest deduction and tax breaks for Individual Retirement Accounts (IRAs).

The federal government has, over time, developed three distinct social policies: asset development for the non-poor, asset *denial* for the poor, and asset *discrimination* for African-Americans and other minorities. Not surprisingly:

■ 10 percent of all families control two-thirds of the wealth;

■ one-third of all American households and 60 percent of African-American households have zero or negative net financial assets; and

■ 40 percent of all white children, and 73 percent of all African-American children, grow up in households with zero or negative net financial assets.[2]

The response to these skewed policies and data is not, however, income redistribution along class and racial lines. Instead, the primary challenge is to expand the reach of the tax code so that every person willing to save, regardless of income, has an opportunity to build the productive assets that lead to lasting economic security; that – unlike public assistance – allows economic well-being and opportunity to be passed on from one generation to the next.

How can this be done? One promising tool has emerged: Individual Development Accounts (IDAs), which are matched savings accounts restricted to first-home purchase, post-secondary education or small business capitalization, and which come with financial education and counseling for the accountholders. Presently, about 4,000 people are saving in their IDAs, all of them with the support of about 200 nonprofit organizations. Nonprofits have been essential to forging partnerships – between accountholders, banks, foundations, policymakers and providers of financial education – that are a hallmark of all successful IDA programs.

One of those 4,000 IDAs is owned by Selina and Duane Darden of Washington, DC. For years, the Dardens and their four children squeaked by on about $25,000 a year, with no savings, no assets, and lots of debt. Owning a home, or owning the beauty shop where Selina worked, were only dreams. Now, almost two years after enrolling in their neighborhood IDA program, the Dardens are just one month away from making a downpayment on a home. Says Selina, "I think the program is excellent. My children learned how to save. We learned how to get credit. We learned how to get life insurance. We learned how to save for retirement…. In the future, after buying a home,

© Earl Dotter

With the help of low-interest loans, this contractor was able to buy one of the houses he helped build.

I would like to own a business. The program has shown me how I can achieve these goals." That which Michael Sherraden argued – that "assets are hope in concrete form" – is turning out to be true.

While IDAs are relatively new, and demonstrating success, people fighting hunger and poverty need to move IDAs beyond demonstration projects to a mainstay of public policy. Neither the wealth gap, nor the opportunity gap, will be overcome without a widely available tool explicitly for low-income people to build assets. IDAs need to be permanently enshrined in the tax code, just as the Earned Income Tax Credit (EITC) and IRAs are.

Encouragingly, Congress is considering two tax-based proposals to begin building assets for the working poor: the bipartisan *Savings for Working Families Act* and President Clinton's *Universal Savings Account* (USA) proposal – the former for IDAs, the latter for retirement. Within 10 years, IDA advocates hope to a see a *universal*

asset-building policy, started at birth, funded throughout life from public and private sources (including families, churches, employers and government), and available for first-home purchase, a small business, post-secondary education and training, and retirement.

In the end, overcoming hunger and poverty requires strengthening existing food and nutrition programs, making work pay, and expanding successful middle-class programs that build assets to all. Asset building is not new to the United States, but it does need to be available to whole classes of people, like the Dardens, who are left behind.

RAY BOSHARA is program director with the Corporation for Enterprise Development in Washington, DC. Web site: www.cfed.org.

[1] Michael Sherraden, *Assets and the Poor: A New American Welfare Policy*, Armonk: M.E. Sharpe, 1990.

[2] Melvin L. Oliver and Thomas M. Shapiro, *Black Wealth/White Wealth: A New Perspective on Racial Inequality*, New York: Routledge, 1995.

expand funding for Individual Development Accounts (IDAs) for low-income people and perhaps seek passage of legislation to establish universal IDAs for all people at birth. These accounts enable people to save and match their funds for paying for education, a home or business development. "Asset Development Strategies that Empower People," (p. 44) explains how IDAs can help people to work and save their way out of poverty.

Working together, government and civil society organizations should also scale up existing asset development activities that enable investors to support economic development (e.g., microcredit, affordable housing) in poor neighborhoods.

Much fresh thinking is going on about how to make it easier for poor people to accumulate assets, and this illustrates a broader point: that there is still plenty of scope for new ideas and innovative approaches toward overcoming hunger and poverty. A national commitment would spawn lots of creativity and experimentation. We stand to learn much more than we know now about livelihood strategies and other ways to reduce hunger and poverty.

Social Investment Strategies: Nutrition Programs, Education and Health Care

Programs that improve nutrition, education, and health help people in need directly and immediately. They are also social investments. They improve people's productivity. Investing in people today will pay off over and over again, for poor people and for society as a whole.

Education

In a more comprehensive attack on hunger, education is also crucial. Low-income people need support to develop the skills to participate more fully in economic opportunities and earn sufficient incomes to meet their needs. A recent Washington Post/ABC News poll found that 79 percent of Americans believe that "improving education" should be the first priority for policymakers.[41] This sends a clear message to policymakers to strengthen public schools, so that all children, including those from low-income families, can benefit from a sound education and pursue jobs that provide a good wage.

Figure 2.5: Percentage of Employees in 1998 Earning Near Minimum Wage

Percentage of Employees Earning Between $5.15 an hour, the minimum wage, and $6.15 an hour.

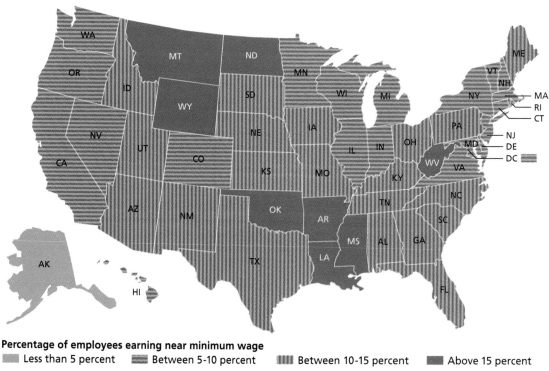

Percentage of employees earning near minimum wage

▨ Less than 5 percent ▨ Between 5-10 percent ▥ Between 10-15 percent ■ Above 15 percent

Source: *The Next Step*, Economic Policy Institute, 1999.

Public schools in impoverished neighborhoods struggle to maintain even basic academic achievement. The degree to which a school is well funded, or under-funded, is strongly associated with family income. While the 10 percent of school districts serving students with the highest household income spent an average of $6,827 per student in 1990, for the next 40 percent of districts the figure was $5,411, for the 40 percent after that, $4,774 and for the lowest 10 percent, $4,375.[42]

The Head Start Program for pre-school children living in poverty should be fully funded. Congress should expand funding to meet the critical nutritional, health and educational needs of an additional 737,000 children in their pre-school formative years.[43] The hosts of retiring baby boomers should consider taking on mentoring and tutoring activities that will contribute to their nation for decades to come.

Specific action should focus on significantly improving literacy, numeracy and high-school graduation rates. One out of six Americans is functionally illiterate.[44] With only 72 percent of its students completing high school, the United States ranks 23rd out of 29 member countries of the Organization for Economic Cooperation and Development (OECD) (see Figure 2.6).[45] In a recent survey of business, government and university leaders, 88 percent claimed that "too many" high school graduates entering college "need remedial education."[46] Students who graduate from high school earn 69 percent more than those who do not.[47]

After-school programs provide valuable skills.

Figure 2.6: Percentage of Students Completing High School in Selected Countries, 1996

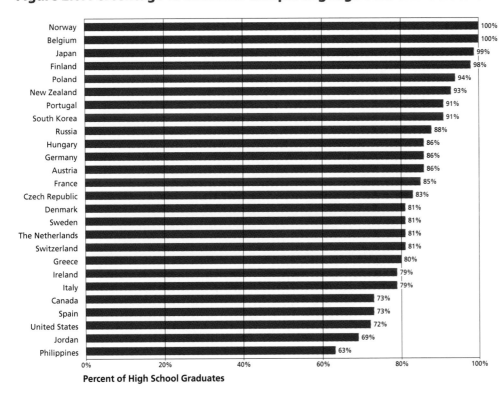

Country	Percent
Norway	100%
Belgium	100%
Japan	99%
Finland	98%
Poland	94%
New Zealand	93%
Portugal	91%
South Korea	91%
Russia	88%
Hungary	86%
Germany	86%
Austria	86%
France	85%
Czech Republic	83%
Denmark	81%
Sweden	81%
The Netherlands	81%
Switzerland	81%
Greece	80%
Ireland	79%
Italy	79%
Canada	73%
Spain	73%
United States	72%
Jordan	69%
Philippines	63%

Percent of High School Graduates

Source: OECD, Education at a Glance, 1998.

The Politics of Welfare Reform

BY STEPHANIE NIEDRINGHAUS

Many people in the United States are excited about the reported success of welfare reform legislation enacted in 1996. Welfare rolls have been cut dramatically and thus it is widely believed that welfare reform is a success.

Individuals and groups who care about the well being of people who are poor are the first to laud programs that work. When people rely on press reports to learn about the efficacy of welfare reform, however, they often receive an incomplete picture.

"Janet" (not her real name) is a typical example. A Chicago mother of five including one foster child, she recently found a job after being dropped from the welfare rolls. However, when we look more closely we see beneath media images. She recently told an interviewer:

> I just enrolled in a work-at-home program stuffing envelopes. It is so depressing...We have less food [since welfare reform], though I look for bargains and sales and try to stretch my money. I end up yelling and fighting with the children, maybe because they aren't getting enough to eat. I don't know. I borrow, but now I owe everyone so I can't borrow anymore.

Janet's struggles are the untold reality of welfare reform. While there are cases of successful transition from welfare to work, many ex-welfare recipients are worse off than before.

NETWORK, A National Catholic Social Justice Lobby, was concerned when *The Personal Responsibility and Work Opportunity Reconciliation Act of 1996* (commonly known as welfare reform) was signed into law because it focused on reducing welfare rolls rather than addressing poverty; and because federal funding to help poor people was drastically cut as part of the package. Afraid that the voices of people most affected by the law would not be heard, NETWORK initiated the *Welfare Reform Watch Project,* designed to monitor the law's implementation.

NETWORK was joined in the project by the Daughters of Charity United States Provinces, The Institute of the Sisters of Mercy of the Americas, the Federation of the Sisters of St. Joseph and Pax Christi USA. Fifty-nine Catholic social service facilities in 10 states agreed to take part in a two-year

in-depth survey of over 2,500 clients. Survey findings, including Janet's story, were published in a deeply troubling report entitled *Poverty Amid Plenty: The Unfinished Business of Welfare Reform.*

The survey focused on ten states with high welfare caseloads: California, Florida, Illinois, Massachusetts, Michigan, New Jersey, New York, Ohio, Pennsylvania and Texas.

The report reveals that, despite this nation's unparalleled economic prosperity, people continue to suffer in poverty as they receive less government assistance. Over the course of the study, the percentage of survey respondents receiving welfare dropped, reflecting national trends, but the number of people with neither jobs nor welfare rose by 27 percent. Even those fortunate enough to find work reported significant hardships. For example, survey respondents with jobs were just as likely as those who were unemployed to report that their children suffered from lack of food and health care. Fifty-two percent of the soup kitchen patrons and 42 percent of those using food pantries reported that their children skipped meals or ate less.

Women with children were especially hard hit. Despite the public perception that people using soup kitchens are generally older single men without children, increasing numbers of women and children are turning to them for help. In fact, 70 percent of the NETWORK survey respondents who relied on soup kitchens were female, and 57 percent had children.

Numbers, however, tell only part of the story. Personal stories put a human face on the suffering. Janet's situation is mirrored, with variations, in the lives of many others, including a teenage boy in New York found slathering chunks of butter on bagels at an after-church coffee. He sheepishly told a bystander that there was no food in the house even though his father had managed to find a job. A Texas mother, after losing her welfare benefits, was only able to afford the rent on her small apartment by skimping on the family's groceries and going without health insurance.

Too many people are content to look at declining welfare rolls without seeking a deeper understanding of what is happening to people after they lose their government benefits. Fully 41 percent of

© Margie Woodson Nea

the NETWORK survey respondents lacked working telephones, making them unreachable by most polls and surveys – as is true for many other people who live in poverty. Their stories and their voices are often unheard.

Poverty is a national problem that demands national solutions. To eliminate the reality of hunger and deprivation among children, the United States needs laws guaranteeing a living wage, universal health care and affordable housing, along with the help that enables people to move successfully from welfare to work: for example, nutrition programs, as well as assistance with child care, transportation and education.

Welfare reform legislation comes up for reauthorization in 2002, and we should carefully consider whether to allow the continued shredding of our nation's safety net. Some may question how we can afford to pay for so many programs, but the more profound question is, how can we afford not to?

Only by moving forcefully to eliminate the debilitating suffering caused by poverty can we truthfully claim to be a nation rooted in justice for all.

STEPHANIE NIEDRINGHAUS is communications coordinator at NETWORK, A National Catholic Social Justice Lobby. For a copy of the executive summary of "Poverty Amid Plenty: The Unfinished Business of Welfare Reform," phone 202-547-5556.
E-mail: network@networklobby.org.
Web site: www.networklobby.org.

States and civil society organizations should provide innovative training, comprehensive programs for the hard to employ, and other work supports, such as counseling; childcare referrals; and help in accessing government assistance programs to enable people to make the transition to work, or to better-paying work.[48]

Health

One in every six persons – over 43 million people – lacks health insurance, an increase of over 5 million people since 1994. One in seven children has no health insurance, yet nine out of 10 uninsured children have at least one working parent.[49] Inadequate health care exacerbates food insecurity and puts children at risk.[50] Having health insurance helps a family to "smooth over" unexpected crises and avoid hunger.

People of color and poor people are the hardest hit. Half of all poor people working full time are uninsured. Uninsured people enter hospitals sicker, receive fewer tests and leave sooner. People of color tend to receive inferior access and treatment.[51] Poverty and poor health are twin sisters.

Most people over 65 get a major part of their coverage through Medicare. Poor people receive health care through Medicaid. Unfortunately, Medicaid covers only about half of all low-income people who live below the poverty line.

As former welfare recipients return to work, many of them are unaware that they are still eligible for Medicaid coverage. Sometimes unable to get health insurance through her new job, and unaware that she can continue with Medicaid, a mother formerly receiving welfare may think she has no choice but to go without, thereby putting her children's health at risk. The Families USA Foundation found that approximately 675,000 low-income people lost Medicaid coverage and became uninsured as of 1997, as an unintended consequence of welfare reform.[52] Therefore improved service and outreach to people making this transition are critical to ensuring that their health insurance coverage does not fall through the cracks.

Moreover, Medicaid itself does not cover all who need it, and should be expanded. In 43 states, working parents are ineligible for Medicaid if their earnings are just enough to bring them to the poverty line, leaving 46 percent of all poor working parents uninsured.[53]

Speaking Truth to Reform

BY JIM HANNA

"My clock is ticking as of today, October 1, 1996. I am haunted by the image of a cardboard box. I know that is where my son and I could end up if we are not really careful. We've been homeless three times in my son's five years. I have often said that I gave birth to hope. I don't want to believe our country has given up on us, but sometimes, that is the way it feels.

"I am currently attending a university full-time, but today, that changes. Under the [welfare] reform law, I am only allowed a one-year certificate and not the four-year degree that I signed on for. How is it that a bad policy can decide my family's potential? How is it that the President, who has intimate knowledge of family violence and its impact, how is it this President has not heard my voice? How is it we do not matter? How can America not hear my voice?" testified Eleanor Williams (not her real name) at her first public hearing.

The Maine legislature's Commission on Poverty among Working Families was looking for answers. Eleanor was asking tough questions, quite aware that we stood on the brink of a new era in our nation's efforts to address poverty.

As executive director of the Maine Coalition for Food Security (MCFS), some of the most personally challenging work I do is identifying, recruiting and supporting the participation of low-income people in our projects. I believe our work has no credibility without the voice and presence of those suffering the oppression of an unjust economic system.

Bread for the World shares our perspective that the answer to hunger is not just food and charity, but justice. Low-income people are not the problem, but part of the solution to poverty. With this in mind BFW Institute created the Transforming Anti-Hunger Leadership (TAHL) program.

Portland's TAHL team first met in January 1996. Working in the shadow of welfare reform, we monitored its progress through Congress, not expecting it would ever pass. We could not imagine our nation making the lives of poor people more difficult than they were already.

Our team reached out to three mothers raising their children with help from Aid to Families with Dependent Children (AFDC), now Temporary Assistance to Needy Families (TANF). The new law has had a dramatic impact on their lives. These mothers have testified at hearings and helped craft legislation based on their lived experience of the welfare system.

We would have preferred continuing to work on solutions rather than spending our energies reacting to the problems created by welfare reform. Thankfully, our efforts have helped create an environment in Maine in which low-income people have some good opportunities.

Positive aspects of Maine's new welfare laws include benefit increases, effective elimination of time limits, support for childcare, maintenance of eligibility for food stamps for all legal immigrants and the "Parents as Scholars" program which allows TANF recipients to complete a four-year degree.

Eleanor has been involved in "Parents as Scholars," starting with her testimony, through helping draft legislation, to participating in the

---

The U.S. government, working with private and non-profit providers, should ensure affordable, universal health care by developing cost-effective solutions. At least 10.7 million children in the United States have no health insurance. Despite federal funding for the Children's Health Insurance Program (CHIP) to provide health insurance to 5 million uninsured children, states have provided only about 1 million children with coverage.[54] At a minimum, the federal government should strengthen state governments' outreach and simplify the enrollment process in

CHIP to ensure coverage of all eligible children without health insurance. Moreover, the federal government should consider other options for providing comprehensive health insurance to all uninsured children. For example, the American Academy of Pediatrics has advocated a new health insurance proposal that would replace Medicaid and CHIP at a cost of $44 billion per year.[55]

State governments, in conjunction with non-profits and religious organizations, should tap into the existing budget surplus (estimated at $4-7 billion) from state welfare programs and use some

Community-based organizations provide career assistance.

new program. This past session, she went back to the legislature to testify against 20 hour-a-week work requirements that combined with class and study time could take mothers away from their kids for 50 or more hours a week. We were successful in modifying those rules. Maine remains one of a few states allowing TANF recipients to complete a four-year degree.

The new time limits were hotly debated. The maximum time period over which any person can receive the federal benefit is five years over a lifetime. Working through a larger coalition, MCFS engaged in dialogue with the Maine legislature and the Department of Human Services. As a result, the legislature passed a law eliminating the cutoff. Anyone who has followed the TANF rules

and is still on the program at the five-year limit can now continue to receive benefits paid with state funds. Most states do much less.

While we have managed to reweave the safety net in our state, unresolved tensions remain. The law was created by policy-makers who believe a woman should stay home to raise her children. And yet the law makes it virtually impossible for a mother to do that. It turns impoverished mothers who received public assistance into impoverished working mothers. Welfare reform can only be successful when all who work can support their children and give them quality care.

Our board of directors constantly discusses internalized oppression as we seek to become ever more inclusive and supportive of low-income people's participation. We challenge ourselves with tough questions about our roles in, and accountability for, perpetuating inequality. We count it a success that the three mothers who began their involvement with the TAHL team have at various points been members of MCFS' board.

The project of eradicating hunger is a powerful lever that can help humanity forge common values. One of the most significant ways to do that is by building platforms from which those directly suffering economic oppression can voice their pain. If MCFS can reveal the institutional violence of an unjust system, the result may help shift collective perceptions that pave the way for the justice, equality and freedom upon which this nation was founded.

JIM HANNA has been executive director of MCFS since 1994. He is grateful to Edith Richardson for her suggestions for this article and her commitment to a better world for all. E-mail: jim@mefoodsecurity.org.

of the funds to improve the nutritional, health and educational status of children (e.g., childcare, after-school and summer programs).[56] Over half of the 50 states did not use the full amounts of their federal welfare block grants in 1998.[57]

Advocacy organizations should hold state governments accountable to ensure that surplus welfare funds are effectively targeting children's basic needs and improving former welfare recipients' capacities to hold jobs. Maine is one state that has done well at helping its former welfare recipients to adjust to the changes in the law. "Speaking

Truth to Reform" (above) illustrates the key role that grassroots advocates have played in bringing this about.

Empowerment Strategies

If hunger is to be overcome, the voices of poor and hungry people must be heard. Hunger will not end until poor people are empowered to participate meaningfully in political and economic processes that affect their lives. Meaningful participation requires appropriate political and economic mechanisms for representing not only

From Farm to Table: Reconnecting Our Food Systems

By Rachel E. Rudy

In 1994, community activists and advocates came together to address the nation's food and farming crises. The founding purpose of the community food security (CFS) movement was to bring together previously disparate members of communities to develop food systems reflecting a regional focus and promoting healthful food for all members of society.

The Community Food Security Coalition, the largest nongovernmental voice in the movement (see p. 109), defines community food security as a situation in which "all people are able to obtain a culturally acceptable, nutritionally adequate diet through non-emergency (or conventional) sources."[1] By concentrating on neighborhoods and areas where hungry and poor people live, community members and others can redirect resources to more effectively meet community needs. While low-income people's needs are certainly a priority, the CFS movement differs from traditional anti-hunger initiatives by broadening out to address food and nutrition deficiencies in all socioeconomic classes. This can be achieved by attending not only to food quantity but also food quality; and to when, where and how that food is produced.

Organizations and projects have sprung up throughout the country. They frequently build on programs that have been in place for years, but have now become a part of a larger movement. Food policy councils have organized in many cities to help facilitate these programs. These local coalitions draw from a wide spectrum, including anti-hunger advocates, nutritionists, educators, community activists, low-income people and civil servants. Sometimes the councils exist under the wing of a local government or as part of an existing non-profit. Programs vary from region to region, as each has a different set of circumstances and resources. Cities can learn from effective models developed in Austin and San Francisco, for example.

Access to suitable retail outlets is crucial to food security. Many supermarkets have followed the flow of money and space from inner cities to the suburbs. Urban transportation systems have not been designed with access to food markets in mind. Consequently, many inner city residents (of whom over 40 percent do not own a car) depend on small corner stores. These stores tend to carry a limited selection of fresh fruits and vegetables along with a wide array of expensive pre-prepared foods high in fat and sodium.

In Austin, Texas two cab companies reported that one-half to one-third of their calls were for travel to and from a food store. The Austin/Travis County Food Policy Council established a Grocery Bus, with a route traveling through neighborhoods with supermarkets at either end of the line. Today 23,000 residents use the Grocery Bus, which has become so profitable that the local transit authority is considering adding extra routes to serve needy neighborhoods.[2]

Communities are working with government agencies to encourage tax incentives for businesses located in low-income neighborhoods. In 1992, President Clinton proposed the development of Enterprise Zones and Empowerment Communities that revitalize distressed areas by providing direct government funding as well as tax incentives.

Frequently, it can be easier to develop systems that connect with local agriculture sources and provide space and resources for people to grow their own produce. San Francisco League of Urban Gardeners has developed an urban youth farm that is increasing the availability of produce to low-income residents in addition to providing teen employment. Vacant lots can be transformed into spaces that not only allow people to grow their own produce, but also provide an engaging outdoor activity and a beautiful green space.

Farmers' markets are a burgeoning institution in this country. Modeled after European counterparts, they can supply a neighborhood with valuable nutrients for a good part of the year. Federal partnerships through the WIC Farmer's Market Nutrition Program and Food Stamps have increased the viability of these markets in low-income neighborhoods.

Food co-operatives and buying clubs create opportunities to obtain food outside traditional outlets. A buying club started by the Missouri Rural Crisis Center allows residents to pool resources and buy pork from local producers below retail price. In Portland, Maine, the Maine

This farmers' market in Washington, D.C. serves both producers and consumers by improving access to fresh, nutritious produce for city residents and helping expand the economic opportunities for area agricultural producers.

Food Security Coalition (a participant in Bread for the World Institute's Transforming Anti-Hunger Leadership program), promotes economic ownership and affordable, nutritious food through a food co-op where the community retains ownership and control.

These creative strategies have attracted the federal government's attention. In 1996, Congress passed the Community Food Security Act and authorized $2.5 million in grants to projects throughout the country. Many of these efforts are strengthened by Americorps*VISTA members who help communities devise transportation systems, start community gardens and make food distribution systems more available and efficient.

In 1999, the USDA launched the Community Food Security Initiative. The USDA has pledged to reach down to communities and support existing CFS programs through information dissemination, technical support and monitoring systems. While the primary activity of grassroots coalitions remains working with constituents, there is a crucial need for communities to organize so they can be more effective advocates.

The USDA has created an opportunity for people in the CFS movement to develop relationships with the federal government and, in turn, help ensure that government programs work for the people. Community leaders can, for example, publicize the Food Stamp and WIC programs among people who may not know they qualify for assistance. Community activists can also reach beyond existing programs to influence policy at state and national levels. Those working on sustainable solutions should be at the table alongside those working to meet immediate food needs.

If our food system can create the variety and selection that many have available in their local supermarket; if we can buy tomatoes from the Netherlands and bananas from Costa Rica, then it is certainly within our grasp to create a more equitable food system in this country.

RACHEL E. RUDY is a research assistant with Bread for the World Institute. E-mail: rrudy@bread.org.

[1] Community Food Security Coalition, *A Guide to Concept, Structure, Content and Implementation*, unpublished.

[2] UCLA Pollution Prevention Education and Research Center in conjunction with the Community Food Security Coalition, *Homeward Bound: Food-Related Transportation Strategies in Low-Income and Transit-Dependent Communities*, Los Angeles, CA: UCLA, undated.

hungry and poor people, but others who are disenfranchised through apathy or through the current inequitable system for financing elections.

Grassroots Organizing

Middle- and upper-income people should join with poor people in advocating for poor peoples' interests at community, state and national levels. To facilitate this, governments and civil society organizations should provide anti-hunger leadership training and support channels through which poor people can be heard. For instance, Bread for the World Institute's Transforming Anti-Hunger Leadership (TAHL) Program has played a catalytic role in strengthening the advocacy capacities of community and statewide anti-hunger organizations across the U.S. (see p. 105).

Volunteers can support voter registration and get-out-the-vote drives in low-income communities. Governments can make it easier for all citizens to register and to vote, for example by opening polling places in the evenings and on weekends. This might especially benefit low-wage workers who often have little flexibility in their work schedules. In 1960, 63 percent of all eligible voters took part in the national elections. By 1996, the figure had declined to 49 percent, with only one in five low-income people voting (see Figure 2.7).[58] Poor people may feel it does not make a difference whether they vote or not because they see precious few changes in their favor.

But voting makes a huge difference in the policies that are enacted and the way funds get spent. Wealthier people have many – too many – ways of influencing their legislators, via direct access, contributions, and membership in interest groups.

© Earl Dotter

Low-income people can make a difference through voting their interests.

Congress should increase funding for legal assistance for poor people through the Legal Services Corporation (LSC). It provides essential legal services to those who are unable to pay and assistance to 258 local programs in every county and congressional district of the United States. LSC should once again be allowed to file class action suits, a right that LSC formerly possessed and which it is now denied by law. As Rep. James Ramstad (R-MN), a key supporter of LSC, has argued: "If our justice system is only available to people with means, that's no justice at all."[59]

With increased cases of eligible poor and hungry people being denied food stamps, welfare, Medicaid and other benefits at the state and local levels, it is critical to ensure that they have equal access to effective legal advocacy and that their rights are protected. For instance, legal advocates for poor people in New York City have taken Mayor Guiliani's administration to federal court for not informing low-income people that they were eligible for food stamp benefits.[60]

To end hunger in the United States, civil society and the private sector must also do their share. The emergency feeding movement, which is comprised of an extensive network of over 50,000 nonprofit organizations, churches, and a cadre of nearly 1 million volunteers nationwide, plays a complementary role in collecting and distributing food to hungry people. Private charity will always be needed to fill gaps and meet needs in a personal way. Moreover, emergency food providers can play a crucial role by helping volunteers connect with the public policy implications of their work.

Figure 2.7: National Voter Participation in Federal Elections, 1960-1996

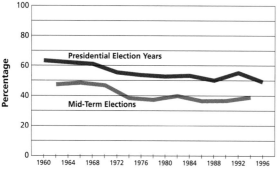

Source: Federal Election Commission.

New partnerships are emerging at the state, county and community levels. World Hunger Year has compiled case studies on many successful grassroots programs.[61] They feed hungry people, help them into the job market, and often also develop the capacity of low-income communities to plan and speak for themselves. Successful programs often combine resources for churches, businesses, foundations and government agencies. World Hunger Year is working with the USDA to replicate successful programs and make it easier for them to obtain government backing. Public-private partnerships of this sort are another area of rapid social innovation.

Campaign Finance Reform

The U.S. Congress should place limits on soft-money and special interest donations for political campaigning. Individual citizens, especially those seeking social justice, have found their voices overwhelmed by the massive political funding provided by special interests representing corporations and other groups.

Those candidates who raised the most money in the 1996 election won 92 percent of House races and 88 percent in the Senate.[62] Fundraising for the elections in 2000 may total a record $2 billion, with few controls on candidates' spending levels.[63] Successful grassroots efforts have helped reform state campaign finance in Arizona, Maine and Massachusetts. Continued advocacy is needed to extend these "clean money" reforms to other states.[64]

Conclusion

The comprehensive approach outlined here – making work pay, investing in human resources, and empowering people – presents a series of complementary policy measures that the federal government can take to end hunger. Such an effort will require much more than the $5 billion investment in federal nutrition programs that would cut hunger in half by simply feeding people. But the comprehensive approach would, in our judgement, be sufficient to end hunger and food insecurity in the United States. It would be a more durable and cost-effective way to end hunger. Healthier, better-educated, better-paid workers would pay more taxes and thus increase government revenues.

We have the opportunity to end hunger in the United States early in the 21st century. Meeting the needs of the changing faces of America – increasingly rich and poor – requires renewed vision and commitment from all sectors of society. But the federal government must do its part. The choice is ours!

DR. JAMES V. RIKER is senior researcher at Bread for the World Institute. E-mail: jriker@bread.org. ELENA MCCOLLIM is a policy analyst at the Institute. E-mail: emccollim@bread.org.

A Program to End Hunger in the United States

Short-Term
■ Strengthen federal nutrition programs – especially Food Stamps and WIC.

Short- and Long-Term

Livelihood Strategy
■ Raise the minimum wage by $1 an hour.
■ Improve EITC outreach to increase the incomes of all eligible people.

Social Investment Strategy
■ Invest in education for low-income areas and improve the high-school graduation rate.
■ Expand the Head Start Program to serve all eligible pre-school children.
■ Provide health insurance to all uninsured children.
■ Increase funding for transportation that helps low-income people.

Empowerment Strategy
■ Increase voting and political participation by low-income people.
■ Reform campaign finance.
■ Support grassroots community organizing among low-income people.

CHAPTER 3

What Developed Countries and International Agencies Can Do

BY ELENA MCCOLLIM AND JAMES V. RIKER

I believe we should…push donor countries to do much more on the development assistance issue. Today, we are talking about debt relief. But debt relief alone will not suffice. If we can get donors to increase official development assistance, and at the same time, increase our own capacity to assist developing country governments in building basic institutions, then the foundations for future development will be laid.

Kofi Annan, Secretary-General of the United Nations.[1]

© World Bank

People in developed countries can powerfully help or hinder the efforts of people in developing countries. Developed country governments dominate the economic, military, and diplomatic affairs of the world. They dominate international agencies such as the World Trade Organization (WTO), the International Monetary Fund (IMF) and the World Bank and some United Nations agencies. Nongovernmental organizations (NGOs) in the developed countries can influence their own governments and also support the burgeoning rise of NGOs in the developing countries.

One immediate and effective *livelihood strategy* for developed countries to help reduce world hunger is to cancel some of the unpayable debt of the world's poorest countries, and to do so in a way that channels the benefits to poor people in those countries. An investment by the United States of $970 million dollars over four years, coupled with what other industrialized countries and international institutions have pledged to do, would leverage an estimated $27 billion dollars in debt cancellation for the poorest countries.

The chief *social investment* strategy of developed nations is increased, poverty-focused aid. If the United States would provide an additional $1 billion in effective, poverty-focused aid each year (including funding for debt relief), the World Food Summit goal of reducing hunger by half by the year 2015 could be achieved.

Developed countries also help *empower* people in developing countries by creating more democratic global institutions and by reforming the WTO, the IMF and the World Bank to be more transparent, accountable and participatory. That way, people in the developing world will be enabled to assert their interests around policies that affect their lives.

The three strategies work together. Debt cancellation must not take place at the expense of international development assistance. Both of these in turn are necessary if the poor majority in developing countries is to benefit from, rather than be harmed by, globalization. And democratization of the international financial institutions is crucial to making them serve, not thwart, the interests of that poor majority.

The three strategies are discussed below. The total cost to the developed countries is small

Citizen advocacy in developed countries promotes debt reduction.

relative to the need and, most of all, to the benefit. And as we will see below, the U.S. public is willing to pay this modest cost. The cost to the developed countries would be $4 billion a year, for a total of $60 billion to be spent between the year 2000 and the World Food Summit target date of 2015.

Livelihood Strategies
Debt Cancellation

Northern (developed) countries should support debt cancellation that channels savings to poor people in the poorest countries. Southern (developing) countries, particularly the most deeply indebted and poorest, stand little chance of making progress in the fight against hunger and poverty as long as they labor under the burden of unpayable debt. The debt crisis of the 1990s affects some of the poorest countries in the world, many of them in Africa, which owe the debt principally to multilateral institutions like the World Bank, the IMF, and the regional development banks, and secondarily to other governments.

Cancellation of the unpayable debt could have an important impact. For example, one researcher observes that canceling the debt of 33 heavily-indebted African countries, if used for the right

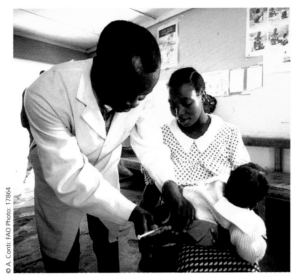

Debt cancellation can free up resources for health and education.

kinds of social investments, "would save the lives of 7 million children per year by 2000 and provide 90 million females with access to basic education."[2]

Partly in response to earlier citizen advocacy, the World Bank and the IMF in 1996 developed an initiative to provide debt relief to the Heavily Indebted Poor Countries (HIPC). In recent years a groundswell of response, stretching from North to South under the banner of Jubilee 2000, has taken the initiative to task for being too little, too late. A fundamental criticism of HIPC is that its central goal is to forgive just enough debt to keep debt service payments flowing to creditors. Creditor agencies have emphasized paying the debt first and then directing anything left over toward basic human needs such as health, nutrition and education.

Bread for the World and other Jubilee advocates argue that poverty reduction should come before debt payments. Otherwise, debt payments will continue to suck the economy dry, compromising the abilities of the poorest and most indebted countries to improve the lives of their most desperate citizens. Countries will be unable to reduce poverty or meet the other global goals agreed at the U.N. conferences of the 1990s (see Table 1.10, p. 29).

But the criticism of HIPC goes deeper. HIPC has conditioned debt cancellation on a country's meeting economic conditions set by the IMF's Enhanced Structural Adjustment Facility (ESAF), which makes loans on easy terms to poor countries. These conditions relate to inflation, tax revenues, government spending, foreign currency reserves, and government external borrowing, and their object historically has been to stabilize the economy so that growth can take place.[3] Critics charge that these conditions often lock into place economic policies that aggravate poverty, for example, by forcing cutbacks in social services.

To their credit, the IMF and World Bank have acknowledged that the HIPC initiative is inadequate. This conclusion grows out of pressure from nongovernmental advocacy groups as well as the devastating impact of the global financial crisis of 1997-1998.[4] The Bank and Fund have now decided to develop a poverty reduction strategy with government and civil society in each highly-indebted poor country. IMF conditions are supposed to be developed within the framework of these poverty reduction strategies.

Northern governments should support civil society organizations in developing countries as they try to get their governments to be more transparent and accountable. Too many of the big decisions are made by elites behind closed doors. It is little surprise, then, that the elites often gain the most from those decisions.

The insistence of people in developing countries that debt cancellation be channeled to human needs could get better results if decision-making processes were more open and participatory. The United States and other Northern governments should cancel the bilateral debt of the poorest countries, and use their voice and vote in the international financial institutions to support cancellation of the multilateral debt of those countries. They should also insist that the World Bank and IMF indeed open their policy dialogue to civil society in poor countries, especially to groups that represent the interests of poor people.

In November 1999, Congress appropriated $123 million for cancellation of debts owed to the U.S. government. This was less than one-third of the $370 million requested by the Clinton administration, but would allow the U.S. Treasury to write off most poor country debts owed to the United States. Much remains to be done to build on this agreement. Increased resources should be

Jubilee Vision: The Power of a Movement[1]

BY LYNNISE PHILLIPS AND SARA GRUSKY

Birth of a Movement

For the Jubilee 2000 movement, Biblical concepts of economic justice are relevant today. In the Hebrew Bible, every fifty years land and animals were to rest; all property restored to its original owners; and all debts cancelled. This would build into society periodic correction of the unjust accumulation of wealth and widening of inequality. Today's Jubilee movement calls for canceling the unpayable debts of the world's poorest countries by the year 2000. It calls for a fresh start in the new millennium.

An astounding 1.5 billion people live in absolute poverty (on less than $1 a day), nearly half of them children. The developing world's foreign debt makes it nearly impossible for them to escape.[2] Sub-Saharan African countries spend more each year repaying debt than on all primary education and healthcare.[3] Yet despite years of payments, debt levels have only increased, due to compounded interest and loan rescheduling. Public attention to the debt crisis has indicted rich governments and the international financial institutions (principally the World Bank and International Monetary Fund), claiming the human cost is too high. Some responsibility rests with the borrowing governments as well, as they incurred the debt in many cases without their people's knowledge or consent, and used it for projects of little use to the majority.

The severe effects of debt on education, health care, infrastructure and the environment have mobilized the development of a broad international Jubilee movement. In 1996, in response to international pressure, the World Bank and the International Monetary Fund (IMF) jointly launched a new initiative to reduce debt, the Heavily Indebted Poor Countries (HIPC) initiative. Bread for the World and other groups have been involved in efforts to reform the HIPC initiative to enable it to provide faster, deeper and broader debt relief.[4]

Since Jubilee 2000's inception, over 60 countries have launched campaigns, involving churches, development and humanitarian assistance groups, environmental organizations, unions, student groups, women's groups, professional organizations, religious leaders and rock stars.[5] Pope John Paul II has called for Christians:

> to raise their voice on behalf of all the poor and to make a call for reducing substantially, if not canceling outright, the international debt which threatens the future of many nations.[6]

The campaign is driven by the conviction that the millennium should offer a fresh start to those burdened by debt.

The Power of a Movement

Once small, Jubilee 2000 (J2000) has achieved international visibility through citizen advocacy. Its activities include popular education, media work, mass mobilization, legislation and lobbying, petitions, sign-on letters and the Jubilee 2000 trademark: mass demonstrations at the annual economic summits of the Group of Seven (G-7) nations. The movement targets the heads of state and finance ministers in creditor countries. Its first major event was a human chain in Birmingham, England during the 1998 G-7 Summit, with a reported 50,000 participants. At the 1999 G-7 Summit in Cologne, Germany, 70,000 people joined in a human chain symbolizing the bondage of foreign debt. Over 400 NGOs supporting debt relief handed over petitions with more than 17 million signatures to German Chancellor Gerhard Schroeder.

Thirty-five demonstrations and marches in other countries coincided with the Cologne event.[7] The J2000/USA coalition formed a human chain around the U.S. Department of Treasury in Washington, DC. In Argentina, advocates organized a demonstration at the Plaza de Mayo, while in Peru, others formed a human chain around the German Embassy and presented a petition with 15,000 signatures.

Since the 1996 launch, Jubilee campaigns around the world have taken different directions. The J2000/USA campaign has focused on popular education – holding workshops and conferences around the country – and on legislative efforts. The U.S. campaign has passed Jubilee 2000 resolutions in city councils and state legislatures, urged citizens to write letters to the media, the U.S. Congress and the U.S. Treasury, and introduced legislation in Congress.

Proclaim Jubilee: Break the Chains of Debt was Bread for the World's 1999 nationwide Offering of Letters. Tens of thousands of citizens urged their members of Congress to support the Debt Relief for Poverty Reduction Act (H.R.1095) in the House of Representatives and the parallel Debt Reduction for Poor Countries Act (S. 1690) in the Senate. This legislation would help cancel poor country debt, and ensure that funds thus freed up go to reducing poverty. Bread for the World's closest lobbying partners on Capitol Hill included the U.S. Catholic Conference, Oxfam, the Episcopal Church (USA), the Presbyterian Church (USA) and the United Methodist Church.

The Jubilee 2000 movement can be credited with making debt a major focus at Cologne, when the G-7 leaders proposed a new reduction plan. The Cologne Initiative is hardly a panacea, but it is an improvement. It proposes deeper debt reduction, for more countries, than does the current (1996) HIPC Initiative. It also shortens the waiting period and calls for stronger links between debt relief and poverty reduction. It still requires countries to make structural adjustments before receiving debt relief, but the IMF and World Bank are instructed to modify structural adjustment in the context of a publicly discussed poverty reduction framework for each country. Jubilee 2000/USA, while welcoming U.S. leadership in the Cologne initiative, insists the relief must go further. Bread for the World's main focus in late 1999 was that Congress approve U.S. funding for debt relief. Otherwise, other countries might also renege on commitments and even the Cologne initiative might fall apart.

Focus on the South

In the developing world (also called the global South), Jubilee campaigns call for debt cancellation not only for the poorest countries but also for

"Our daily bread is not ours" – a popular education workshop on debt takes place in Nicaragua's Atlantic Coast.

some heavily-indebted, middle-income countries with large populations of poor people, such as South Africa, the Philippines, and Brazil. The Southern Jubilee campaigns also point to broader issues. Some raise the issue of "odious debts," contracted under *apartheid* or inherited from former dictators. They emphasize popular education, advocacy training and the rights of citizens to participate in government decisions. Statements from Southern regional gatherings have raised common demands: total cancellation of foreign debt, with national processes to determine how proceeds will go to meet basic human needs and restore the environment; a rejection of structural adjustment as a condition of debt reduction; and calls for a more egalitarian global economic order.

One of Jubilee's key elements is its global nature. Latin American regional Jubilee conferences have been held in Honduras and Peru, and a Foreign Debt Tribunal was held in Brazil. There have been major regional gatherings in Ghana, South Africa and Zambia. And Asian debt campaigners have produced a Philippines-Asia Declaration.

The launch of debt campaigns in Africa is particularly important because 35 of the 41 most heavily-indebted poor countries are in Sub-Saharan Africa. The Uganda Debt Network (UDN) was launched in 1996 to:

> Advocate for reduced and sustainable debt levels, accountability and effective use of national resources for the benefit of all the people of Uganda.[8]

UDN is a coalition of Ugandan institutions formed to monitor debt cancellation. The group mobilizes, educates and informs the grassroots and also encourages democratic consultation and participation in contracting new loans. UDN has participated in monitoring the Poverty Action Fund in Uganda and implementing the Uganda Poverty Eradication Action Plan of 1997, two initiatives that channel resources from debt relief to poverty reduction.

Reflecting priorities of the Poverty Eradication Action Plan, the government's 1999 budget raises primary healthcare spending almost fourfold, rural road maintenance more than three times and primary education spending by one-third.[9] Primary school enrollment has more than doubled in the last two years.

In Nicaragua the Jubilee 2000 coalition comprises 23 organizations, including women's groups, environmental organizations, religious associations, youth groups and development NGOs. In the wake of Hurricane Mitch, the movement to cancel the debt grew even broader. While half of the debt of Nicaragua's government was cancelled in 1995, this portion of the debt was not being serviced anyway. So Nicaragua's poor majority has not seen any benefits. This experience leaves Jubilee keenly aware of the need for citizen participation and government accountability.

Moving Forward and Looking Ahead

Jubilee 2000/UK, the movement's founding coalition, has outlined its post-Cologne strategies. Ann Pettifor, coordinator of J2000/UK, says future advocacy will be directed toward "pushing the G-7 to go outside their usual negotiating framework and use the expectation around the millennium to radicalize their position."[10] The group will continue to mobilize mass opinion to force G-7 leaders into action. They will continue to discuss the debt crisis in terms of "debt bondage," using the imagery of chains and slavery; and they are committed to reorienting the U.K. campaign toward empowering the South.

The movement is currently setting strategies for the 2000 G-7 Summit in Okinawa, Japan. It proposes a pre-2000 G-7 Summit, ideally in Africa, focused exclusively on foreign debt.

Jubilee 2000's strength is that it is both visionary and practical. The vision is expansive – a new global order of greater transparency, democracy, accountability, and equity – but the immediate goal is concrete: a new start in the next millennium for one-sixth of the world's population.

LYNNISE PHILLIPS is a research assistant in BFW Institute's Debt and Development Project. E-mail: lphillip@bread.org.
DR. SARA GRUSKY was project manager. To contact Jubilee 2000/USA, call 202-783-3566, or visit their website at: www.j200usa.org.

[1] For more on the debt relief campaign, see Kathy Selvaggio, "Citizen Advocacy Reduces Debt," in *The Changing Politics of Hunger: Hunger 1999*, Bread for the World Institute, Silver Spring, Maryland: 1998.

[2] The foreign debt of the developing world is US$ 2 trillion. Center of Concern.

[3] *Jubilee 2000/USA Coalition*, at: www.j2000usa.org.

[4] The broader agenda also includes redefining the concept of sustainable debt to provide for larger debt relief packages, and de-linking debt relief from compliance with structural adjustment packages.

[5] *Jubilee 2000/UK Coalition*, at: www.jubilee2000uk.org/main.html.

[6] *Tertio Millennio Adveniente*, Paragraph 51, cited in *Swiss Coalition News*.

[7] Fred Rosen, "Doing Battle against the Debt," *NACLA: Report on the Americas*, Volume XXXIII, No.1, July/August 1999, 42.

[8] Mission Statement of the Uganda Debt Network, undated brochure.

[9] "Uganda: Economic Growth Bringing Social Gains, But Slowly," UN Office for the Coordination of Humanitarian Affairs, April 28, 1999, at www.reliefweb.int/IRIN/.

[10] J2000/UK Strategy Paper, August 4, 1999.

The Fight Against Corruption

Transparency and accountability must become international norms if corruption is ever to be curtailed. No one suffers more than ordinary citizens when the prices of essential goods, such as utilities, are artificially inflated due to bribe-taking by public officials; when a country incurs massive debt to finance "white elephant" projects; or when, under privatization, state-owned companies are sold not to the most qualified bidder but to friends and relations of the head of state. It is cause for hope that in recent years, the issue of corruption (often under the euphemism of "good governance") has received attention at the highest levels. "These are not good days for the old argument, widely popular even five years ago, that a little corruption in developing countries is probably good for greasing the wheels of commerce."[5]

In December 1997, ministers of 34 countries (29 of them members of the Organization for Economic Cooperation and Development, or OECD) signed an agreement against the bribery of foreign officials.[6] Though only a beginning, it represented a significant recognition of the importance of fighting corruption at the highest levels. There has been a parallel recognition and action on the part of ordinary citizens: many developing-country debt campaigns are advocating for transparency and accountability in administering funds from debt cancellation.

allocated, and efforts made to ensure that debt cancellation is targeted to meeting basic needs in poor countries. The U.S. government should invest $970 million over four years toward canceling the debt of the poorest countries.

International trade is another area that shapes the destinies of developing countries. More open trade can increase jobs and income, but can also harm poor countries which have less clout in the international negotiations which shape trade (see "Developing Country Perspectives on Trade Negotiating," pp. 72-73).

Social Investment
Participatory, Poverty-Focused Aid

In addition to canceling the unpayable debt of the poorest countries, the developed countries should also expand participatory, poverty-focused and results-oriented development assistance.

U.S. funding levels for official development assistance (ODA) are at a fifty-year low, lagging behind those of Germany, Japan, and France even when measured as a total sum of money.[7] The United States' aid level, at 0.09 percent of GNP, ranks dead last among the industrialized nations.[8] Most of the other rich countries also fall short of the 0.7 percent goal set at the 1995 Social Summit in Copenhagen. And although U.S. foreign assistance levels increased in 1998, the overall declining trend since 1990 has been dramatic – not only in the United States but also in most of the wealthy countries.[9]

For starters, the United States should pay its $1.7 billion in arrears to the United Nations.[10] Economist Jeffrey Sachs says, "The failure of the U.S. to pay its U.N. dues is surely the world's most significant default on international obligations, far more egregious than any defaults by impoverished HIPCs (Heavily Indebted Poor Countries)."[11]

The U.S. Public is Willing to Pay

A study by the University of Maryland's Program on International Policy Attitudes (PIPA) finds that 60 percent of the U.S. public favored paying U.N. dues in full. When the hypothetical payment of those dues is made conditional on U.N. financial reforms, the figure rises to 78 percent.[12]

The United States' failure to fulfill its obligations undermines its credibility at the United Nations. As Secretary of State Madeleine Albright points out, "American dollars leverage the contributions of others…[I]t is far easier to persuade others to do their part when we are clearly doing ours."[13] Although she was referring to aid for national security and reconstruction, the same could be said of humanitarian and development assistance.

The current low levels of development aid in no way reflect the U.S. public's will. On the contrary, PIPA finds that "an overwhelming majority supports aid in principle and only a small minority would eliminate it. An overwhelming majority feels the U.S. spends too much on foreign aid, *but this attitude is based on gross exaggerations of the actual amount*"[14] (emphasis added).

Fifty-eight percent of respondents agreed with the following statement: "If I knew that most foreign aid was going to the poor people who really need it rather than to wasteful bureaucracies and corrupt governments, I would be willing to pay more in taxes for foreign aid."[15] Respondents were also asked,

> Imagine that the U.N. called a conference of leading scientists and experts to develop a plan and determine how much it would cost the developed countries, working together with the poor countries, to virtually eliminate hunger in the world in 5 years. If you were confident that this plan probably could work, and that people in other countries, as well as the U.S., would pay their fair share, would you personally be willing to pay ($50 or $100) each year for the next five years to virtually eliminate hunger?[16]

Half the sample was asked about paying $50 for five years, and 78 percent of that half said they would be willing. The other half was asked about paying $100 for five years, and 75 percent of them agreed.[17] While the five-year time span is, as we know, too short, these figures do indicate the U.S.

public's willingness to pay for a program to end hunger. Fifty dollars per person would amount to $12.5 billion a year, more than enough to contribute the fair U.S. share to cut hunger in half by 2015.

Improving the Quality of Aid

Unfortunately, more than half of U.S. foreign aid goes not to poverty reduction, development and humanitarian aid but to military and security assistance and economic support (see Figure 3.1). In 1996, 53 percent of U.S. aid went to relatively well-off countries – Egypt and Israel and the countries in transition of Eastern Europe and the former Soviet Union.[18]

Since the Cold War ended, anti-poverty advocates have hoped that USAID would be more poverty-focused. Cold War motives distorted the priorities of donors and recipients alike. Now that the Cold War is over, democratic regimes have replaced many dictatorships, and international aid agencies have new opportunities to become more effective in reducing poverty and hunger.

On the other hand, aid is increasingly going toward emergency needs – responding to economic crises, natural disasters and the fallout from civil strife. This is true of emergency aid both

Figure 3.1: U.S. Foreign Assistance Budget, 1999, Estimated

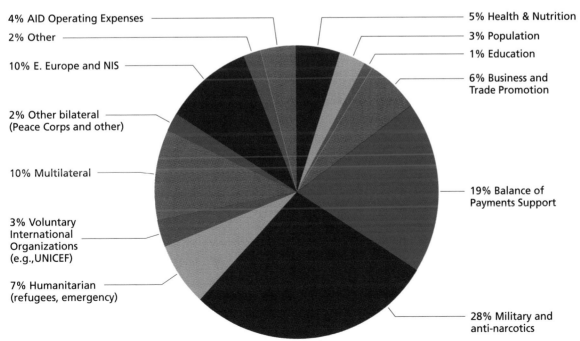

4% AID Operating Expenses
2% Other
10% E. Europe and NIS
2% Other bilateral (Peace Corps and other)
10% Multilateral
3% Voluntary International Organizations (e.g., UNICEF)
7% Humanitarian (refugees, emergency)
5% Health & Nutrition
3% Population
1% Education
6% Business and Trade Promotion
19% Balance of Payments Support
28% Military and anti-narcotics

Source: InterAction, 1999.

International Agencies Fight Hunger

BY ELENA MCCOLLIM AND JAMES V. RIKER

The 1996 World Food Summit in Rome mandated that countries create Plans of Action to cut world hunger in half by 2015. To date, only two – the United States and Canada – have completed their Plans of Action, although a number of countries are nearing completion.

The United States government announced its Plan of Action in March 1999 with little public fanfare.[1] The U.S. Plan will be difficult to implement because no new funding is added. To address the funding gap, the United States Agency for International Development (USAID) sponsored an independent study that recommended the additional appropriation of $685 million to fund a Presidential Initiative to meet the goal of reducing hunger by 50 percent internationally.[2]

The General Accounting Office (GAO) of the U.S. Government, however, predicts that existing efforts by governments and international donors are not sufficient to meet the World Food Summit goal.[3]

Several international agencies are leading the fight against hunger through research and policy analysis on agriculture, food security and nutrition. The Consultative Group on International Agricultural Research (CGIAR) is an association of public and private sector members that supports a network of sixteen international agricultural research centers.[5] The International Food Policy Research Institute (IFPRI), an affiliated research center of the CGIAR, specializes in food and agricultural policy. Also, the Administrative Committee on Coordination's Sub-Committee on Nutrition (ACC/SCN) coordinates information exchange on nutrition issues across the UN agencies.[4]

Four global-level United Nations agencies located in Rome specialize in issues of food and agriculture. The oldest, largest, and most influential of the four food agencies in Rome is the Food and Agriculture Organization of the United Nations (FAO), established shortly after World War II largely at the behest of the United States government. FAO's Committee on Food Security (successor to the World Food Council, which was established following the World Food Conference) is now charged with follow-up to the 1996 World Food Summit. The World Food Programme (WFP), established in 1961, also on U.S. initiative, provides food aid for disaster relief and long-term sustainable development. The International Fund for Agricultural Development (IFAD) was also established as an outcome of the World Food Conference.[6] IFAD (p. 67) finances projects to combat rural poverty.

We pledge our political will and our common and national commitment to achieving food security for all and to an ongoing effort to eradicate hunger in all countries, with an immediate view to reducing the number of undernourished people to half their present level no later than 2015.

— ROME DECLARATION ON FOOD SECURITY,
NOVEMBER 1996.

Tracking Progress

FAO has launched a yearly report on the state of world food insecurity. The series reports on progress toward meeting the World Food Summit goal at the global and national levels. FAO also coordinates the Inter-Agency Working Group (IAWG) established to develop the Food Insecurity and Vulnerability Information and Mapping Systems (FIVIMS).

FIVIMS links existing information systems across a range of areas including crop forecasting, early warning systems, and nutrition information.[7] Among the linked databases are, for example, the Global Information and Early Warning System (GIEWS). GIEWS, also a part of FAO, monitors food supply and demand in all countries. It uses satellite images to track crops and predict drought or other production problems; monitors world food trade with attention to its interplay with food security; and gathers economic, political and agricultural information from governmental and non-governmental sources and local and international media.[8]

Attacking Rural Poverty

IFAD works to improve household food security and nutrition through agricultural and rural development. The majority of IFAD projects help rural poor people to raise their incomes through farming and non-farm employment.

Poor households seek to have more secure sources of food and income. For IFAD, therefore, household food security is a fundamental analytic tool in designing anti-poverty programs. Gender and household food security are inextricably linked since women play a key role in ensuring their families' capacity to get adequate food. Specific poverty-focused strategies are needed. Development initiatives that aim at economic growth may not "trickle down" to poor and food insecure people, especially women.

IFAD played a lead role in starting the Popular Coalition to Eradicate Hunger and Poverty, a network of international agencies and non-governmental organizations that aims "to eradicate hunger and poverty by empowering the rural poor through agrarian reform and access to productive resources."[9] The Coalition gives special emphasis to the role of civil society in this effort.

2020 Vision

In response to "considerable disagreement on the magnitude and nature of the world's food and environmental problems combined with complacency that global food surpluses were a sufficient guarantee of global food security," IFPRI launched the 2020 Vision Initiative to promote food security.[10] The 2020 Vision develops a shared vision and strategy for action on how to meet future world food needs by 2020 while reducing poverty and protecting the environment. IFPRI is actively monitoring global trends and regional strategies for reducing food insecurity.

A Variety of Actors

Each of these plans – the World Food Summit Plan, the Popular Coalition and IFPRI's 2020 Vision – is distinct. The plans also assume a variety of actors: Southern governments; Northern governments, especially the U.S. government; intergovernmental organizations; the international system of agricultural research institutions; and universities, land grant colleges and agricultural extension systems. Finally, and to varying degrees, the plans also recognize the vital and fundamental role of rural people, farmers' associations and civil society organizations in combating hunger.

[1] See Mary McGrory, "Hunger: An Issue with Edge," *Washington Post*, March 25, 1999, A3.

[2] J. Dirck Stryker and Jeffrey C. Metzel, *Meeting the Food Summit Target and the United States Contribution*, APAP III Research Report 1038, Prepared for the U.S. Agency for International Development, September 1998.

[3] General Accounting Office, U.S. Government, *Food Security: Factors that Could Affect Progress Toward Meeting World Food Summit Goals*, Washington, DC: GAO, March 1999.

[4] *SCN News*, U.N. ACC Sub-Committee on Nutrition, New York, NY: 1999, 1.

[5] "What is the CGIAR?" at: www.cgiar.org/whatis/htm

[6] Ross B. Talbot, *The Four World Food Agencies in Rome*, Ames, Iowa: Iowa University Press, 1990, 3-4.

[7] FAO, *The State of Food Insecurity in the World*, Rome, Italy: FAO, 1999, 1.

[8] At: www.fao.org/giews/english/giews.htm

[9] The Popular Coalition to Eradicate Hunger and Poverty, "Empowering the Rural Poor Through Improved Access to Productive Assets," Rome, Italy: IFAD, May 1999, 2.

[10] IFPRI website, at: www.ifpri.org, and IFPRI, *A 2020 Vision for Food, Agriculture, and the Environment: The Vision, Challenge and Recommended Action*, Washington, DC: IFPRI, 1995.

as a total sum and as a proportion of total aid (see Table 3.1, p. 66). According to the International Food Policy Research Institute (IFPRI), "In the mid-1980s, about 80 percent of [World Food Programme] assistance was spent on development projects with the remainder being allocated to emergency relief. Ten years later, these proportions were reversed."[19] The U.N.'s budget has been similarly affected, starting in the early part of this decade. In 1992, 45 percent of that budget went toward emergency and refugee operations, a 25 percent increase since 1987.[20]

During the Cold War, developing countries became proxy battlegrounds for the East/West conflict. Once the Cold War was over, old ethnic tensions were revived, leftover weapons were plentiful and some poor nations began to struggle in earnest for a new, post-colonial, post-Cold War identity. Internecine conflict erupted and the number of emergencies has increased.

Emergency assistance operates differently from long-term aid. In an emergency, the first priority is rightly to save lives – as quickly as possible. This often results in a top-down approach, very different from development work that relies on local ingenuity and allows for the nurturing of local capacity. Sometimes, "the delivery of large quantities of assistance via centralized, top-down,

Emergency aid can help re-establish food security. Rwandan farmers receive coupons for seeds.

donor-dependent interventions may actually undermine longer-term development efforts by 'decapitating' local administrative capacity."[21]

Development practitioners have found that participatory principles can be followed even in emergency situations. Bread for the World Institute has advocated that relief aid should, whenever possible, move quickly into recovery and development "through such activities as helping people restore assets and livelihoods, and food-for-work and other job creation projects that rebuild infrastructure."[22]

Table 3.1: Trends in Bilateral and Emergency Aid: 1985/86 – 1995/96
In millions of 1995 U.S. dollars

	1985/86			1995/96		
	Column A **Bilateral Disbursements**	Column B **Emergency and Relief**	Ratio of B to A **1985/86**	Column A **Bilateral Disbursements**	Column B **Emergency and Relief**	Ratio of B to A **1995/96**
Germany	5,198.00	145.00	0.028	4,762.00	415.00	0.087
Japan	7,364.00	156.00	0.021	9,954.00	240.00	0.024
Netherlands	1,999.00	78.00	0.039	2,302.00	516.00	0.225
USA	10,520.00	741.00	0.070	6,200.00	977.00	0.158
Four-Country Average	6,270.25	280.00	0.045	5,804.50	537.00	0.093

Source: John Hoddinott, "The Shift from Development to Emergency Assistance and its Impact on Poverty and Nutrition: A Conceptual Framework," February 1999.

Participation for Sustainability in Rural Ghana[1]

BY THE INTERNATIONAL FUND FOR AGRICULTURAL DEVELOPMENT

The International Fund for Agricultural Development (IFAD) was established as a specialized agency of the United Nations in 1977 in response to a resolution adopted at the 1974 World Food Conference. Its purpose is to fund programs for the advancement of rural poor people, principally through farming and off-farm employment. Responding to the expectations of rural poor people, and incorporating their active participation, are key to the programs' success.[2]

One successful example is the Upper-East Region Land Conservation and Smallholder Rehabilitation Project in Ghana. This $15 million, seven-year project, financed jointly by IFAD, the Ghanaian government, and the World Food Programme, and with cooperation of the UN Office for Project Services. It was designed to help small-holding farmers achieve food security and to earn a living from their land during the dry season. The project was also designed to halt land degradation and alleviate poverty.

With a six-month-long dry season, erratic rainfall, poor-quality soil and one of the highest population densities in western Africa, the Upper-East Region is undoubtedly Ghana's most impoverished area. To achieve food security and allow farmers to earn a living from their land during the dry season, one solution stands out above all others: use low-lying lands as reservoirs by building dikes and dams. Many such structures were built in the years shortly following independence, from 1957 up through 1965. However, the lack of maintenance had left them in poor working condition or totally inoperative. IFAD launched the project with an eye to halting any further deterioration.

A key innovation was the involvement of poor farmers in setting an agriculture research agenda that reflected their needs. The project set up a research team locally which worked closely with the farmers to identify and prioritize problems and conduct on-farm trials of new agricultural techniques. Extension agents were part of that team, thus forming a link between research and its application.

Forming small groups was critical to the full participation of the small-holding farmers affected by the project. More than 1,200 credit groups and 27 water users' associations were formed, as well as 1,470 and 400 groups respectively for agriculture and livestock services. In this way, 67,255 poor households were reached, compared with the 51,400 expected at the design phase.

In the region, few women have title to land, much less access to credit. Most cultivate small patches on their husbands' farms or on plots belonging to other relatives – which is one reason why land, newly irrigated as part of the Upper East project, was allocated first to qualifying female-headed households, then other women farmers. This was, and still is, an uphill battle given the existing social norms. A rural credit project was also set up to finance crop production and farm-related small businesses. Almost 70 percent of the project participants were women, and they also received technical assistance to increase their income-generating capacity, mainly in food processing.

The program has so far helped the farmers increase their yields of peanuts and corn by between 150 and 200 percent. In addition, new varieties of soybean were introduced. So successful was the credit project that those participating in it almost doubled their income, and employment increased by 36 percent. With the increased income, the farmers were able to start sending their children to school.

Because the project was based in part on building infrastructure – the irrigation dikes and dams – maintaining these facilities over the long haul was a key priority. For the project to be sustainable, associations of water users needed to be created at each dam site that would assume long-term responsibility for maintaining the irrigation ditches and all facilities rebuilt under the project. With the aid of project officers and local extension services, these associations gradually took charge of the 43 sites scheduled to be rehabilitated by the end of 1997. The sense of ownership and responsibility taken on by the water users during the project has become stronger now that there is water for their plots during the dry season and their incomes have increased. By supporting the development of such associations, the project also allowed for the formulation of a standard procedure for community mobilization around rehabilitated sites – a model that can be successfully replicated elsewhere.

[1] Adapted from *Partners for Success: Rural Women in IFAD's Projects*, IFAD. Used with permission.

[2] International Fund for Agricultural Development, *Annual Report 1999*, 3.

Oxfam highlights a number of principles for helping to ensure that emergency assistance empowers its beneficiaries, rather than increasing their dependency. For example, relief work should be held to the same standards as development work, and be designed to support and improve local capacities. Development work in turn should be geared toward preventing or at least mitigating future disasters. Lastly, "[b]oth relief and development should be more concerned with increasing local capacities and reducing vulnerabilities than with providing goods, services or technical assistance."[23]

While emergency assistance has been increasing, food aid has been declining, as the developed countries have reduced subsidies to their farmers. Despite the overall downward trend, U.S. food aid spiked in 1999. In response to a domestic farm crisis, the United States multiplied its volume of food aid five times over the previous year, shipping about 8.5 million metric tons worth $1.7 billion, compared with 1.6 million tons 1998.[24]

If implemented with care, food aid can be part of a web of programs to help impoverished people toward greater self-sufficiency.[25] But food aid can also push down local prices and depress local agriculture. Because food aid is budgeted in money rather than volume, when world market prices are high, imports fall and food aid needs rise. Unfortunately, that is exactly when food aid volumes fall because the budgeted amount can only buy a smaller volume since prices have risen. It seems likely that food aid allocations will continue to be countercyclical – least generous in times of greater need and higher cost, and most generous in times of low food prices. In part, that is what happened in 1999, with aid volumes increasing in the wake of low prices.

Increased international assistance – not just any assistance, but programs single-mindedly focused on reducing poverty – is essential to rapid progress against world hunger. Private voluntary organizations – such as Church World Service, World Relief, and Oxfam – promote increased funding by Northern governments for international assistance that is participatory, poverty-focused, results-oriented and well coordinated.[26] Some of this assistance should go through private voluntary organizations, since they have a strong record of poverty-focused, participatory assistance.

Not least, donor governments should coordinate their aid in such a way that borrowing-country governments are in the center of the aid process, rather than being pulled in different directions by donor demands. One effort at donor coordination that has been underway for some time is the U.N.'s Donor Assistance Framework (UNDAF), which coordinates assistance from the constellation of U.N. agencies. The UNDAF "serves as the planning framework for the country programs and projects of participating United Nations system organizations."[27] The World Bank's new Comprehensive Development Framework (CDF) (p. 70) similarly strives to coordinate donor assistance via consultation with governments, civil society and the private sector.

The USAID-commissioned study of what it would take to cut hunger in half looked at the needs in each group of poor countries and the types of projects that have done most to reduce extreme poverty and hunger. That study suggests how hunger-focused aid might be deployed (see Table 1.8, p. 25). Most notably, the study suggested devoting two-fifths of this hunger-focused aid on improvements in agriculture, which has suffered from declining attention by international aid agencies until very recently.

Empowerment

Reform of International Economic Institutions

It may seem paradoxical that the holders of power can be agents of empowerment for poor countries and people. But, rich countries and international development agencies do have an important role to play in responding to calls for change from below. Northern governments and civil society organizations alike must reform, or in some cases continue to reform, international economic institutions to make them more transparent, accountable, and participatory. These institutions include the World Bank, the IMF, the regional development banks, and trade and investment negotiation fora, principally the World Trade Organization (WTO).

Democratizing the World Bank and the International Monetary Fund

The World Bank and the International Monetary Fund have considerable influence in the economic decisions of many developing countries. But their analysis and policy dialogue with governments has traditionally been confidential. Opening this process to the public in developing countries, especially to poor people and their representatives, would shift some power from elites to the people. Poor people will have a better chance to defend their interests.

Both institutions have already made some improvements. The World Bank has steadily since the mid-1980s responded to NGO activism by opening channels for dialogue and participation. In the past two years, in the wake of the financial

> # The **macroeconomic framework** may require more **detail** and flexibility to accommodate the needs of the **poverty reduction** strategy.
>
> – THE WORLD BANK AND IMF.

crisis that began in Asia, the IMF has significantly increased the transparency of its operations (by, for example, posting on its web site various documents outlining its agreements with borrowing governments). The U.S. Congress has been decisive in requiring this transparency.[28] But the task of improving transparency, accountability, and participation is not yet completed.

For years, civil society advocates have maintained that certain macroeconomic policy reforms – specifically, structural adjustment programs (SAPs) – have greatly exacerbated hunger and poverty. In recent years, the World Bank and

some of the regional development banks have put more emphasis on poverty reduction as they develop economic policy recommendations for borrowing governments. They have, for example, recommended new and carefully targeted safety nets to mitigate poverty caused by economic shocks.

As pointed out on p. 58, the World Bank and IMF have unveiled plans to develop a poverty reduction startegy for highly-indebted poor countries. They have done so in response to the Asian crisis and to those elements in the global Jubilee campaign, especially U.S. groups, which have insisted that the proceeds from debt cancellation be channeled into poverty reduction.

The World Bank and IMF are supposed to develop this poverty reduction framework together with the national government and representatives of civil society. Economic policies are to be tailored to the poverty reduction goal. The Bank and Fund have told their boards:

> On the one hand, specific programs and expenditure plans initially included in the poverty reduction strategies may need to be modified to ensure fiscal viability. On the other hand, the macroeconomic framework may require more detail and flexibility to accommodate the needs of the poverty reduction strategy.[29]

The World Bank now asserts that even when budgets must be cut, social spending – for example on health, education, rural infrastructure and microcredit – should be protected, perhaps at the expense of military spending. As to safety nets:

> In a short-turn crisis situation, the focus should first be on programs that already exist and can be scaled up quickly. These programs should deliver the services the poor need (for example, transfers to buy food) and reach the poor (even though they may reach some who are not poor).[30]

This analysis reflects some of the positions taken by civil society advocates over the years. Governments must not shirk one of the chief duties that falls clearly within their realm of competence: effective social service provision. "Safety nets should not be confused with what the market

International trade must include safeguards for labor rights, the environment, and food security.

or the state is expected to deliver; namely, economic growth and production in the first case and basic social services in the second."[31]

The Bank still needs to translate this analysis into its routine operations. Moreover, it is the IMF that sets budget targets. That is why it will be so important for the new joint Bank/Fund poverty reduction strategy to balance fully the needs of poor people with needed economic reforms.

The international financial institutions should conduct social assessments of loan transactions tied to macroeconomic policy, in order to identify benefits and losses.[32] At the project level, each project should include participatory stakeholder analyses – that is, analyses by those most affected by the project.[33] Civil society organizations, for their part, must monitor both the policies and the practices of these institutions in terms of their impact on hunger and poverty.

In fact, they are already doing so in a variety of ways. One example is the Structural Adjustment Participatory Review Initiative (SAPRI), jointly undertaken by the World Bank and an international network of over 1,200 citizens' organizations in 10 developing countries and economies in transition. SAPRI will assess the impact of structural adjustment programs on the people of those countries. This endeavor was launched in mid-1997 and is being implemented in Ghana, Mali, Uganda, Zimbabwe, Bangladesh,

El Salvador, Ecuador, and Hungary, with Bolivia under consideration.[34] According to the U.S. NGO, Development GAP, which is helping to coordinate the SAPRI effort:

> The breadth, challenge, and objectives of SAPRI are without precedent. Never before have the Bank and client governments engaged civil society, much less the Bank's major critics, in such a far-reaching exercise.[35]

Another promising new World Bank initiative is the Comprehensive Development Framework (CDF). Analogous to the UNDAF (see p. 68), the CDF seeks to place the borrowing country, rather than the Bank, at the center of development planning.[36] The borrowing-country government is to develop a national plan in consultation with civil society. Subsequently, donor countries help to fund and implement the plan by working in partnership with the government, private sector and civil society.[37]

The World Bank says that the CDF is needed to achieve better donor coordination as well as an improved sense of "ownership" – a sense of commitment to the development plan – by the borrowing country. The CDF also seeks to coordinate the functions of the IMF and World Bank – especially important at a time when the lines between the two are becoming increasingly blurred. World Bank President James Wolfensohn states, "What is key is that the two parts, namely macroeconomic aspects on the one side and the social, structural and human on the other, must be considered together."[38] However, as with debt relief, success of this new initiative seems to depend at least partially on the role of IMF conditionalities. It remains to be seen to what extent these conditionalities (p. 58) will prevent ordinary people from having a true say in their country's development plan.[39]

New developments in thinking and practice at the World Bank and, to a lesser extent, the IMF, give cause for hope. It is up to Northern NGOs, civil society organizations and governments, to join with Southern counterparts in monitoring and evaluating the development policies and practices of international financial institutions in terms of their transparency, participation and accountability.

Democratizing Trade and Investment Regimes

Since the end of World War II, the nations of the world, led by the United States and other developed countries, have steadily reduced tariffs and other obstacles to international commerce. The rapid growth of international commerce has been key to sustained economic growth worldwide, which is itself a necessary precondition for helping people escape from poverty and hence from hunger. But global competition has also widened the gap between rich and poor worldwide and disrupted the livelihoods of many groups who have been unable to compete.[40]

Northern governments and institutions should promote international trade that includes safeguards for labor rights, the environment and food security, and opens developed country markets to developing country exports of processed products. When trade negotiations become more transparent, it gives poor countries and poor people a chance to defend their interests. Trade agreements can and should protect the rights of vulnerable people – the right of workers to form unions, for example, and the intellectual property rights of tribal groups to traditional knowledge that is commercially valuable.

The previous trade negotiating round, the Uruguay Round (1986-1994) was noteworthy not only as the most extensive and inclusive one to date, but also as the first to pay significant attention to agriculture. It culminated in the creation of the World Trade Organization (WTO), which replaced the General Agreement on Tariffs and Trade (GATT). A meeting of trade ministers in Seattle, Washington in December 1999 is expected to launch a new round of trade talks, called the Millennium Round. Agriculture is an important part of Millennium Round negotiations just as it was under the eight-year-long Uruguay Round.

Meanwhile, a number of changes have taken place in the world trade arena during the five years since the Uruguay Round ended. The Uruguay Round trade agreements included the Marrakesh agreement, which pledged to mitigate any possible negative effects of trade liberalization on low-income countries in Africa and elsewhere. But the Marrakesh agreement was left vague, and the signatory countries have lacked the political will to implement it.

Plunging grain prices in 1998 triggered a crisis in U.S. farming, resulting in pressures to undo recent changes in agricultural policy. Specifically, the 1996 Freedom to Farm Act is phasing out farm subsidies and ended the Farmer-Owned Grain Reserve, established in 1977. But when commodity prices collapsed in 1998, Congress responded with the Agricultural Relief Package, comprising a total $6.6 billion of assistance.[41] In the fall of 1999, Congress passed an even larger package of $8.7 billion.[42] It remained an open question whether U.S. agricultural policy would revert back to price supports after 2002, when they are due to be phased out.[43]

The financial crisis that began in Southeast Asia in mid-1997 and subsequently spread to Russia and Brazil has somewhat abated in terms of its impact on financial markets and GNP growth rates for some – though not all – of the

When workers are **free** to organize and defend **their rights**, they can negotiate for wages and terms **appropriate** to their situations.

affected countries. Yet its impacts on middle-income and poor people in the affected countries are likely to continue for a long time to come, unfortunately largely outside the awareness of policymakers and the public in the rich countries. Financial implosion not only contributed to the U.S. farm crisis described above, but also is certain to resonate deeply during the Millennium Round, because of its impacts on the affected countries' capacity to participate in international commerce.

Developing Country Perspectives on Trade Negotiating

BY EUGENIO DÍAZ-BONILLA

Since the first round of trade negotiations under the General Agreement on Tariffs and Trade (GATT) after World War II, developing country participation has been limited. However, in the last round (the Uruguay Round, 1986-1994) those countries began to play a larger role. In particular, members of the Cairns Group of agricultural net exporters influenced negotiations.[1]

Since the Uruguay Round, developing country accession to the World Trade Organization (WTO) has continued apace. Of the 134 WTO members, about 80 percent are developing countries, including 29 of the 48 countries that the United Nations classifies as least developed countries.[2]

Late in 1999, trade ministers from member countries of the WTO were meeting in Seattle to decide whether to launch a new round. It is in developing countries' interest to be active and informed participants. If only because of their numbers, they could have a unique opportunity to influence the negotiations.

There is currently a heated debate on the impact of trade and agricultural policies in developing countries, as well as on the role and performance of the WTO. The concerns are that opening up agricultural markets may hurt poor countries, and also vulnerable groups within them. According to this view, higher and more volatile food prices hurt consumers, while poor farmers may be displaced by imports of cheap food. Also, those opposed to the WTO argue that placing decision-making in an international agency encroaches on national sovereignty. Some have called for a halt to negotiations for agricultural liberalization and for restrictions to the WTO.

Others believe that these proposals, however well intentioned, could inflict decisive damage on the same groups and countries they seek to help. In this view, continuing the negotiations will address agricultural protectionism in developed countries, which along with other trade restrictions such as in textile products, have hurt income and employment in developing countries. These analysts also view agricultural protectionism as a tax on food consumption (i.e., protectionism keeps prices of agricultural products artificially high). This hits poor families especially hard and mostly benefits larger agricultural producers.

According to this view, the process begun in the Uruguay Round should continue, completing the unfinished agenda while considering the needs of the vulnerable.

For example, unfair competition from subsidized, developed-country agricultural exports, which hurts poor agricultural producers in developing countries irrespective of their net agricultural trade position, should be banned. Producers in developing countries cannot compete against the treasuries of industrialized countries.

Also, if the developing countries are to diversify their agricultural sectors, they need expanded access to markets in developed countries. When processed products are taxed more than raw materials, it harms employment possibilities in developing countries. Therefore, eliminating or reducing tariff escalation (as this practice is called) is important.

Future negotiations also need to address the special situation of least developed countries and net food-importing countries. This means giving enough food aid, particularly avoiding cycles that tend to reinforce, instead of counteract, situations of oversupply and shortages. Future negotiations should also prioritize technical assistance and financial support to agriculture in these countries. Lastly, the special financial facilities that exist to help buy imported food must be continued and expanded. Food aid should be in grants, focused toward poor countries and social groups, and delivered in ways that do not displace domestic production in these countries.

Agricultural price volatility must also be carefully monitored. The expansion of world agricultural trade should limit overall fluctuations by spreading supply and demand shocks over larger areas. But the global decline in world public stocks of agricultural commodities may work in the opposite direction. Improving early warning of possible food shortages and providing better targeted food aid programs and financial facilities for emergencies should help allay those concerns.

Developing countries, as more disadvantaged players in the global arena, need an international legal system that limits the ability of larger countries to act unilaterally. Moreover, there is room for improving transparency and participation at the national as well as the international level. The implementation of internationally negotiated rules that limit the power of special interests and arbitrary government measures, can strengthen domestic legal and institutional frameworks in developing countries.

The emphasis therefore should be on improving the WTO. This institution applies rules that have been approved by the legislative bodies in each of the member countries, and a great deal of work is carried out directly by officials from those same governments. At the same time, despite the WTO's formal structure based on one-country-one-vote, and consensus method of decision-making, much of the negotiating takes place in informal contexts from which developing countries are excluded.

Agricultural and trade policies, however, are only part of the comprehensive international framework needed to promote economic and social development in poor countries and groups. Attention must also be given to canceling the unpayable external debt of the poorest countries, further liberalizing trade in textiles, and adequately managing capital flows.

At the same time, improved international conditions should go hand in hand with a better domestic framework in developing countries. This includes stable macroeconomic policies, open and effective markets, good governance and the rule of law, a vibrant civil society, and programs and investments that expand opportunities for all, with special consideration for disadvantaged groups and especially poor women. Internal peace and reconciliation are a prerequisite in conflict-torn countries.

Developing countries can secure some gains for themselves by pushing toward a transparent, rule-based trading system.

DR. EUGENIO DÍAZ-BONILLA is a Research Fellow at the International Food Policy Research Institute (IFPRI). He has been a member of the Argentine government delegation to several agricultural trade negotiations. He also worked for many years in rural poverty alleviation projects as a consultant for international organizations, governments and NGOs in Latin America and the Caribbean.

[1] Current members of the Cairns Group are Argentina, Australia, Brazil, Canada, Chile, Colombia, Fiji, Indonesia, Malaysia, New Zealand, Paraguay, the Philippines, South Africa, Thailand and Uruguay.

[2] This is as of February, 1999. In addition, 6 least-developed countries are in the process of accession, and three are observers.

Labor Rights

The lowering of trade barriers makes it easier for companies to move to countries with low labor costs and lax, or seldom enforced, environmental regulations. This in turn causes developing countries to compete for foreign investment, and makes it difficult for any one country to maintain standards in the face of transnational corporations' threats to move elsewhere, in a "race to the bottom" for lower standards.

Preventing such a race requires minimum labor and environmental safeguards. This does not mean mandating a global minimum wage, because wages and conditions will vary from place to place. It does mean building trade agreements that respect labor rights. Basic labor rights include the right to organize, and bans on slave and child labor, as set out by the International Labor Organization (ILO), the specialized U.N. agency that formulates international labor standards.[44] When workers are free to organize and defend their rights, they can negotiate for wages and terms appropriate to their individual situations.

Critics charge that such safeguards could be used for protectionism. Objections arise not only from developing country governments, but also from some academics and NGO representatives in the developing countries.

Certainly, developing country critics of social clauses endorse the involvement of the ILO in enforcing labor standards, as they also endorse the

involvement of the United Nations Environment Program (UNEP) in protecting the environment.[45] Moreover, the late Tanzanian president Julius Nyerere pointed out the interdependence of universal social standards and anti-poverty measures:

> The reality is that universal social standards are not possible, and certainly would not be compatible with justice, unless they are linked to, *and are conditional upon*, the parallel implementation of a deliberate, coherent and internally consistent anti-poverty programme – both nationally and internationally.[46]

Environmental Safeguards

Policy-making regarding the environmental impacts of trade liberalization is complicated by the fact that international law in one area may conflict with international law in another. For example, the WTO forbids "unjustified discrimination." The rationale is that this interferes with the goal of a "transparent, equitable, and predictable trading system." But much of national environmental law, and multilateral environmental agreements (MEAs), are based on trade measures considered discriminatory by some.[47]

The new rules on intellectual property rights provide incentives for innovation, yet those who have a margin for risk – relatively wealthy farmers and agribusiness – can most easily capture the benefits. This was too often the case with the Green Revolution technologies of capital-intensive agriculture in the 1960s and 1970s. As agricultural ecologist and Rockefeller Foundation president Gordon Conway observes,

> Too often the new technologies have been injected into communities with rapidly growing populations already dominated by excessive inequalities where, in the absence of countervailing policies, the powerful and the better-off have acquired the major share of the benefits.[48]

The same could occur today if policies to prevent it are not implemented.

Therefore at a minimum, agreements on trade in intellectual property rights (TRIPs) should not be permitted to push aside the public sector's role

Job hunters seek employment at Amazon.com in Kentucky. Many workers had lost their jobs when a garment firm relocated its operations to Central America.

© Billy Suratt/Newsmakers

Environmental standards must be upheld.

in agricultural research. When profit considerations alone drive agricultural research, the result may tend toward advances in crops of little relevance to the developing world.

Fortunately, awareness is growing of the nature of knowledge as a "global public good," and consequently of the importance of international cooperation in reducing the knowledge gap between rich and poor nations. This is especially important given the need to devise new ways of protecting traditional knowledge developed by local, sometimes indigenous people in developing countries.

Efforts are underway to restructure the current patent system to correct this imbalance. For example, recently a number of environmental organizations submitted comments to the U. S. Patent and Trademark Office (PTO) calling for changes in the patent application process that, within the framework of existing law, would give recognition to knowledge created by traditional cultures.[49]

Public institutions, like the Consultative Group for International Agricultural Research (CGIAR), can put their research expertise at the service of staple crops that are suited to the majority population in developing countries (for example, cassava or sweet potatoes in some African countries). For that reason, the affiliated research centers of the CGIAR must continue to receive public support (see p. 64).

Capital Flows

While public monies for foreign assistance have been decreasing, private investment is another matter. Private capital flows in developing countries have increased dramatically over the past decade – from $43.9 billion in 1990 to a peak of $299 billion in 1997, then falling again to $227.1 billion in 1998 in the wake of the global financial crisis.[50] However, most of these flows go only to middle-income countries, leaving the poorest countries behind.

Furthermore, as the global financial crisis of the past two years has shown, the wild spikes and dips of capital flows present very real risks for the countries in which that capital is invested. Capital flows are related to the trade debate because the agreement on trade-related investment measures (TRIMs) requires nations to phase out requirements on the locally-produced content of goods, thus removing a tool for directing economic development policy.[51] The proposed Multilateral Agreement on Investment encountered a veritable tsunami of public opposition in 1998 and was ultimately dropped from consideration (at least for the time being). Many NGO advocates believe that the global community does need an agreement on investment of some sort. But their assessment was that the MAI as it stood placed excessive emphasis on the rights, but not the responsibilities, of investors without a corresponding emphasis on the rights and responsibilities of national governments to protect labor and the environment.

Figure 3.2: Capital Flows to Developing Countries, Official and Private, 1990-1998

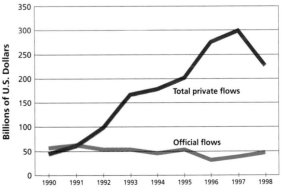

Source: World Bank, Global Development Finance, 1999.

Some maintain that allowing the free market rather than government policy to shape capital flows imposes a healthy discipline on governments by making them follow sound economic policies. But one economist points out that this sort of discipline should be imposed by the political system instead.

> In most democratic societies, the discipline needed by governments is provided by electoral accountability…Governments that mess up the economy are punished at the polls…[M]arket discipline empowers financial markets – domestic and foreign – over other constituencies in society, creating serious problems for democratic governance.[51]

Thus, in their negotiations with other industrialized nations, Northern governments, especially the U.S. government, should coordinate policies with other nations to foster full employment at a living wage and with provision for social services.

Through their participation in international trade negotiations, particularly the third ministerial meeting of the World Trade Organization (WTO), Northern governments, especially the U.S. government, should encourage transparency, participation, and accountability in international trade negotiations. They should also make trade liberalization reciprocal by reducing barriers to developing country imports and by reducing tariff escalation (higher tariffs charged on manufactured products than on raw materials). Northern governments should uphold labor and environmental safeguards in trade agreements. Finally, they must support greater definition and implementation of the Marrakesh decision. This means making resources available for food aid and also for technical and financial assistance for agriculture. These policies would indeed empower poor countries and poor people in these countries.

Conclusion

Much of what developed countries and international institutions can do to promote the livelihoods, social investment, and empowerment of poor people in poor countries lies in the realm of policy. Some as we have seen, depends on reversing the shamefully low levels of funding for foreign assistance. The needed policy shifts and funding are modest, but the payoffs potentially tremendous.

ELENA MCCOLLIM is a policy analyst at Bread for the World Institute. E-mail: emccollim@bread.org.
DR. JAMES V. RIKER is senior researcher at the Institute. E-mail: jriker@bread.org.

Africa: Seeds of Hope Act – Revitalizing Agriculture

By James V. Riker and Ray Almeida

A major victory was achieved for rural peoples of Sub-Saharan Africa in late-1998. Despite considerable political odds, Bread for the World led a broad-based coalition of over 200 development organizations, churches and denominations, land grant universities, U.S. farmers' groups and citizens to gain passage of the *Africa: Seeds of Hope Act* of 1998.

Persistent grassroots activism by citizens, which generated over 250,000 calls, letters, e-mail messages and visits to Congress, combined with effective last-minute lobbying led to unanimous bipartisan support for this bill one day before the 105th Congress adjourned. On November 13, 1998, President Clinton signed the *Africa: Seeds of Hope Act* (now Public Law 105-385), ensuring "a brighter future for the people of Africa."[1] This measure has the potential to revitalize agriculture and improve the lives of rural people, especially women, in Sub-Saharan Africa.

The premise behind this pioneering bill was clear. As Rep. Tony Hall (D-OH), a co-sponsor of the bill, argued: "Without a strong and vibrant agricultural sector, Africa cannot thrive" (see "The Critical Role of U.S. Leadership," pp. 20-21). This bill establishes an innovative framework for collaboration among U.S. government agencies, land-grant universities, international agricultural research centers, nongovernmental organizations (NGOs) and businesses to advance sustainable agricultural and rural development in Sub-Saharan Africa. Passage of the bill reaffirmed the U.S. government's commitment to improving the food security and incomes of small-holder farmers, the majority of whom are women.

Bread for the World, working with coalition partners, is actively advising the U.S. government and monitoring its efforts. Working jointly with NGO partners in Malawi and Mozambique, Bread for the World Institute is now evaluating the impact of U.S. policies on food security and rural incomes.

The U.S. Agency for International Development (USAID) is expanding its Africa Food Security Initiative to three new countries; improving coordination for agricultural research and extension efforts that provide improved techniques and seeds to small-holder farmers; reviewing effective

ACDI/VOCA

microenterprise and credit activities to expand their benefits to rural entrepreneurs and farmers; supporting farmers' cooperative development activities; expanding Title II NGO development programs that provide humanitarian food aid; and developing an integrated agricultural sector strategy for Africa. Together these elements offer renewed hope and promise for revitalizing agriculture and ensuring food security in the region.

This legislative victory represents only a first step in a long-term process to transform Sub-Saharan Africa's agricultural landscape and to realize the aspirations of its peoples. U.S. government agencies, businesses, universities, private voluntary organizations and advocacy groups need to ensure that the legislation is carried out effectively. Strengthening the efforts of farmers, grassroots groups, indigenous NGOs and government agencies in Africa is critical to a hunger-free future.

Dr. James V. Riker is senior researcher with Bread for the World Institute. E-mail: jriker@bread.org.
Ray Almeida is an international policy analyst with Bread for the World. E-mail: ralmeida@bread.org.

[1] Statement by the President, The White House, November 13, 1998, at: library.whitehouse.gov.

CHAPTER 4

What Developing Countries Can Do

BY JAMES V. RIKER AND ELENA McCOLLIM

The human family has achieved outstanding progress in the 20th century. Developing countries have covered as much ground over the past 35 years in challenging poverty, hunger, disease, and ignorance as the industrialized nations covered in more than a century. The developing countries have doubled school enrollments, halved infant mortality and adult illiteracy, reduced malnutrition by a third, and extended life expectancy at birth by 20 years.[1]

Ismail Serageldin, chairman of the Consultative Group on International Agricultural Research (CGIAR), and Vice President for Special Programs at the World Bank.

© F. Faidutti, FAO Photo: 17506

Developing countries, too, play a fundamental role in ending hunger. Despite the challenges they face, many of the poorest countries can take significant actions to reduce and ultimately end massive hunger.

These countries can foster comprehensive economic growth strategies that improve poor people's *livelihoods* by increasing incomes and assets, promote *social investment* in poverty- and gender-focused policies and programs, and lead to the *empowerment* and participation of poor and hungry people. Most important, it requires the political commitment at all levels of government and the broader society to eliminate hunger.

Livelihood Strategies

Broad-based economic growth is a critical first step to creating income-earning opportunities that give people the means to meet their basic nutritional needs. In the poorest developing countries, the agricultural sector holds the best promise for spurring sustainable economic development. The key is to increase agricultural productivity while protecting and enhancing the natural resource base. Access to productive resources (e.g., credit, land) and income-generating opportunities enable poor people to improve their livelihoods. Poor and hungry people must have a chance to help find solutions and generate sustainable livelihoods.

Promote economic growth opportunities

From the national to the local levels, broad-based economic growth should be promoted in ways that give priority to the needs of hungry and poor people. Increased economic growth alone does not ensure that the benefits of that growth reach all members of society. Policies and programs are needed both to increase the incomes and the buying power of hungry and poor people. Research in India has shown that increased wages, incomes and agricultural productivity are most likely to reduce absolute poverty.[2] "Strategies that increase the income of the poor are the most sustainable means of improving household food security."[3]

Facing page: Ugandan women's cooperative produces palm leaf crafts.

Developing country governments, the private sector and farmers each play a critical role in promoting broad-based agricultural growth with strong rural-urban linkages. Agriculture is the main source of income and employment for the majority of poor people who live in rural areas. Sound government policy can spur private sector investment in the agricultural sector that can contribute to a wide range of productive farm and farm-related activities. Improving the productivity of smallholder farmers can expand agricultural exports and help reduce poverty.[4]

Broad-based agricultural growth promotes growth and poverty alleviation in other sectors. IFPRI estimates that every $1 dollar increase in agricultural production leads to $2.32 in growth for the overall economy.[5] Developing countries should therefore prioritize small-scale agricultural production and the impoverished small-scale producer.

Livelihood strategies that increase the access of vulnerable households to sufficient food by improving people's incomes should be complemented with nutrition, health and educational opportunities. "Deliberate efforts aimed at reducing and preventing malnutrition are needed, in tandem with policies aimed at increasing national and household income."[6]

Promote international trade

Developing countries can use their increasing role in the world trade system to support international trade that increases market access for their exports. Trade liberalization can affect developing country prosperity both positively and negatively. Liberalized trade opens up opportunities, but also risks.

Uganda is a frequently cited example where economic opportunities have paid off. Uganda has seen growth rates of 6.5 percent over the past 10 years and has managed to get inflation down into single digits.[7] A principal architect of the reforms states that:

> Africans need to be more aggressive in their approach to international trade. We need to exploit our comparative advantages by diversifying into new product lines…We must also improve the quality of our exports to meet new sanitary and phytosanitary

standards…. [w]e should also exploit the new market opportunities arising from regional trade agreements, which are the future areas of growth for Africa.[8]

But developing countries need access to developed country markets, particularly for products with high economic value, for such strategies to work. According to the U.N. Research Institute for Social Development (UNRISD), reducing such developed country barriers to developing country imports by half would result in income to the developing countries equal to what they currently receive in aid.[9] "Developing Country Perspectives on Trade Negotiating," pp. 72-73, analyzes the prospects of such market opening for developing countries.

Safeguard food security

During negotiations leading up to the latest round of trade agreements, known as the Uruguay Round, some developing countries raised concerns about possible adverse impacts of trade liberalization on food security. They were particularly concerned about the impacts on low-income countries that do not produce enough food to meet their needs and must import the rest (Low-Income Food Deficit Countries, or LIFDCs). Developing country representatives feared that food prices would become increasingly volatile, and that domestic shortfalls would not be made up by greater access to developed-country markets. They were also concerned that more efficient food production could lead to lower carryover stocks in the developed countries, resulting in

Natural resource management: Madagascar farmers' committee implements anti-erosion measures.

© H. Wagner, FAO Photo: 17418

both higher prices and lower food levels in the event of global shortfalls and greater need. These developments raise important concerns for ensuring people's food security.

Improve agriculture and natural resource management

In those countries that remain overwhelmingly rural, agricultural development provides the foundation for broad economic growth. Governments must recognize the context in which agricultural production occurs – the human scale and natural resources critical to a sustainable development process. Agricultural research and extension that improves agricultural productivity and assures sound natural resource management should be relevant and responsive to the needs of small-scale farmers and hungry people. Environmental degradation and inappropriate agricultural practices can ruin the land upon which people rely for their survival. For example, in some villages of Africa, poor farmers unexpectedly found they could no longer grow bean crops, second only to maize in dietary importance, because soil fertility had been depleted. Working with bean researchers at the International Center for Tropical Agriculture (CIAT), the farmers have incorporated new bean varieties, green manures, improved soil conservation measures and sustainable farming practices that have assured stable food production.[10] Farmer participation in the research process is crucial to designing effective technologies and practices for sustainable agriculture in fragile, resource-poor lands.[11]

The ultimate challenge, especially in Sub-Saharan Africa, is to identify sustainable agricultural practices and policies that both enhance the natural resource base and the local society, and are also productive and profitable.[12] Strengthening the agricultural research networks and extension efforts by governments, NGOs and farmers' groups offers the best prospects for developing profitable and sustainable farming practices.

Southern governments and civil society organizations should invest in gender-sensitive and poverty-focused rural development (including off-farm employment) and agricultural research and extension. All over the developing world, but particularly in Africa, where up to 80 percent of

© Margie Woodson Nea

Nigerian women food farmers are the producers. Without them, there is no national food security. If we do not address this holistically – empower women economically, socially and politically – there is no future for Nigeria.
– CHIEF BISI OGUNLEYE [14]

food production is in the hands of women, agricultural extension should train and employ women as extension agents so that they might better reach women farmers.

> The world still needs to invest more in agricultural research, in agricultural infrastructure, and in providing credit to small farmers, especially women in agriculture. [13]

Promote access to productive assets

Southern governments and civil society organizations should promote access to productive assets such as land and credit, so that poor people have the means to develop economically secure livelihoods and thereby promote broad-based economic growth. Government and NGOs' credit mechanisms for hungry and poor people in the developing world have often spurred job creation, business activity and economic growth. Nearly 30,000 savings associations in rural India have enabled 300,000 poor women to pool their meager financial resources to transform their lives. This alternative source of credit has enabled women like Battan, a seamstress, to break the grip of moneylenders who charge 120 percent interest, to feed her family and to embrace her aspirations, saying: "I want to make my daughter (financially) independent." [15]

Improving poor people's access to land can lead to a wide range of productive enterprises that enhance livelihood security. For rural poor people, land can make all the difference between grinding poverty and the opportunity for a better life. Making sure that people have access to land is an important livelihood strategy for developing countries to pursue in the fight against poverty. Research has found that because it is more costly to hire and supervise extra labor to run large farms, family-operated smaller farms can actually be more efficient. [16] Moreover, land-poor persons lack assets that can serve as collateral for investments – such as education or productive assets like wells or draft animals – which could improve their lives. Such persons are poor "not because they are inherently less productive or lack the necessary skills, but because…they never get the opportunity to utilize or fully develop their abilities." [17]

Land reform has been a contested issue in many countries. For East Asian countries, such as Japan, South Korea and Taiwan, successful land reforms were building blocks of a successful development strategy. [18] However, in much of Latin America, South Asia and Southern Africa, land reform remains a hotly contentious issue. [19] Discussing the pressing need for land reform in India, one author goes so far as to say:

> [S]ubstantive agrarian reform: land redistribution, tenancy reform and labor protections…is a precondition to India's rural poor ever emerging from poverty. This is so because land redistribution transforms their material conditions by providing them with a productive asset, at the same time emancipating them socially and politically. Only then can India's poor benefit from democracy, from greater public investments in education or health, or from economic growth. [20]

Credit can transform the lives of rural women.

Today, a network of international agencies has organized itself into the Popular Coalition to Eradicate Hunger and Poverty. It is led by the International Fund for Agricultural Development (IFAD) and includes the World Bank as well as non-governmental organizations and networks both Northern and Southern (including Bread for the World Institute). Formed at a 1995 conference in Brussels, the Popular Coalition seeks to put land reform again at the center of the development agenda. It does so in a context in which traditional models of land reform are being replaced by market-based land reforms.

Land reform has traditionally consisted of three types. One, redistribution, has meant expropriating land from large landowners (usually with, but sometimes without, compensation) and handing it to the landless. Another, resettlement, has moved people from areas of high population density to supposedly unused land. Finally, tenurial reform has involved redefining tenure arrangements–i.e., typically granting security of tenure to people who had previously worked as sharecroppers or tenants.[21] Many of these efforts have failed:

> [L]and reform…has been fraught with political difficulties and obstruction from the vested interests of politicians, government bureaucrats, and local elites. Without participation of the rural poor in implementation programs, and without effective organizations of the rural poor acting as countervailing forces to the vested interests, it is unlikely that much progress will be made.[22]

In theory, the new model of market-based or negotiated land reform relies on voluntary transfers between a willing buyer and a willing seller. The government, rather than expropriating land (with or without compensation) from large landholders, limits its role to establishing the framework and, in some cases, making available a land purchase grant.[23]

Market-based models are replacing the different kinds of traditional models in many places. In Brazil, a project of negotiated land transfers has run into opposition from civil society groups. The groups charge that in a setting where power is as unequal as it is in the Brazilian northeast, landless peasants stand little chance against powerful landowners' ability to bid up prices and/or to favor their own workers in the negotiations.[24]

The Popular Coalition, recognizing the complexities of the issue, is creating knowledge networks to disseminate accurate knowledge about land reform, including case studies of market-assisted reforms. The Coalition is documenting best practice, showing what works and what fails.

Social Investment Strategies

Developing country governments must take the lead for sound public investment that enhances human capacities. Investing in basic education, nutrition and health care will improve people's capacities to meet their nutritional needs and contribute to society.

Literacy empowers women.

Improve women's education and legal status

Throughout the developing world, women play a key role in the fight against poverty and malnutrition. Women too often bear the greatest load when cuts in social spending shift more of the burden of care onto their backs. Investment in educating women and improving their legal, social and educational status will have a significant impact on their health and nutrition, and that of their children, especially those under age 5.[25] Primary and secondary education for women in the developing world has led to a dramatic improvement in life opportunities for both women and their children. Experience throughout the developing world has shown that: "the higher the educational level of women, the better the educational and nutritional level of their children."[26] Overall, improving women's education has made the greatest contribution (43 percent) to reducing child malnutrition in the developing world from 1970 to 1995 (see Figure 4.1).[27] Governments should invest in primary and secondary education for girls, and training and adult education for women to have the greatest impact on reducing child malnutrition.

Better-educated women tend to have greater autonomy and control over their lives, making it possible for them to make more choices. They make informed choices for themselves and their families, have fewer but healthier children and become more effective contributors to society.[28] Thus, a key step to reducing hunger is to remove legal and cultural barriers that discriminate against girls and women and prevent them from gaining an education. Gender discrimination in South Asia is a big factor in undernutrition and child malnutrition.

Southern civil society organizations should lobby for, and Southern governments should implement, reforms of legal codes to improve the status of women and their ability to own land. In many developing societies, women's rights to hold property, own a business and vote are limited, thus preventing them from being full members in their communities. As one woman who lived in the slums of Nairobi starkly characterized what pivotal change would free her from the life of poverty: "I would be born a man."[29] In Bangladesh, where many women have assumed

Figure 4.1: Key Factors that Reduce Child Malnutrition, 1970-1995

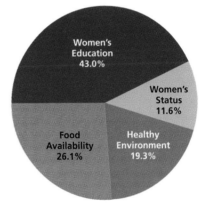

Source: Lisa Smith and Lawrence Haddad, "Explaining Child Malnutrition in Developing Countries: A Cross-Country Analysis," FCND Discussion Paper No. 60, Washington, DC: IFPRI, Food Consumption and Nutrition Division, April 1999, 59.

leadership roles in their communities, they have sought to improve social conditions and create entrepreneurial opportunities through joint savings, credit and community associations. These efforts have enabled many poor women to improve their livelihoods and status in their communities.

Invest in nutrition and social programs

Developing country governments and civil society organizations should give high priority to providing potable water, sanitation, primary health care, nutrition and education. Access to safe water and sanitation is a key factor affecting a person's health and nutritional well being. Some of the most effective basic human needs programs actively involve and empower poor people.

Nutrition education can help improve women's and children's health.

UN peacekeepers safeguard an election in the Central African Republic.

One of the most cost-effective ways to reduce child mortality and improve nutrition is by targeting micronutrient deficiencies (see "Corporations Fighting Hunger," pp. 92-93).[30] Effective targeting of micronutrient malnutrition in South Asia should begin with improving people's access to vitamin-rich foods.[31] Innovative research in Thailand has demonstrated that local women leaders can effectively improve the nutritional status of vulnerable people by providing multiple micronutrients simultaneously at the community level.[32]

Even in cases where poor women have little education, training in childcare and health practices can have a major impact on reducing childhood malnutrition. For example, providing women with special childcare training (healthcare and feeding practices) prior to childbirth has reduced malnutrition in Accra, Ghana.[33]

Urban agriculture activities by low-income people have led to improved nutrition for children in Kampala, Uganda.[34] Government and non-governmental organizations (NGOs) can support such informal initiatives and not overregulate legal barriers to urban agriculture.

Foster peace-building

Authoritarian governments, anarchic nation-states, international conflict, and civil war spawn severe hunger around the world. Concerted efforts are required at multiple levels to foster democracy, engage in effective conflict prevention and resolution, and nurture lasting peace. At the local level, poverty and violence unravel the social fabric and contribute to undernutrition.

Developing country governments, working with international humanitarian and relief organizations, should emphasize conflict resolution and prevention, peace education, and reconstruction and rehabilitation. They can promote preventative and timely humanitarian assistance by increasing financial support for refugee assistance programs. Developing country governments should cooperate in international community efforts to agree upon rules and triggers for international intervention. Governments should ensure that uprooted people themselves participate in all phases of designing, implementing and monitoring programs, and should better address the needs of women and children, who comprise 70 to 80 percent of uprooted people.

Sensational news coverage at times of exceptional violence has convinced many people that some developing countries are hopeless. But *Countries in Crisis*, Bread for the World Institute's annual report on world hunger for 1996, found that much can be done by local people and concerned outsiders to prevent conflict and recover from it.

Empowerment Strategies

> Economic empowerment leads to political empowerment. When you have money, you have the ability to negotiate good health, you can be more productive, you can invite yourself to the table.
> – Chief Bisi Ogunleye, Nigeria[35]

Overcoming hunger requires addressing the fundamental issue of power and politics. In order for developing country governments to reduce hunger, they must tap the energies of grassroots people through participatory processes and responsive institutions at all levels of society.

Promote civic participation

Effective initiatives to reduce hunger and poverty will require that hungry and poor people, especially women, are actively engaged in defining solutions from the grassroots to the national levels. Strengthening the voice of hungry and poor people is essential to ensure the success of these efforts and to hold government and other institutions accountable. Rafiatou Karim in Benin said: "Our grandmothers and mothers suffered to educate us. The women food farmers make the country survive, but are never considered when plans are made."[36] Clearly citizens and grassroots groups cannot just wait for government officials to invite their participation. They will have to organize themselves and insist on democratic participation.

Peter Williams, WCC

Seeking to improve their lives, poor people organize at a Dalit Solidarity Peoples meeting in India.

Civic participation shapes the possibilities for ending hunger.

UN/DPI/M

Effective citizen participation and public advocacy in democracies generally leads to enhanced food security initiatives by governments that are held accountable (see *The Changing Politics of Hunger: Hunger 1999*). Jean Drèze and Nobel laureate Amartya Sen argue that mobilizing citizen advocacy can be an effective tool to influence a government to act against famine, hunger and poverty.[37]

In the eastern Indian state of Orissa, citizen advocacy groups have put pressure on the state and district governments to address massive hunger and poverty since the mid-1980s. But the government has often deflected public advocacy and not acted to improve social services. "The result has been a widening implementation gap between public expectation and government delivery and, indirectly, an erosion in legitimacy of government authority."[38] Grassroots advocacy is just the first step to building effective and responsible leadership that serves hungry and poor people.

People will act if they are given the political means to shape their future. Farmers in Senegal have formed an effective national federation that

A Regional Network for Sustainable Food Security in Africa

By Jean B. Bakole

Africa faces the daunting task of overcoming hunger, malnutrition, starvation and abject poverty in the 21st century. Starvation and the chronic decline of agriculture are some of the most important challenges that African governments and peoples have been facing since independence. Despite two decades of economic reforms, Africa is the only region in the world where the number of undernourished people will continue to increase in the early 21st century.

It is clear that the goals of the 1996 Rome Declaration on World Food Security and the Food Security Action Plan (see Chapter 1, p. 28) cannot be effectively achieved without putting into place effective instruments for its implementation by African people themselves. Hunger on the African continent cannot be eradicated unless and until African peoples and their leaders refuse to live with this scourge any longer. Improved voice and influence by civil society in the media on food security is bound to raise the awareness and consciousness of public officials to make policies that promote food security and nutrition.

Across Africa, thousands of local unions, regional associations and civil society organizations are working to eradicate hunger and poverty. Until 1996, these disparate groups had no continental platform for collaboration, advocacy and the exchange of information on best practices for achieving food security and sustainable development. Recognizing the need for concrete action, the Coalition of African Organizations for Food

Security and Sustainable Development (COASAD), a regional network of African civil society organizations, was founded at the 1996 World Food Summit to coordinate education, research, advocacy and action for achieving sustainable food security for all African peoples.[1] Today, COASAD consists of 170 African organizations (NGOs, farmers' groups, professional unions, doctor's associations, women's associations) from 37 countries engaged in advancing food production, nutrition and sustainable development in Africa.

COASAD's strength lies in the breadth of its work: from reinforcing the institutional and strategic capacities of member organizations to voicing their concerns and recommendations in policy discussions. For the first time, local, national, regional and international policy makers are hearing the unified voice of an African regional network to achieve "sustainable food security and the eradication of hunger and poverty on the African continent."[2]

Jean B. Bakole is international representative for the Coalition of African Organizations for Food Security and Sustainable Development (COASAD). E-mail: coasad@skynet.be

[1] COASAD is the French acronym for "Coalition des Organisations Africaines pour la Securité Alimentaire et le Développement Durable."

[2] The COASAD Declaration on Sustainable Food Security, Dar es Salaam, Tanzania, 23-26 November 1998.

---

has improved the government's agricultural policies.[39] Despite the threat of violence, a remarkable 98.6 percent of the people registered to vote in East Timor turned out for the referendum on Indonesia rule in August 1999; 78.5 percent of the people defied the odds and voted for independence from Indonesia.[40]

Regional Challenges

Most of the world's hungry people are in South Asia, Sub-Saharan Africa and China, each of which faces special challenges.

South Asia: alleviating hunger and poverty

While IFPRI projects that the number of people affected by malnutrition in South Asia will decline by 20 million people by 2020, it expects that 2 out of 5 pre-school children will still be malnourished by 2020.[41] Governments and civil society organizations in South Asia need to focus especially on the rights, nutrition and health status of women and children; potable water and sanitation for rural and urban communities; and increased educational and employment opportunities for hungry and poor people. The Indian government should also provide improved agricultural research, extension and technologies that are appropriate and responsive to the circumstances of smallholder farmers in low-potential rainfed areas.

Revitalizing agriculture in Sub-Saharan Africa

If current trends continue, the number of people affected by malnutrition in Sub-Saharan Africa is projected to increase by 50 percent, or an additional 43 million people, by 2020.[42] The primary challenges facing the region are to revitalize agricultural production and stimulate broad-based economic growth.[43] Africans need to focus especially on building stable, democratic institutions. Many Africans are convinced that a shift away from government management and toward reliance on markets is needed, but making that shift is often difficult and traumatic.

Sub-Saharan Africa needs more agricultural research and extension that is appropriate to the ecological, economic and social realities of its smallholder farmers.[44] Also needed are improved infrastructure, transport and marketing facilities throughout rural Africa to reduce food marketing costs and improve availability and access.[45] And finally, targeted programs are needed for prevention of AIDS, health care for infected persons, and support for orphaned children (i.e., education, foster homes and community-support networks) affected by this health crisis.[46]

China: food, population and environment

Given China's potential impact on world food markets, a range of expert opinion concurs that it is imperative to monitor and analyze the food, population and natural resource balance over the next 20-25 years.[47] The government has massively subsidized grain production leading to bumper crops. However, China's environmental crisis may threaten national development and long-term food security.[48] Projections vary as to whether China will be able to sustain high yields of food grains in the 21st century.[49] To enhance food security, rural development and environmental protection, China needs to increase investment for agricultural research, extension and technologies

that are ecologically sound, resource-conserving and appropriate for semi-arid and marginal food-growing regions of the country.[50]

Conclusion

The solutions for overcoming hunger will ultimately be tested and hammered out in the developing countries. No one solution, by itself, will reduce hunger and undernutrition in the developing world. A comprehensive set of policies and programs that is suited to each country's realities will be required to turn the tide. The onus is now on developing countries to assess seriously their needs and act on improving poor and hungry people's livelihood opportunities, investing in poverty reduction and empowering them. "There now needs to be more serious and aggressive dialogue on how these pieces best fit in a given country environment."[51] In order to define the best plan, government, civil society organizations and the private sector must collaborate to reduce and end undernutrition in the developing world. Renewed leadership and new forms of collaboration among all sectors are essential to develop lasting solutions to overcoming undernutrition.

DR. JAMES V. RIKER is senior researcher with Bread for the World Institute. E-mail: jriker@bread.org. ELENA MCCOLLIM is a policy analyst with the Institute. E-mail: emccollim@bread.org.

The **solutions** for **overcoming hunger** will ultimately be tested and hammered out in the **developing countries**.

CHAPTER 5

Transforming the Politics of Hunger

BY DAVID BECKMANN

It is possible to feed…all. We have the wisdom and the resources. I wonder if we can find the compassion and the international political will to accomplish it.[1]

Christine Vladimiroff, prioress of the Benedictine Sisters of Erie, chair of Bread for the World's board of directors, and co-chair of the U.S. Food Security Advisory Committee.

C hapters 1-4 argue that the U.S. government could reduce by half the number of people who suffer hunger and food insecurity – and do its part to cut world hunger in half for roughly $6 billion a year, plus policy shifts that would make it easier for poor people to make a living and speak up for their interests. This chapter is about the cultural and political changes that would be required to achieve an anti-hunger program on this scale in the United States and worldwide. The changes required are substantial, but achievable.

The U.S. Government Is Pivotal

U.S. government leadership is crucial to rapid progress against hunger. However, the U.S government cannot do all that is required, even to end hunger in the United States itself. State and local governments, churches and charities, businesses, and poor and hungry people themselves all have roles to play in overcoming hunger. But experience with welfare reform between 1996 and 1999 confirms the crucial role of the federal government.

The private economy has boomed, making it easier than ever for low-skilled workers to find jobs. Churches and charities have increased private food distribution by 10-17 percent a year.[2] All state governments have adopted new anti-poverty policies, including some promising innovations. But the welfare reform act of 1996 by itself slashed funding for food stamps and welfare by an estimated $57 billion. That one decision took away an average of more than $1,600 for every man, woman and child below the poverty line. More generally, the federal government has reduced funding and policy attention during this period and, for that reason, hunger and food insecurity have not significantly declined.[3] If the federal government were more actively working with states,

Internet Organizing

BY DAVID BECKMANN

George Michael, Celine Dion, Bono and other celebrities challenged the world to commit itself to ending poverty through NetAid, by participating in a worldwide web event on October 9, 1999. Concerts in London, New Jersey and Geneva were simultaneously broadcast globally by television, radio and a new web site called NetAid.org. Cosponsored by the U.N. Development Programme and CISCO Systems, Inc., an Internet company, the event raised money for Kosovo refugees and African countries, and also recruited support for needed changes in public policy, notably debt relief for poor countries.[1]

Another novel use of the Internet is being promoted by the Environmental Defense Fund. Their web site **www.scorecard.org** allows anybody with a modem to get specific information about the top ten polluters in his or her own community. EDF taps into a vast reservoir of scientific data on sources of pollution and through **www.scorecard.org** gives grassroots activists information that can help them take on environmental problems locally.[2]

Bread for the World is finding the Internet a powerful aid to grassroots activism on hunger issues. People who visit **www.bread.org** can write their members of Congress directly from our web site.

Travel author Rick Steves, who connects by listserve to 30,000 of his customers every month, sometimes urges these internationally minded people to write Congress about debt cancellation for poor countries. A click on one of Rick's monthly e-letters puts any interested customer on the write-your-own-letter page of Bread for the World's website.

Bread for the World is developing listserves too – to give activists throughout the country up-to-the-minute information on legislative developments, to link activists who focus on local media, and to share information and perspectives with like-minded groups throughout the world.

DAVID BECKMANN is president of Bread for the World and Bread for the World Institute.
E-mail: institute@bread.org.

[1] "NetAid New York, London and Geneva Concerts Generate Hits to Fight Extreme Poverty," *NetAid Press Release*, October 9, 1999.

[2] "www.democracy.com," *The Economist*, April 3, 1999, 28.

charities and business, the United States could have enjoyed a sharp decline in hunger during this economic boom time.

U.S. government leadership is also crucial for rapid progress against hunger globally. The U.S. government certainly cannot solve the world's problems, but the U.S. government plays a leadership role in international affairs. This role is especially so in the post-Cold War world. The U.S. economy accounts for over 27 percent of the global economy.[4] The developed countries of North America, Western Europe and Japan even more clearly dominate the world, with 73 percent

U.S. government leadership is **crucial** for rapid progress against hunger globally.

of global economic production, and the U.S. government often plays a lead role among the developed country governments.[5] In stark contrast, the total economic production of the remaining 174 countries is roughly equal to the United States' share.

Hungry people themselves struggle constantly to survive and improve their situation, and they will exert most of the effort required to make mass hunger a thing of the past. Change at the national level in developing countries is also important; Chapter 4 discusses what developing countries can do to make progress against hunger. But the United States and the other developed country governments dominate international decisions about trade and finance, war and peace, and the policies of international institutions. Chapter 3 describes developed country and international agencies' policies that would make it much easier

for hungry people around the world to improve their livelihoods and meet the basic needs of their families.

The United States plays a major role in shaping this global framework for international development. The pivotal role of U.S. leadership is illustrated by the evolution of global policy toward developing country debt. When Mexico defaulted in 1982 and commercial banks suddenly retreated from lending to developing countries, U.S. Treasury Secretary Baker diagnosed the crisis as a short-term liquidity problem. He proposed additional lending, mainly by the World Bank and International Monetary Fund, to tide the indebted countries over. This additional lending was conditioned on major changes in developing country economies, including a sharp shift toward free-market and free trade policies. The other developed countries supported the Baker Plan, and the developing countries had to live with it.

A few years later, another U.S. Treasury Secretary – Nicholas Brady – concluded that some rescheduling of debt would be required. The other developed countries supported the Brady Plan, the World Bank and International Monetary Fund implemented it, and the developing countries again had to live with the global policies the U.S. government favored.

This pattern has continued ever since. In 1999, church and humanitarian groups around the world, including Bread for the World, joined together in the Jubilee movement for debt relief for the world's poorest countries (see pp. 59-61). The Jubilee movement was stronger in the United Kingdom and several other countries than in the United States. But when the developed country heads of state met in June 1999, their agreement closely reflected the debt policy reforms that President Clinton brought to the summit.[6] Six of the G-7 countries have parliamentary governments, so their prime ministers could make firm commitments. But the U.S. funding contribution to the plan – and, thus, the deal as a whole – depends on approval by the U.S. Congress.

Another factor that makes the U.S. government pivotal to anti-hunger politics is that U.S. policies toward the developing countries tend to be less progressive than those of most other developed countries. U.S. development assistance, for example, is only a meager 0.09 percent of U.S. national income – lower than any other donor country.[7] The United States owes $1.7 billion to the United Nations, and consequently risks losing its vote in the General Assembly.[8] The United States is among only a few states that have not ratified treaties such as the International Convention on the Right of the Child or the International Land Mine Treaty. Since the United States is so often a hold-out against progressive international initiatives, a shift in the U.S. stance could quickly lead to a series of international decisions that would accelerate global progress against hunger.

If the United States would offer to commit another $1 billion a year to overcoming hunger and severe poverty worldwide – as this report recommends – the other developed countries would probably be willing to commit at least $3 billion more as well. This effort would follow well-established patterns of "burden sharing" among the developed country allies.

A U.S.-led push to reduce world hunger would also influence the priorities of developing countries and the use of local resources. When the developed countries and international institutions put some emphasis on poverty reduction, especially rural development in the 1970s, many developing country governments shifted their priorities and budget allocations. In the 1980s, the developed countries and international institutions pushed hard for more reliance on free-market economics, and many developing countries shifted their policies and budgets again in keeping with what aid donors were now thinking. Many aid-funded projects also include funding from local sources and, thus, directly shift the allocation of domestic resources. Developing countries do have substantial resources of their own, so they could and would add funding to a global effort to overcome world hunger.

So this chapter focuses on how to change U.S. politics – partly because Bread for the World Institute is a U.S.-based organization – but, more fundamentally, because more positive U.S. government leadership is pivotal.

The Needed Political Change is Possible

We do not need a revolution

The needed shift in U.S. government's domestic priorities is substantial, but not radical. $5 billion a year is a lot of money. But it is not much at all when compared to the $792 billion tax cut Congress approved in 1999, or even the $250 billion tax cut President Clinton favored.

In the 1970s and 1980s, the environmental movement succeeded in moving environmental protection from a fringe issue to a mainstream, bipartisan issue. One very crude indicator of the influence environmental groups have on national policy is the budget of the Environmental Protection Agency (EPA), now just over $7 billion a year. Ending hunger would cost a bit less than that, so the political effort required to end hunger might be similar to the level of effort the environmental movement has achieved.

How much effort is currently devoted to lobbying Congress to do its part to end hunger? Bread for the World's budget for lobbying is about $3 million a year, and all other lobbying on hunger issues (RESULTS, America's Second Harvest, InterAction, church offices, and others) may come to another $1.5 million.[9]

By contrast, the budgets of all the nation's charitable feeding agencies probably total at least $2.5 billion. International private voluntary organizations (PVOs) manage another $3.2 billion each year in grant funds every year.[10] These figures for advocacy and assistance are all rough, but U.S. people are contributing about 1,000 times more to assisting hungry people than to winning the changes in policy that could end hunger.

If concerned people and organizations would double or, at the most, triple the relatively small effort they devote to transforming the politics of hunger, we could end hunger.

Now is the time

Last year's report on world hunger, *The Changing Politics of Hunger: Hunger 1999*, analyzed worldwide trends in how political decisions are made. On balance, right now is an opportune time to push for political changes to dramatically reduce hunger.

Corporations Fighting Hunger

BY DON WALTER AND DAVID BECKMANN

Fourteen business corporations (including Kellogg, Proctor & Gamble, Land O'Lakes, BASF, and Monsanto) are now working together with international aid agencies to eliminate Vitamin A deficiency, a nutrition problem that debilitates more than 250 million children worldwide. This initiative is tapping into the huge resources of talent, research, money and power wielded by business. It provides a terrific example of how businesses can make a difference in addressing social problems, while at the same time helping themselves.

Vitamin A deficiency (VAD) is a common problem in the developing world. A few milligrams of Vitamin A per day is essential to people's healthy development. Insufficient intake of Vitamin A can contribute to night blindness, a weakened immune system, learning disabilities, impaired work capacity, and sometimes total blindness or even death. Unfortunately, VAD affects millions of children in 90 countries. More than 400,000 children go blind every year due to a lack of the vitamin in their diets.

VAD is easily preventable. Vitamin A can be found in a number of common foods such as meats, eggs, leafy greens, and grain products. But many developing country policy-makers need to be made aware of the problem and how to address it. Public education programs, systems to deliver nutrition supplements, and management and information systems have to be set up.

Since the mid-1970s, the U.S. Agency for International Development (USAID) has supported VAD research. In 1984, USAID clearly established a link between VAD and child mortality. In 1997, USAID launched its first projects to reduce the prevalence of VAD. In countries where Vitamin A projects were implemented, infant mortality rates fell by an average of 23 percent over a five to seven year period.

USAID then forged an alliance with other countries' aid programs, UNICEF and private corporations. This international public-private partnership will:

- Develop and market Vitamin A enriched and fortified foods;
- Help companies expand their manufacturing and distribution of fortified foods;
- Enhance the quality and safety of foods produced in developing countries to meet international standards, thereby increasing the number of potential partners for joint ventures;
- Improve delivery systems to ensure that more people will receive help;
- Support nutrition education programs; and
- Increase awareness of the importance of VAD programs.

Addressing VAD is one of the most cost-effective tactics for improving child survival. The cost of fortifying food is literally pennies per year and dramatically cuts illness and deaths. A USAID study concluded that every dollar invested in Vitamin A supplementation results in an estimated $146 gain through increased productivity, averted health care and lower worker disability costs.

The Vitamin A initiative is a "win-win" partnership in which everyone benefits. The recipient countries' benefits are obvious – healthier children. Healthier children learn better, develop properly, work harder and are more likely to succeed. This intervention helps not only the individual but society as a whole. Healthier children means lower future health care costs and increased productivity. The benefits of Vitamin A intervention are felt for many years, even lifetimes.

Participating companies have an opportunity to make a major social contribution and also build new markets for themselves. Participating governments help remove barriers to the commercial distribution of fortified foods. Families learn about and become accustomed to new fortified foods. These families are likely to be customers of these and other food products for years to come.

This is only one example of how businesses help to overcome hunger. American Express, Block Buster Video, United Parcel Service, Philip Morris, General Mills and many restaurants are very active in raising and giving funds to assist hungry people. These companies want to help and also find that this cause enhances their public image and employee morale. Many charities that help hungry people receive important financial contributions from businesses and business people.

Monsanto has divested its chemical operations to focus on technological innovation in agriculture. They see their work as necessary to help the world feed its growing population. Some aspects

Farmers in Malawi raise palms to process into oil, rich in Vitamin A.

of biotechnology are controversial, and Monsanto recently decided to delay indefinitely the possible use of "terminator" crops – improved varieties that are genetically engineered to be sterile, so that farmers have to rely on the commercial supplier for seeds. Monsanto is actively urging government policies that will encourage openness to genetically engineered crops worldwide. To their credit, Monsanto has also supported RESULTS' promotion of microenterprise programs.

Agricultural producers and agribusiness have a self-interest stake in ending hunger. When hungry and poor people enjoy some increase in income, they spend the bulk of that extra income on food, perhaps including some imported food. For that reason, economic and social progress in Asia and the Middle East has made these regions a rapidly growing market for U.S. agricultural exports. So why aren't agribusiness companies such as Cargill and ADM speaking out more strongly for U.S. policies to help end hunger in the world? They do lobby the U.S. government to provide free trade in agriculture, but are not strong voices for poverty-focused aid.

General Mills, the American Association of Grocery Manufacturers, and some other food industry organizations support the Food Research and Action Center (FRAC). FRAC is the most stalwart lobby for the Food Stamp Program, and grocers and some food producers have a self-interest stake in the Food Stamp Program. It is surprising these corporations have not done more in response to the dramatic shrinkage of the Food Stamp Program since 1995.

In general, corporate lobbying focuses mainly on immediate self-interest issues, such as industry-specific regulations. Ben & Jerry's is the best known company that has made support for social reform part of its business. Ben Cohen, the CEO, is currently leading a creative campaign to shift U.S. budget priorities from military to social spending.

Haworth, Inc., Europe Through the Back Door, and Mastercard International have been among the corporate pioneers in support of advocacy for hungry people. If a few more companies would provide leadership toward ending hunger – not just helping hungry individuals, but supporting social change – that would be an important new development in the politics of hunger.

DON WALTER, a Mickey Leland Hunger Fellow with the Congressional Hunger Center, served a policy placement with Bread for the World Institute in 1999. E-mail: dwalter@yahoo.com.
DAVID BECKMANN is president of Bread for the World and BFW Institute. E-mail: institute@bread.org.

Hunger in a Global Economy: Hunger 1998 discussed the powerful effect that economic globalization is having on hunger and politics everywhere. The global economy is pushing down the wages of working people in the developed countries, and global competition is also disruptive for many vulnerable people in developing countries.

But the growing, increasingly interdependent global economy is also conducive to economic growth and new opportunity for many poor people. Politically, the global economy makes people in the developed countries more aware of their interdependence with developing countries and, thus, provides new reasons to help address developing country problems.

The sustained expansion of the global economy has brought extraordinary prosperity to many people in the United States and other developed countries, and this prosperity may make people more inclined to share. Sustained growth in the 1960s set the stage for President Johnson's War on Poverty. It is hopeful that presidential candidates from both U.S. political parties in 1999 are sounding themes of compassion and fairness.

The Changing Politics of Hunger: Hunger 1999 also noted two other international trends in politics – the dramatic spread of democracy around the world since the early 1980s and the increasing power of mass media. In 1988, 66 countries were electoral democracies. In 1998, 117 countries were electoral democracies, and democracy helps to make governments responsive to social needs.[11] The growing power of the media is a two-edged sword. It has made advertising and, thus, money more important in politics everywhere, but strong mass media also improve the level of public knowledge about social issues and foreign affairs. Dramatic improvements in electronic technology open new opportunities for grassroots organizing and advocacy (See "Internet Organizing," p. 89).

What is different this time?

Many people realized in the 1970s that hunger could be ended. A National Academy of Sciences study and a Presidential Commission on Hunger both confirmed this conclusion.[12] At the World Food Conference of 1974, Secretary of State Henry Kissinger promised, "that within a decade, no child will go to bed hungry."[13]

This new awareness spawned many anti-hunger groups, including Bread for the World. Another anti-hunger group, The Hunger Project, committed itself to ending hunger by the year 2000 and convinced tens of thousands of people to join them in that commitment.

A series of studies and statements since then have confirmed that hunger could indeed be ended. But it has not happened. So what is different this time?

The Hunger Project was over-optimistic that hunger would be ended by 2000. The world's experience since the 1970s has provided more evidence about approaches that effectively reduce hunger. So we can now say with even more confidence that ending hunger is feasible. But unless many people and key nations take action to end hunger, hunger could well persist.

And this report's program to end hunger is different than earlier reports along these lines, mainly in that our program includes actions to empower hungry people and, in other ways, build political will. Early steps toward ending hunger must build political capacity to push for further change. Otherwise, the rest of the needed investment will never be secured.

© Margie Woodson Nea

Ten Priority Areas for Action[14]

As Bread for the World and BFW Institute have repeatedly analyzed strategies to change how U.S. politics affects hungry people, we have become convinced that the following ten lines of action are especially promising. These priority areas are where we suggest concerned people invest their efforts:

1. *Religious communities can teach social concern and active citizenship.* U.S. churches and other religious communities are mobilizing massive efforts to help hungry people, mainly direct assistance. But they could do much more to teach that God requires social justice as well as individual charity. Bread for the World is a Christian citizens' movement, and the size and persistence of our membership confirms that religious faith can indeed inspire people to push for social justice – and keep at it for a lifetime.

2. *Individuals and agencies assisting hungry people can expand what they do to influence government policies.* The U.S. private feeding movement (food pantries and charitable feeding agencies) is very large. America's Second Harvest network alone includes 189 affiliated food banks, 50,000 agencies, with more than one million staff and volunteers, and feeds about 26 million hungry Americans 1 billion pounds of food each year.[15] During the 1990s, food banks have begun to speak out on public policies that are important to hungry people. The new president of America's Second Harvest, Deborah Leff, is committed to further expanding the network's efforts in public education and public policy.

Some U.S. PVOs that channel humanitarian and development assistance to developing countries have also become increasingly involved in advocacy. They have made advocacy the top priority of InterAction, the association of about 160 private voluntary organizations that work for international development. But these agencies, both domestic and international, still do far too little to speak up for the people they serve. Their leaders often realize the importance of public policy, and some of the best leaders of charity are involving their agencies and supporters in advocacy. The size, commitment and credibility of U.S. assistance agencies give them the potential to transform the politics of hunger.

Workers demonstrate for livable wages and welfare-to-work jobs with dignity.

3. *Anti-hunger advocacy agencies can be strengthened.* Bread for the World, RESULTS, and the Food Research Action Center (FRAC) are the main anti-hunger advocacy organizations at the national level. There are also anti-hunger and anti-poverty coalitions in many states. Investing volunteer time and financial contributions in advocacy organizations is a high-impact way to reduce hunger.

4. *Low-income people's organizations can be strengthened.* We will not end hunger until more poor and hungry people become politically active in defense of their own interests. Voter registration drives and low-income community organizing are of fundamental importance. Similarly, grassroots groups and representative governments in developing countries are key actors in the global politics of hunger. They speak with authority about their own needs and priorities. Concerned individuals and groups can invest in organizations that empower struggling people.

Achieving a Victory Over Hunger

By J. Larry Brown

During the early decades of this century, the United States and other industrial nations experienced unprecedented success in lowering the rates of disease and death among their populations. Many of the great killer diseases of previous centuries were corralled sufficiently to reduce mortality rates more dramatically than any time in human history. Babies were far less likely to die at birth, and the life spans of adults increased by decades.

What is most notable about this progress, however, is not that it happened but *how* it happened. Surprisingly, the synthesis of sulfas and other miracle drugs played only a small role. Rather, this astounding period of progress occurred as the direct result of governmental actions that we now refer to as public health measures: purified water, flush toilets, garbage pick-up, refrigeration of foods, workplace safety rules, pollution measures, and regulation of food handling. In short, this miraculous time was due not to the magic of wonder drugs but to the magic of human endeavor – thousands of people in thousands of communities in many nations working in concert to achieve a common goal: the passage of laws to protect human life. This national effort worked, and it greatly improved the quality of life for all time.

With this record of human progress, it is difficult to understand why we do not extend similar life-sustaining protections to all citizens. It is especially hard, for example, to explain why we have a world where people still go hungry, especially when there is a global abundance of food. And it is even more difficult to explain the existence of the disease we call hunger in the world's most wealthy and most scientifically advanced nation. After all, assuring that all Americans have access to an abundant food supply is not nearly as daunting as was reducing disease and death in the early part of the century.

It is not that we Americans do not care about hunger; after all both public opinion polls and the existence of charitable food programs in virtually every community speak of great compassion and concern. But perhaps we think about the problem incorrectly. We are so accustomed to mounting "emergency food programs" in community after community that the sheer human effort it entails, and the satisfaction derived by the modern-day saints who handle its operations, may have obscured cause and effect, problem and solution.

The simple truth is that no modern nation has ever solved the problem of hunger through charitable efforts, one community at a time. It is not the way to protect the well-being of a democratic people in a wealthy democracy. Some protections inevitably are more properly within the governmental domain, particularly when we understand government as the collective manifestation of public will. We recognize, for example, that the defense of the nation is the responsibility of the

5. *Organizations of people of color can be strengthened, and other organizations that help low-income people can more fully engage people of color.* Within the United States, hunger is especially prevalent among people of color. So when racial groups win fair treatment and advancement, that helps reduce hunger. African-Americans can also be strong advocates for Africa. The Congressional Black Caucus is already the strongest defender of African interests within the U.S. government. Latinos will probably become a strong advocacy voice for Latin America. As Figure 5.1 shows, African-Americans and especially Hispanics are becoming larger elements in the U.S. population and will become more important politically in the years to come.

6. *The media can move beyond stories of pity and charity to explain the causes of hunger, and people and organizations concerned about hunger can make a bigger effort to influence the media.* U.S. mass media do not devote much attention to hunger, and their stories are most often stories of pity and charity. This narrow, human-interest viewpoint is partly because the organizations that are working to overcome hunger do not usually make much effort to influence the media, and what effort they do make is typically organizational self-promotion. Additional resources invested in anti-hunger media work could make a big difference. Almost any person, with training from an organization such as Bread for the World or RESULTS, can influence how newspapers,

© Earl Dotter

federal government. It would make no sense to abolish the Defense Department and tell every community to defend itself and its families through volunteer militias. Similarly, it makes no sense to leave the nutritional well-being of our population to the vagaries of local charity. Defending against hunger is no less important a governmental responsibility than is defending against other threats to the well-being of our people.

To be certain, charitable food efforts are vital currently, but precisely because governmental leaders are not doing their jobs. But the genuine love evinced by the efforts of charitable food volunteers must not cloud the fact that charity is an indignity to the hungry. Charity is not a reciprocal act like love; love binds but charity distances. Love arouses passion, charity suspicion. Love enables, charity disables. Love personalizes, charity depersonalizes. No matter how well-meant the effort, it is an indignity for an adult to have to rely on others to feed his family.

We would do well to re-focus our vision from that of a nation which pitches in to feed the hungry to that of a nation which has no hungry to feed. The well-meaning efforts of food charities have become the hydra that obscures our vision of a nation whose people are protected from both the threat and reality of hunger. While charity feeds the hungry today, it has become the basis for governmental complacency in ending hunger tomorrow. Governmental leaders speak about the "limits of government" and the "miracles of the voluntary sector" as the excuse for not promulgating public policies to end hunger as other industrial nations have done so successfully. The existence of charity has corrupted politics, turning public officials from hunger fighters into timid pacifists who urge that we let the poor glean leftovers from the fields. Political leaders have become cheerleaders for charity, and charity has become the public pablum that excuses their lack of leadership.

The challenge before us – churches and synagogues, business and labor, Republicans and Democrats – is to recognize that emergency food programs are not a sign of success but of political failure. Our challenge is to compel our leaders to lead so that America can join the sisterhood of modern nations that protect their people from hunger, the world's original public health threat.

DR. J. LARRY BROWN is Professor of Nutrition and Health Policy and Director of the Tufts University Center on Hunger and Poverty. Web site: www.tufts.edu/nutrition/centeronhunger

Figure 5.1: The Changing Face of the U.S.

The U.S. Hispanic population rose from 4 million in 1950 to 27 million in 1995 – about one in every 11 Americans. It will rise to 95 million in 2050, or about one in every four Americans.

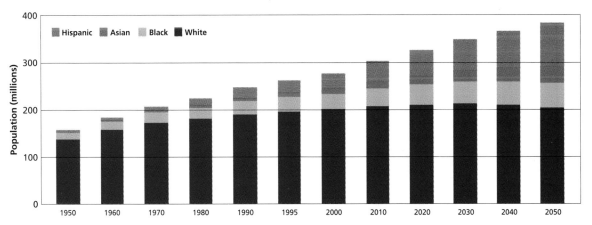

radio and television stations in his or her community cover the problem of hunger.

7. *Students, colleges, and universities can be enlisted in the struggle against hunger and poverty.* Students, colleges and universities have been active in nearly every successful movement for social change. While many of today's students are involved in community charities, they tend to have an even more skeptical view of politics and government than the U.S. population in general. Political conservatives have invested heavily in influencing students. For example, the InterCollegiate Studies Institute, the leading right-wing campus umbrella group, has an annual budget of over $5 million. The Institute works to persuade students that government anti-poverty programs are ineffective or even harmful.

Bread for the World, the Student Campaign Against Hunger and Homelessness, and others are working – but on a much smaller scale – to engage students in civic action on hunger issues. Since 1996, the AFL-CIO's Union Summer has placed almost 2,000 students in union internships across the country – and, as an unexpected by-product, inspired a spontaneous and surprisingly strong

© Rick Reinhard

We need...to create a **political** environment where the parties will compete to **convince** the **voters** of the **merits** of their approach to ending hunger.

anti-sweatshop movement at campuses across the country.[16] This example suggests what an expanded anti-hunger organizing effort among students might achieve.

8. *Voters and political leaders can inject hunger and poverty concerns into electoral politics, so that elected officials more often provide leadership in overcoming hunger.* Under President Clinton's leadership, much of the Democratic Party's leadership stopped talking very much about poverty. During the same period, the Republican leadership of Congress became much more vocal about the purported moral irresponsibility of poor people and the corrupting influence of government assistance. We need instead to create a political environment where the parties will compete to convince the voters of the merits of their approach to ending hunger – as they do now on the issue of education. This result will happen if people committed to overcoming hunger get active in electoral politics, contributing time and money to candidates who want to help end hunger.

9. *A clear and fresh anti-hunger policy agenda should be developed that can draw people from across political and ideological lines.* This report is a step forward in this area. In the past, Bread for the World and the Institute have shown how a wide range of policy issues affect hungry people, but we have never before proposed a program to

© Celia Escudero-Espadas

end hunger. Doing so has entailed making judgments about which plausible policy changes would have the biggest impact. We hope this report will help develop a clear and compelling policy agenda for the anti-hunger movement as a whole. We hope it will convince people across the political spectrum that the costs of ending hunger are not prohibitive. We mean this report to be a step in the broader discussion, and welcome alternative proposals from various ideological perspectives. We also expect to learn from innovation and experience with anti-hunger efforts in the years ahead.

10. *People and organizations working against hunger and poverty should think of themselves as part of a large, potentially dynamic movement.* Tens of thousands of U.S. organizations are helping hungry and poor people. Virtually every church in the country is running food drives and taking up offerings to help hungry people. Hundreds of large agencies, both domestic and international, seek donations from the U.S. public. These efforts usually go on independently, and the people involved often feel overwhelmed by the needs they face. But these dispersed efforts could coalesce into a mighty movement. That depends on people and organizations coming to think of themselves as part of a larger movement of social concern and together working for a shift in U.S. culture and politics.

The movement will not be tidy or neatly defined. We can each pray for and work for a movement, but no one can organize a true movement or be in charge when it happens. Millions of people are gripped by the scandal of widespread hunger and might think of themselves as an anti-hunger movement. Others focus on children, poverty or fairness. But these issues are all interrelated and complementary.

A number of national anti-hunger organizations are talking together about the possibility of a campaign to end hunger. This initiative would be bigger than any one organization. The campaign could include coordinated efforts along the ten lines of action outlined here.

Whatever happens at the national level, it is crucial that individuals across the country commit themselves to help overcome hunger and begin taking action. Chapter 6 is about what each of us can do.

DAVID BECKMANN is president of Bread for the World and Bread for the World Institute.
E-mail: institute@bread.org.

Law as Catalyst in the Eradication of Hunger

BY JOHN TETON

A small network of activists is pushing, with some success, for an eventual treaty that would make it illegal, under international law, for national governments to allow widespread hunger to persist. This proposed treaty would formalize global awareness that hunger can be ended and put added pressure on governments that neglect the problem.

The International Food Security Treaty (IFST) would establish an enforceable international legal guarantee of the right to be free from hunger, and oblige governments to establish and implement their own related national laws. The treaty (accessible at **www.treaty.org**) specifies legal responsibilities nations share to prevent starvation and malnutrition, and associated monitoring and enforcement mechanisms. For example, the deliberate use of starvation as a weapon – a tactic that led to the simultaneous famines in Bosnia and Somalia in 1992 – would be prohibited. The draft IFST also calls for creating a global food reserve and resource center for emergency assistance, and allows both individuals and nongovernmental organizations to bring complaints to U.N. agencies when governments fail to uphold the right to be free from hunger.

The IFST is now seven years into an estimated period of twenty to thirty years necessary for its evolution from initial conception to near-universal acceptance. Attention is now focusing on what steps must be taken to make the Treaty a reality. The history of existing global agreements on such issues as armed conflict (e.g., the Geneva Conventions) and the environment (e.g., the Law of the Sea and treaties on biodiversity and endangered species), suggest the five-phase process illustrated in the figure on p. 101. The timeline reflects an estimate of how long will be necessary for each phase, as well as a "fast-track" alternative, recognizing the potential for swift historical change, like the collapse of the Soviet Union and the end of apartheid.

The Five Phases of IFST Evolution

Phase 1: Concept Development (7 years)

Phase I, recently completed, focused on constructing and circulating the IFST Principles, gathering a critical mass of expert opinion, drafting the principles into Treaty form, and organizing a network of supporters among leading figures in the United Nations, anti-hunger organizations, government officials, religious groups and grassroots volunteers.[1]

Phase 2: Proposal to the United Nations (1-2 years)

The IFST must be formally brought to the table that counts in treaty-making: the global community of national governments. Formal sponsorship will be established by one or more governments and/or by an intergovernmental organization like the U.N. Food and Agricultural Organization, and debate begun within the United Nations.

Phase 3: Initial Ratifications (2-3 years)

The IFST would come into force when 20 governments have ratified it. Once one or more nations have committed to the Treaty through the act of sponsorship, recruiting the next nineteen could prove a relatively easy matter.

Phase 4: Early Treaty Era (3 years)

This is the only phase with a pre-set time limit built into the draft Treaty. Within three years after coming into force, individual nations must: (1) establish their own laws criminalizing the use of hunger as a weapon and insuring access to food for those unable to obtain it on their own; (2) participate in the functioning of the world food reserve and resource center; (3) file the first round of triennial reports to the United Nations on their progress and plans to implement the IFST; and (4) support any food security monitoring or enforcement actions proven necessary within the United Nations. At the same time, governments, organizations, and individuals will continue urging all nations to support the Treaty.

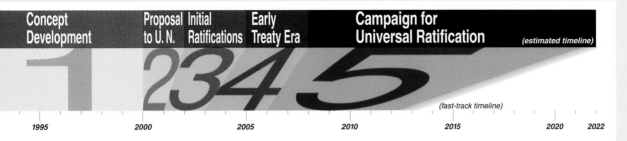

| Concept Development | Proposal to U.N. | Initial Ratifications | Early Treaty Era | Campaign for Universal Ratification | (estimated timeline) |

(fast-track timeline)

1995   2000   2005   2010   2015   2020   2022

Phase 5: Campaign for Universal Ratification (7-14 years)

In order for the right to be free from hunger to be fully protected, all remaining countries must be persuaded to sign and support the Treaty.

Prescription for Individual Action

Individual citizens in every country can contribute to the effort in small and large ways:

1. *Lobbying* government officials to urge their active support of the IFST, and

2. *Spreading the word* about the IFST among neighbors, relatives, schoolmates, co-workers, and fellow members of religious and community organizations.[2]

History has shown that such citizen pressure – not the leadership of politicians – represents the primary source and engine for successful social change movements.

U.N. Under-Secretary General Maurice Strong – himself a principal initiator of the Laws on the Environment and Biodiversity among others – sees the IFST "as the centerpiece of a whole system by which the capacity of the Earth to feed its people is translated into a real commitment to do something, because there's no fundamental need for hunger now, and certainly none for starvation." But his optimism is tempered by this sage advice to IFST supporters:

> The timing for this kind of treaty won't get right unless people like you campaign for it. Initiatives like this – you could equate it to abolishing slavery or any one of a number of things – they do not occur overnight. They need to be championed by small groups of people who have strong connections and are prepared to prevail against a general mood of apathy.

JOHN TETON, director of the International Food Security Treaty Campaign, participated in the NGO Forum at the World Food Summit, and served as coordinator of the 1998 International Conference on Consensus Strategy for the Right to Food in Law. E-mail: treaty@worldnet.att.net.

[1] IFST supporters now include United Nations Under Secretary-General Maurice Strong, former U.N. Assistant Secretary-General Robert Muller, Chilean U.N. Ambassador Juan Somavia (Coordinator of the 1995 U.N. World Summit on Social Development), U.S. Senator Dianne Feinstein, and African anti-hunger leader Jean B. Bakole (International Representative for COASAD, le Coalition des Organisations Africaines pour la Souveraineté Alimentaire et le Developpement Durable).

[2] The International Food Security Treaty campaign serves as a resource and network for such activities.

History has shown that... **citizen pressure** ...represents the **primary** source and engine for **successful** social change movements.

CHAPTER 6

What You Can Do

BY MICHAEL RUBINSTEIN

Governments can be counted on to do the right thing, but only after they have exhausted all other possibilities.

Attributed to Abba Eban, Israeli statesman, 1915-

© Earl Dotter

Hunger, which affects more than 790 million people worldwide, is perhaps the most grievous moral blight on the conscience of the world. This report has stressed steps that governments, especially the U.S. government, could take to cut in half the worst aspects of hunger and poverty worldwide by 2015.

There has been incremental progress in the fight to end hunger. But currently the political will to implement a program to end hunger is missing.

If it is possible to end hunger, why is it not happening? After all, isn't the purpose of government to take action against the most serious problems faced by the people of this country? Isn't that why we elect leaders to represent us?

The sad truth is that the knowledge of how to end hunger by itself is insufficient. The ability to eradicate killer diseases like measles and polio is not enough to see them disappear. The ability to prevent nutritional deficiencies among children does not mean that children will no longer suffer from them. The amazing success of anti-poverty strategies like microcredit, does not mean that such programs will be implemented.

Without the political commitment to use the tools at hand, they will not be used – and this program, mere words on a paper, will be nothing more than a collection of good ideas. We could say that the program to end hunger begins with government. But because we live in a democracy, it really begins with you.

Every lasting political change in this country spawning a new era of social justice – from women's suffrage to the 1960s civil rights legislation – was spearheaded by ordinary people who organized for action. That is what it takes to get our political process to respond.

But with the increasing power of money in politics, it is very easy for the ordinary person to feel that he or she cannot have an impact on the political process. It is not hard to believe that our individual vote does not really matter, that we are powerless to influence the process.

In reality, you – as a single individual – do not make a difference. Sitting in your living room, complaining about all of the world's problems, you cannot change anything. Only when you join forces with others who share your commitment, can you make a difference. Working within an effective social justice organization, you get to vote, not just every two years, but every time you take action. Every letter you write, every meeting with an elected official, every piece you get published in your local newspaper represents your vote for a socially just world.

Of course, our ability to have an impact is not limited to political action. We also express our values through what we buy and how we invest our

> Every **lasting** political change in this country spawning a new era of **social justice**... was spearheaded by **ordinary** people who **organized** for **action**.

money. Every time you purchase clothing that was manufactured under a certified code of conduct, you vote for fair wages and good working conditions. With each investment you make in a socially responsible mutual fund, you vote for corporations that uphold environmental and labor standards.

The following list of organizations and companies address one or more of the issues raised in this report. You can contact any of them to participate in their work. This list is by no means complete; space would only allow us to choose a few representative organizations in each category. The World Wide Web is a powerful tool for you to find more organizations in which you can get involved. Use this information to turn these good ideas into action.

And remember: vote early and vote often.

MICHAEL RUBINSTEIN is local media associate with Bread for the World. E-mail: mrubinstein@bread.org

Advocacy and Community Organizing

Bread for the World (BFW)

Bread for the World is a nonpartisan Christian citizens' movement that seeks justice for the world's hungry people by lobbying our nation's decision makers. Its mission is to bring about changes in public policy to address the root causes of hunger and poverty in the United States and overseas. Bread for the World focuses on using the power its members have as citizens in a democracy to influence how government decisions affect hungry people. Its 44,000 members contact their members of Congress about legislation that affects hungry people in the United States or worldwide. Bread for the World is the largest grassroots advocacy network on hunger issues.

BFW members have won many legislative victories. In 1998, due to the work of Bread for the World, Congress passed the *Africa: Seeds of Hope Act*, a bill that targets aid to support the efforts of small-scale farmers in sub-Saharan Africa to increase their incomes and crop production (see p. 77). That same year, Congress restored food stamps to 250,000 legal immigrants, due to the lobbying of Bread for the World and other organizations.

There are four ways to participate in Bread for the World.

Become a member

Bread for the World's newsletter and action alerts offer concise, reliable information on legislation in Congress that is important to hungry people. Members are informed when their representatives sit on key committees and how they vote on hunger issues. To become a member, contact the BFW office nearest you.

Involve your church

Every year, hundreds of churches across the nation generate tens of thousands of letters to their members of Congress, calling on them to support specific anti-hunger legislation. A letter-writing event during or after a service allows your church to connect its spiritual life with effective social justice action. To find out how to do an Offering of Letters in your church, contact the national office to order the Offering of Letters handbook.

Sen. Sam Brownback (R-KS) meets with constituents from the Kansas City Church of God in Christ. The group encouraged him to support debt relief and introduce a companion bill in the Senate.

Become an activist

Bread for the World is a lively grassroots presence in hundreds of local communities. You can join or form a BFW group in your church or community. BFW members who meet together learn and draw strength from each other. They become more active. Some BFW groups meet monthly for worship, study or action. Others meet just a few times a year to take specific action – to see their member of Congress, for example, or to plan a workshop for local congregations on BFW's main campaign for the year. Contact your regional organizer to find out about groups in your area. In most congressional districts, volunteers have organized telephone trees at key points in the legislative process.

Contribute financially

It takes money to educate and organize people effectively on hunger issues.

National office:

Bread for the World
1100 Wayne Avenue, Suite 1000
Silver Spring, MD 20910
Phone: (301) 608-2400 or (800) 82-BREAD
E-mail: bread@bread.org
Web site: **www.bread.org**

Regional offices:

Pasadena, CA
Phone: (625) 568-3233
E-mail: breadca@igc.org

Charleston, SC
Phone: (843) 579-9900
E-mail: breadsouth@igc.org

Chicago, IL
Phone: (312) 629-9529
E-mail: breadchicago@igc.org

Minneapolis, MN
Phone: (612) 871-9084
E-mail: breadmn@igc.org

Transforming Anti-Hunger Leadership (TAHL)

Bread for the World Institute supports Transforming Anti-Hunger Leadership programs in many communities and 14 states. These programs bring together leaders from various organizations that deal with hunger and poverty for leadership training, collective planning and coalition building. TAHL has improved the racial and income diversity of leadership in the anti-hunger movement. It is also helping to build state and local coalitions that speak up for hungry people in state capitals.

Local TAHL groups include: Detroit, MI, Milwaukee, WI, Minneapolis, MN, Missoula, MT, New Orleans, LA, Philadelphia, PA, Phoenix, AZ, Portland, ME, Tampa Bay, FL, and Wichita, KS.

Transforming Anti-Hunger Leadership Program
Bread for the World Institute
1100 Wayne Avenue, Suite 1000
Silver Spring, MD 20910
Phone: (301) 608-2400 or (800) 82-BREAD
E-mail: transforming.leadership@bread.org
Web site: **www.bread.org**

RESULTS

RESULTS is an international grassroots lobby creating the political will to end hunger and poverty. With groups in the United States, Australia, Canada, Japan and the United Kingdom, RESULTS influences hundreds of members of Congress and Parliament to support effective anti-hunger and poverty programs. In the United States, RESULTS has about 80 "global" groups that lobby for child survival and microcredit programs and work to improve the policies of the World Bank and IMF. Approximately 50 "domestic" groups in the United States work for federal support for WIC, Head Start and U.S.-based microcredit programs. RESULTS' volunteers receive extensive training to learn how to lobby members of Congress and to generate editorials in their local newspapers. Partly because of the work of RESULTS volunteers, Congress has dramatically increased funding for child survival and microcredit programs.

Microcredit Summit

Over 2,900 people, representing 1,500 organizations from 137 countries, participated in the Microcredit Summit in Washington, DC, on February 2-4, 1997. Organized by RESULTS Education Fund, the Summit launched a nine-year campaign to reach 100 million of the world's poorest families, especially the women of those families, with credit for self-employment and other financial and business services by 2005. People can participate in the Microcredit Summit fulfillment campaign by enrolling the institution where they work or volunteer to support the goals of the summit. Examples of institutions that can join include schools, clubs, professional and civic associations, places of worship, corporations, banks and local governments.

RESULTS
440 First Street, NW, Suite 400
Washington, DC 20001
Phone: (202) 783-7100
E-mail: results@action.org
Web site: **www.action.org**

Microcredit Summit Project
c/o RESULTS Educational Fund
440 First Street, NW, Suite 460
Washington, DC 20001
Phone: (202) 637-9600
E-mail: microcredit@igc.org
Web site: **www.microcreditsummit.org**

Jubilee 2000/USA Campaign

Part of an international campaign to cancel the unpayable international debts of the world's highly indebted poor countries, Jubilee 2000/USA works to influence U.S. policy on debt relief. Jubilee2000/USA supports the advocacy and media efforts of grassroots groups across the nation. Bread for the World is a member of Jubilee 2000/USA.

Jubilee 2000/USA
222 East Capitol Street, NE
Washington, DC 20003
Phone: (202) 783-3566
E-mail: coord@j2000usa.org
Web site: **www.j2000usa.org/j2000**

Industrial Areas Foundation (IAF)

The Industrial Areas Foundation builds on the work of the renowned community organizer Saul Alinsky. The IAF empowers volunteers in communities to have an impact on local issues that affect the quality of life. Volunteers are trained in the nuts and bolts of community organizing, including relationship-building, influencing legislators and media work. The IAF approach to organizing stresses building powerful local organizations that include religious congregations representing a diverse cross-section of the community.

IAF has affiliated organizations in metropolitan areas throughout the United States. For example, BUILD, an IAF-affiliate in Baltimore, successfully lobbied for a requirement that contractors for the city government be required to pay workers a living wage.

Industrial Areas Foundation
220 West Kinzie, 5th floor
Chicago, IL 60610
Phone: (312) 245-9211

Workers' Rights

National Labor Committee (NLC)

By focusing pressure on corporations, the National Labor Committee strives to end labor and human rights violations, ensure a living wage, and help workers and their families live and work with dignity. The NLC works with a strong network of local, national, and international groups to build coalitions that use popular campaigns to promote labor rights and pressure companies to adhere to existing national and international labor and human rights standards.

The NLC exposed the appalling working conditions of factories that made clothing for the Kathie Lee label and prompted Kathie Lee Gifford to monitor and improve the treatment of workers.

National Labor Committee
275 7th Avenue, 15th floor
New York, NY 10001
Phone: (212) 242-3002
E-mail: nlc@nlcnet.org
Web site: **www.nlcnet.org**

Protecting labor rights is key to winning a livable wage.

United Students Against Sweatshops (USAS)

With activities on over 150 university campuses nationwide, United Students Against Sweatshops has sparked a growing wave of student activism. USAS targets companies that produce clothing for colleges and universities. Students pressure their schools to purchase college gear only from companies that abide by Codes of Conduct guaranteeing the protection of the basic human rights of workers. Students advocate for four important provisions that enable a Code to truly protect workers' basic rights: full public disclosure, enforcement of the rights of women, independent monitoring, and a living wage.

USAS has won remarkable concessions, for example:

- As of September 1999, students at over 15 major universities have won full public disclosure of factory locations, a necessary step for monitoring the compliance of factories.

- Seventeen universities have added living wage language to their Code of Conduct – agreeing to devote resources to determining and implementing a living wage to meet their workers' basic human needs. This step would allow many workers who produce college apparel offshore to receive increased wages.

United Students Against Sweatshops (USAS)
1413 K Street, NW 9th floor
Washington, DC 20005
Phone: (202) NO SWEAT or (202) 667-9328
Web site: **www.umich.edu/~sole/usassy1/
index.html**

Socially Responsible Investing/ Shopping

EthicalShopper.com

EthicalShopper.com is an on-line shopping mall that sells socially and environmentally responsible products. The company carefully screens all products offered to ensure the manufacturing processes, conditions of the workers, and environmental impact of the products are in keeping with EthicalShopper.com's mandate. Its goal is to provide Internet users with a one-stop shopping site where their consumer dollars will support only good causes by companies committed to preventing environmental pollution or social harm.

Founded in 1999, the company's web site sells clothing and products for baby care, kids, body and spa, travel, the kitchen, and the garden. It also offers an "eco-supermarket" that includes cleaning supplies (including environmentally-safe cleaners and insecticides), pet care and food.

The site provides detailed information on each product, revealing why EthicalShopper.com chose to feature it to consumers.

> **EthicalShopper.com**
> 2330 Westwood Blvd., Suite 107
> Los Angeles, CA 90064.
> Phone: (310) 475-2492 or (877) 4-e-ethic
>   (877-433-8442)
> E-mail: rachel@ethicalshopper.com
> Web site: **www.ethicalshopper.com**

SocialFunds.com

SocialFunds.com is an Internet-based business that serves the investment needs of socially responsible investors and empowers them with the resources they need to make informed decisions regarding their investments. Its web site provides financial education, investment research, investment analysis and recommendations, professional financial services and industry news.

SocialFunds.com, together with the Interfaith Center on Corporate Responsibility, has developed the Shareholder Activism Center, an interactive web-based tool which provides extensive coverage of shareholder resolutions pertaining to the environment, corporate governance, global finance, human rights, militarism, health, and equality. If you own stock in a company, the Shareholder Activism Center can assist you in the process of voting, and it provides all of the information you need to quickly and easily contact the company and let management know how you feel about a particular issue, policy or behavior.

In 1999, socially concerned investors – including religious shareholders, foundations, mutual funds, social investment managers, pension funds, and others – filed approximately 220 resolutions with over 150 major U.S. companies.

> **SocialFunds.com**
> 41 Beetlestone Hill Road
> Williamsville, VT 05362
> Web site: **www.socialfunds.com**

Calvert Social Investment Foundation

With Calvert Community Investments from the Calvert Social Investment Foundation, you can invest in community development programs that assist impoverished communities in becoming vital and strong again. By purchasing a Community Investment Note at an amount of $1,000 or higher, you earn a financial rate of return of up to three percent.

Through microcredit programs, your money is lent to help people start or strengthen their own businesses. Through affordable housing programs, your money builds and refurbishes housing that people can afford to buy or rent. Through community development loan programs your money is lent to create more jobs, provide good daycare and reinforce locally-owned businesses in troubled communities.

The foundation also offers a way to invest in development programs in Bangladesh. With Grameen Investments, your investment helps to build upon the microcredit success of the Grameen Bank, which has disbursed $2.5 billion in small loans to over 2 million families, with a cumulative repayment rate of 98 percent. Grameen investments supports a broad-reaching and visionary group of Grameen projects such as microcredit, health and sanitation facilities, renewable sources of energy for unpowered villages, and affordable village cellular pay phone networks. With these projects, you can earn up to three percent on your investment.

The Calvert Social Investment Foundation is a nonprofit organization, not to be confused with Calvert Group, socially-responsible mutual funds.

Calvert Social Investment Foundation
4550 Montgomery Avenue
Bethesda, MD 20814
Phone: (800) 239-5911
E-mail: foundation@calvertgroup.com
Web site: **www.calvertgroup.com/foundation**

Campaign Finance

Common Cause

Common Cause is a nonprofit, nonpartisan citizen's lobbying organization promoting open, honest and accountable government and the right of all citizens to be involved in shaping our nation's public policies.

The organization has been a leader in developing support for legislation to ban the use of "soft money," donations to political parties that indirectly support candidates for national office. Political fund-raisers use soft money to get around limits on the size of donations that can legally be given to individual candidates, allowing corporations, unions and wealthy individuals to make substantial contributions to political parties to benefit candidates of a particular party.

Common Cause has been lobbying for passage of the Shays-Meehan bill, which passed the U.S. House of Representatives on September 14, 1999. A companion bill in the U.S. Senate, sponsored by Senators McCain (R-AZ) and Feingold (D-WI), was defeated. Both bills would end the soft money system by prohibiting candidates and national political parties from raising soft money, and by prohibiting state political parties from spending soft money on activities that affect federal elections.

Common Cause
1250 Connecticut Avenue, NW, #600
Washington, DC 20036
Phone: (202) 833-1200
Web site: **www.commoncause.org**

Public Campaign

Public Campaign is a nonprofit, nonpartisan organization dedicated to sweeping reform that aims to reduce dramatically the role of special interest money in America's elections and the influence of big contributors in U.S. politics. Public Campaign works with state and local organizations, particularly citizen groups, which are fighting for campaign finance reform in their states. Its goal is to build a network of state-based efforts and create a powerful national force for federal reform.

Public Campaign provides support to groups to lobby for "Clean Money Campaign Reform." This approach provides a model for both federal and state races. Various Clean Money Campaign Reforms have already passed in Maine and Vermont. Here is how it works: candidates agree to limit their spending and reject contributions from private sources. In return, the candidates receive a set amount of public funds to run for office. Federal candidates would also receive a prescribed amount of free and discounted TV and radio time.

Public Campaign offers a variety of resources, including:

- Educational materials on the pros and cons of various reform measures, how a Clean Money system works, passage of the Clean Elections Act in Maine, and related reform activities in other states and in Congress;

- Organizers' and Citizen Activists' Tool Kits filled with materials for people who want to promote Clean Money-type reform in their states and communities; and

- Technical assistance in organizing public education and drafting Clean Money Campaign Reform legislation at the state and local levels.

Public Campaign
1320 19th Street, NW, Suite M-1
Washington, DC 20036
Phone: (202) 293-0222
E-mail: info@publicampaign.org
Web site: **www.publicampaign.org**

Sustainable Agriculture and Community Gardening

The Community Food Security Coalition

The Coalition's mission is to promote comprehensive community-based solutions to the nation's food, farming and nutrition problems. Community members work together to find local solutions to problems of hunger and nutrition (see "From Farm to Table," pp. 52-53). Contact the coalition to find out how you can get involved in efforts in your community.

> **The Community Food Security Coalition**
> P.O. Box 209
> Venice, CA 90294
> Phone: (310) 822-5410
> E-mail: asfisher@aol.com
> Web site: **www.foodsecurity.org**

American Community Gardening Association (ACGA)

The most comprehensive community gardening association in the United States, ACGA is a national nonprofit membership organization of professionals, volunteers and supporters of community greening in urban and rural communities.

> **American Community Gardening Association (ACGA)**
> 100 N. 20th Street, 5th Floor
> Philadelphia, PA 19103-1495
> Phone: (215) 988-8785
> E-mail: smccabe@pennhort.org
> Web site: **www.communitygarden.org**

We stand by as children starve by the millions because we lack the will to eliminate hunger. Yet we have the will to develop missiles capable of flying over the polar cap and landing within a few hundred feet of their target. This is not innovation. It is a profound distortion of humanity's purpose on earth.

— MARK HATFIELD,
FORMER U.S. SENATOR (R-OR)

Appendices

The Costs of Ending U.S. Hunger: A Technical Note

BY JOHN T. COOK

A Food Assistance Approach

An estimate of the "food gap" can be derived by comparing food expenditures made by households with incomes at 185 percent of poverty to those for households with incomes below this level. The U.S. Bureau of Labor Statistics' (BLS) Consumer Expenditure Survey (CES) provides data on annual expenditures for food by households at different income levels.[1] Using these CES data on average annual food expenditures, estimates were produced of the additional value of food expenditures that would be made if all food-insecure households in poverty purchased food at the level of an average household with income at 185 percent of poverty. Carrying out these calculations also for food-insecure households with incomes between 100 percent and 130 percent of poverty, and between 130 percent and 185 percent, and combining the additional food expenditures projected if all these food-insecure households had incomes at 185 percent of poverty provides an estimate of the cost of the additional food needed to bring all food-insecure households up to food security. **That total "food gap" cost is $5.997 billion.**

Under the Food Assistance approach, the additional food would have to be collected or purchased, stored and distributed. These processes would involve operations costs. Assuming these costs would be the same as for the food bank network, additional operations costs of $906.499 million would be incurred to get the food into the needy households. **Combining the estimates for the "food gap" costs and additional operations costs yields an estimated total additional cost of $6.903 billion to make all food-insecure households food secure**.

This additional cost of $6.903 billion would be added to the costs of the existing national public and private food assistance system. Based on information from USDA reports,[2] the House Ways and Means Committee's 1998 Green Book,[3] and analyses conducted by Cook and Brown,[4] estimates of the overall costs of the public (federal and state) and private food assistance components were produced for 1997, the latest year for which necessary data are available. In 1997, combined federal and state expenditures on food assistance activities amounted to $40.411 billion.

Accurate estimates of the total costs of the private food assistance component do not exist. However, using data from the 1997 Second Harvest Research Study,[5] the 1998 International Food Bank Directory,[6] Second Harvest's 1995 Network Activity Report,[7] and the USDA website's Food Recovery and Gleaning page State Resource List,[8] an estimate of the total dollar value of this component in 1997 was produced. This estimate (details available from the author) amounts to $2.512 billion for 1997.

Combining the estimates of the total costs of the public and private components of the national food assistance system yields a combined total of $42.923 billion in 1997. Yet, even with the efforts and activities of this extensive hybrid national food assistance system, in 1998, more than 10 million American households containing over 31 million people – 12 million of whom were children – were food insecure. In 3.6 million households, with 6.1 million adults and 3.2 million children, there was measurable hunger. Clearly the existing national food assistance system is not able to provide sufficient food to eliminate food insecurity and hunger, though without it these problems would undoubtedly be far worse.

Combining the estimates of the dollar cost of the "food gap" from above with the estimate of the total dollar cost of the existing hybrid national food assistance system yields an estimate of the total cost of eliminating food insecurity and hunger in the short term. **That sum amounts to approximately $49.826 billion.** However, it should be noted that only about $6.9 billion of this amount is in addition to costs that are already being incurred.

A Food Security Income-Deficit Approach

Another approach to estimating the cost of ending food insecurity and hunger in the U.S. arises from federal poverty, food insecurity and hunger estimates derived using data from the Census Bureau's Current Population Survey (CPS). Results from the USDA's recent report on activities of the Food Security Measurement Project provide estimates of the level and prevalence of food insecurity and hunger for households by ratio of income to poverty (e.g., for households with incomes below 50 percent of poverty, below 100 percent of poverty, below 130 percent, below 185 percent, and 185 percent and above).[9] These food insecurity and hunger level and prevalence estimates are shown in Table A.1. Note that household income of 185 percent of

poverty appears to be a threshold beyond which the prevalences of food insecurity and hunger are very low. For households with incomes at or above 185 percent of the poverty threshold, the estimated prevalence of overall food insecurity is only 3.7 percent. Included among the 3.7 percent of households that are food insecure at some level are 1.2 percent of households in which measurable hunger occurred.

These data suggest that achieving the target of reducing hunger to zero and food insecurity without hunger to 5 percent of the U.S. population in five years time could be nearly achieved by ensuring that all households have incomes at or above 185 percent of the poverty threshold. Though this would certainly not be a trivial accomplishment, and would be tantamount to eliminating poverty in the U.S., an estimate of the cost of bringing food-insecure households up to that level of income can be derived using data on "income deficits" from the Census Bureau's latest poverty report.[10]

The empirical observation, emerging from the USDA Food Security Measurement Project, that very few households with incomes at or above 185 percent of their poverty thresholds are food insecure is consistent with findings from analysis of data from the National Health and Nutrition Examination Survey (NHANES III). In a study

---

Table A.1: Household Food Security, Food Insecurity and Hunger in the U.S. In 1998 by Ratio of Income to Poverty: All Households

Household Income-to-Poverty Ratio	Total (1000s)	Total Food Secure (1000s)	(%)	Total Food Insecure (1000s)	(%)	Total Food Insecure with Hunger (1000s)	(%)
Under 50%	5,205	3,187	61.2	2,018	38.8	816	15.7
Under 100%	12,358	7,980	64.6	4,378	35.4	1,666	13.5
Under 130%	18,018	12,261	68.0	5,757	32.0	2,127	11.8
Under 185%	29,540	21,985	74.4	7,555	25.6	2,685	9.1
185% and Over	61,775	59,482	96.3	2,293	3.7	735	1.2
Income Not Known	12,165	11,505	94.6	660	5.4	269	2.2

Source: USDA estimates based on data from the Food Security Supplement to the CPS.

using data on the USDA food sufficiency questions from the NHANES III to measure household food insufficiency (based on responses that the food eaten in the household is "sometimes or often not enough to eat"), Aliamo et al. found that only about one percent of households with incomes above 185 percent of poverty were food insufficient.[11] In another study examining income levels that enable families to achieve "self-sufficiency" under contemporary social welfare and tax policies, Pearce found that a typical family was able to meet basic needs with an income of 185 percent of the poverty threshold.[12]

The "income deficit," sometimes referred to as the "poverty gap," is a measure of the amount of money needed to raise a poor household's income up to 100 percent of the poverty threshold. It is the difference in dollars between a household's income and its' poverty threshold. Data on income deficits for different kinds of families are available from the Census Bureau's annual poverty report.[13] Though the income deficit varies for families of different types and sizes, the average deficit for all families with incomes below the poverty line in 1997 was $6,602. Inflating this average income deficit by the same percent used by the Census Bureau to update the 1997 poverty thresholds to preliminary 1998 thresholds yields an average income deficit for 1998 of $6,705. Applying this average value to the number of food insecure households with incomes below poverty from Table A.1 yields an estimate of the cost of bringing these households up to the poverty threshold. Using the preliminary poverty thresholds for 1998 published by the Census Bureau on its Internet web site (**www.census.gov**), it is also possible to calculate the average (for families of different sizes) amount of money representing 185 percent of poverty for food-insecure households.

Since the poverty thresholds vary by household size, it is necessary to estimate the average number of members in food-insecure households. Using estimates of the total number of individuals in all food-insecure households from the USDA's 1998 report on food security in the U.S., it is possible to calculate the average number of members of households that are food insecure without hunger, and a separate average for households where hunger was experienced. These calculations yield averages of 3.86 persons per household that is food insecure without hunger, and 2.70 people per household in which hunger is experienced. Taking a weighted average of these two household sizes, using the proportions of all food-insecure households that are food insecure without hunger and food insecure with hunger as weights, yields a weighted average household size of 3.54 people per food-insecure household. Extrapolating then between the values of 185 percent of poverty for households with three and four members yields a weighted average value of $27,689 for 185 percent of poverty for a food-insecure household. The difference between this value and the weighted average value of 100 percent of poverty for food insecure families ($14,967) is then **$27,689 – $14,967 = $12,722**.

Adding this amount to the inflated average 1998 "income deficit" of $6,705 yields an estimate of the amount of money needed to bring the average food-insecure household whose income is below 100 percent of poverty up to 185 percent of poverty. The result of this calculation is $12,722 + $6,705 = $19,427. Multiplying this value times the number of food-insecure households with incomes below 100 percent of poverty in 1998 from Table A.1 (4,378,000), yields an estimate of the total amount of money required to raise these households' incomes up to 185 percent of poverty. That amount is 4,378,000 households × $19,427 per household = $85.05 billion.

As Table A.1 indicates, there are also food-insecure households with incomes above the poverty threshold, though very few above 185 percent of poverty. Taking the differences between the numbers of food-insecure households below each value of the ratio of income to poverty in Table A.1 yields the number of food-insecure households with incomes between each ratio level (i.e., with incomes between 100 percent and 130 percent, and between 130 percent and 185 percent of poverty). Applying the same averaging and extrapolation procedures to these two groups of food-insecure households, and the dollar amounts representing incomes at the indicated ratios of income to poverty for average food-insecure households in these groups, provides similar estimates of the amount of money needed to bring the incomes of food-insecure households with incomes between 100 percent and 130 percent, and between 130 percent and 185 percent of poverty up to 185 percent of the poverty line. Without showing the details of these calculations (which are carried out in exactly the same manner as those for households with incomes below 100 percent of poverty), the results are $4,490 and $8,232 per household respectively.

Multiplying these two dollar amounts by the number of food-insecure households with incomes between 100 percent and 130 percent of poverty and between 130 percent and 185 percent respectively yields an additional amount of income needed to bring these households' incomes up to 185 percent of poverty. These calculations yield $17.54 billion and $16.47 billion. Adding these two values to the $85.05 billion estimated above provides an estimate of the total cost of raising all food-insecure households with incomes below 185 percent of poverty up to that level. This value represents an estimate of the cost of reducing the prevalence of overall food insecurity to about 3.7 percent, and that for hunger to about 1.2 percent by eliminating the "food security income-deficit." **The total cost of achieving this is $119.06 billion**.

If food-insecure households' incomes were raised to 185 percent of poverty, however, the need for food assistance would be reduced and the national food assistance system could be reduced in size. Thus part of the cost of this system ($42.923 billion from above) could be subtracted from the $119.06 billion "food security income-deficit." If we assume the need for food assistance disappears altogether and subtract the total cost of the existing food assistance system from $119.06 billion, it leaves a net income-deficit of $76.14 billion. If half the national food assistance system could be retired, the net cost would fall to $97.60 billion. These three values (i.e., $76.14 billion – $97.60 billion – $119.06 billion) thus represent an estimated range of the net costs of eliminating hunger in the U.S. using a "food security income-deficit" approach, assuming 100 percent, 50 percent, and 0 percent reductions in the cost of the existing food assistance system.

DR. JOHN T. COOK is assistant professor in the Department of Pediatrics at Boston University School of Medicine. E-mail: j.cook@bmc.org

[1] U.S. Bureau of Labor Statistics (BLS), *Consumer Expenditure Survey (CES), 1997*. Information and data taken from the BLS/CES web site at: www.bls.gov/text%5Fonly/csxhome%5Ftxt.htm.

[2] V. Olivera, "Spending on Food Assistance Programs Decreased in 1997," *Food Review*, 21(1): 16-22, January-April 1998.

[3] U.S. House of Representatives, Committee on Ways and Means, *1998 Green Book*, Washington, DC: U.S. Government Printing Office (GPO), 1998.

[4] J. T. Cook, and J. L. Brown, *Analysis of the Capacity of the Second Harvest Network to Cover the Federal Food Stamp Shortfall from 1997 to 2002*, Medford, MA: Center on Hunger, Poverty and Nutrition Policy, Tufts University, July 1997.

[5] Second Harvest, *Hunger 1997: The Faces & Facts*, Chicago, IL: Second Harvest, 1997.

[6] C. J. Consentino, ed., *1998 International Food Bank Directory, Including Food Recovery Programs*, Phoenix, AZ: International Food Banking Services, Inc., February 1998.

[7] Second Harvest, *Second Harvest National Food Bank Network, Network Activity Report, 1995 Edition*, Chicago, IL: Second Harvest, April 24, 1996.

[8] USDA, Food and Nutrition Service, "USDA Gleaning and Food Recovery Web Site, State Resource List," 1998, at: www.fns.usda.gov/fns/MENU/gleaning/SUPPORT/CitzGuide/APPB.HTM.

[9] G. Bickel, S. Carlson and M. Nord, *Measuring Food Security in the United States: Household Food Security in the United States, 1995-1998 (Advance Report)*, USDA Food and Nutrition Service and Economic Research Service, Washington, DC, July 1999. The report is available on the USDA/FNS/ONAE Internet web site.

[10] J. Dalaker and M. Naifeh, *Poverty in the United States: 1997*, U.S. Bureau of the Census, Current Population Reports, Series P60-201, Washington, DC: U.S. GPO, September 1998.

[11] K. Alaimo, R. R. Briefel, E. A. Frongillo and C.M. Olson, "Food Insufficiency Exists in the United States: Results from the Third National Health and Nutrition Examination Survey (NHANES III)," *American Journal of Public Health*, 88(3): 419-429, March 1998.

[12] D. M. Pearce, *When Wages Aren't Enough: Using the Self-Sufficiency Standard to Model the Impact of Child Care Subsidies on Wage Adequacy*, Report prepared for the Pennsylvania Family Economic Self-Sufficiency Project and the Women's Association for Women's Alternatives, Inc. (WAWA), March 1998.

[13] J. Dalaker and M. Naifeh, *Poverty in the United States: 1997*, U.S. Bureau of the Census, Current Population Reports, Series P60-201, Washington, DC: U.S. GPO, September 1998.

TABLE 1: Global Hunger – Life and Death Indicators

| | Population | | | | | | Life expectancy at birth 1995-2000 | | Infant mortality rate per 1,000 live births 1997 | % infants with low birth weight 1990-1997 | % 1-year-old children immunized (measles) 1995-97 | Under-5 mortality rate per 1,000 live births | | Maternal mortality rate per 100,000 live births 1980-97 | Refugees as of December 31, 1998 | |
	Total (millions) 1999	Projected (millions) 2025	Projected growth rate (%) 1995-2000	Projected total fertility rate 1995-2000	% population under age 15 1998	% population urban 1997	Male	Female				1960	1997		Country of origin	Country of asylum
Developing Countries	**4,793.2**	**6,608.8**	**1.6**	**3.08**	**35**	**40**	**62.1**	**65.2**	**65**	**18**	**79**	**104**	**96**	**491**	**..**	**..**
Africa (Sub-Saharan)	**596.7e**	**1,244.1e**	**..**	**..**	**..**	**32**	**..**	**..**	**105**	**15**	**52**	**..**	**170**	**979**	**..**	**..**
Angola	12.5	25.1	3.2	6.80	48	32	44.9	48.1	170	19	78	297	292	1,500	303,300	10,000
Benin	5.9	11.1	2.7	5.80	46	40	51.7	55.2	102	..	82	185	167	500	..	3,000
Botswana	1.6	2.2	1.9	4.35	42	65	46.2	48.4	39	11	79	62	49	250	..	..
Burkina Faso	11.6	23.3	2.7	6.57	47	17	43.6	45.2	110	21	33	196	169	930	..	..
Burundi	6.6	11.6	1.7	6.28	47	8	41.0	43.8	106	..	50	180	176	1,300	281,000	5,000
Cameroon	14.7	26.5	2.7	5.30	44	46	53.4	56.0	64	13	43	125	99	550	..	3,000
Cape Verde	0.4	0.7	..	3.56	40	54	65.5	71.3	54	9	82	73	73	..	..	..
Central African Republic	3.6	5.7	1.9	4.90	43	40	42.9	46.9	113	15	46	177	173	700	..	47,000
Chad	7.5	13.9	2.6	6.07	46	23	45.7	48.7	118	..	17	198	198	900	15,000	10,000
Comoros	0.7	1.2	..	4.80	43	31	57.4	60.2	69	8	49	120	93	..	..	..
Congo, Dem. Rep.	50.3	104.8	2.6	6.43	48	29	49.2	52.3	128	15	63	207	207	870	136,000	220,000
Congo, Republic	2.9	5.7	2.8	6.06	46	83	46.3	50.8	81	16	18	110	108	890	..	20,000
Côte d'Ivoire	14.5	23.3	1.8	5.10	44	45	46.2	47.3	90	12	68	150	150	600	..	128,000
Djibouti	0.6	1.0	..	5.30	41	83	48.7	52.0	111	11	47	164	156	..	3,000	23,000
Equatorial Guinea	0.4	0.8	..	5.58	43	45	48.4	51.6	109	..	82	206	172	..	..	..
Eritrea	3.7	6.7	3.8	5.70	44	18	49.3	52.4	73	13	53	160	116	1,400	323,100	3,000
Ethiopia	61.1	115.4	2.5	6.30	46	16	42.4	44.3	111	16	52	190	175	1,400	39,600	251,000
Gabon	1.2	2.0	2.6	5.40	40	52	51.1	53.8	85	..	32	164	145	500	..	..
Gambia	1.3	2.2	..	5.20	40	30	45.4	48.6	66	..	91	127	87	1,100	..	13,000
Ghana	19.7	36.9	2.7	5.15	44	37	58.3	61.8	68	8	59	127	107	740	11,000	15,000
Guinea	7.4	12.5	0.8	5.51	44	31	46.0	47.0	126	13	56	237	201	880	..	514,000
Guinea-Bissau	1.2	1.9	2.2	5.75	43	23	43.5	46.5	130	20	51	246	220	910	11,150	5,000
Kenya	29.5	41.8	2.0	4.45	44	30	51.1	53.0	57	16	32	97	87	650	8,000	192,000
Lesotho	2.1	3.5	2.2	4.75	40	26	54.7	57.3	95	11	43	148	137	610	..	..
Liberia	2.9	6.6	8.2	6.31	44	45	46.1	48.5	157	..	28	235	235	..	310,000	120,000
Madagascar	15.5	29.0	3.0	5.40	44	28	56.0	59.0	96	5	39	168	158	660	..	..
Malawi	10.6	20.0	2.4	6.75	47	14	38.9	39.6	135	20	87	230	215	620	..	..
Mali	11.0	21.3	2.4	6.60	46	28	52.0	54.6	145	16	56	254	239	580	3,000	5,000
Mauritania	2.6	4.8	2.7	5.50	44	54	51.9	55.1	120	11	20	183	183	800	30,000	20,000
Mauritius	1.2	1.4	0.8	1.91	26	41	67.9	75.1	20	13	84	25	23	112	..	..
Mozambique	19.3	30.6	2.5	6.25	45	36	43.9	46.6	130	20	57	250	208	1,500	..	..
Namibia	1.7	2.3	2.2	4.90	42	38	51.8	53.0	58	16	58	84	75	220	..	2,000
Niger	10.4	21.5	3.2	6.84	48	19	46.9	50.1	191	15	42	320	320	593	..	3,000
Nigeria	108.9	183.0	2.4	5.15	43	41	48.7	51.5	112	16	38	190	187	1,000	..	5,000
Rwanda	7.2	12.4	7.7	6.20	46	6	39.4	41.7	105	17	66	161	170	1,300	13,000	36,000
Senegal	9.2	16.7	2.6	5.57	45	45	50.5	54.2	72	4	65	147	124	510	10,000	30,000
Sierra Leone	4.7	8.1	3.0	6.06	44	35	35.8	38.7	182	11	26	323	316	1,800	480,000	10,000
Somalia	9.7	21.2	4.2	7.25	48	26	45.4	48.6	125	16	25	215	211	1,600	416,600	..
South Africa	39.9	46.0	1.5	3.25	35	50	51.5	58.1	49	..	76	73	65	230	..	29,000
Sudan	28.9	46.3	2.1	4.61	40	33	53.6	56.4	73	15	71	125	115	370	352,200	360,000
Swaziland	1.0	1.8	..	4.70	43	33	57.9	62.5	66	10	82	115	94	..	..	..
Tanzania	32.8	57.9	2.3	5.48	46	26	46.8	49.1	92	14	69	150	143	530	..	329,000
Togo	4.5	8.5	2.6	6.05	46	32	47.6	50.1	78	20	38	142	125	640	3,000	11,000
Uganda	21.1	44.4	2.8	7.10	50	13	38.9	40.4	86	13	60	165	137	550	12,000	185,000
Zambia	9.0	15.6	2.3	5.55	47	44	39.5	40.6	112	13	69	192	202	230	..	157,000
Zimbabwe	11.5	15.1	1.4	3.80	42	33	43.6	44.7	53	14	73	81	80	280	..	..
South Asia	**1,340.3**	**1,971.7e**	**..**	**..**	**..**	**27**	**..**	**..**	**78**	**33**	**78**	**135**	**116**	**551**	**..**	**..**
Afghanistan	21.9	44.9	2.9	6.90	43	20	45.0	46.0	165	20	58	260	257	1,700	1,547,200	..
Bangladesh	126.9	178.8	1.7	3.11	36	19	58.1	58.2	81	50	62	140	109	850	..	53,100
Bhutan	2.1	3.9	2.8	5.50	43	6	59.5	62.0	78	..	84	166	121	1,600	115,000	..
India	998.1	1,330.4	1.6	3.13	34	27	62.3	62.9	71	33	81	131	108	437	15,000	292,100
Maldives	0.3	0.5	..	5.40	43	27	65.7	63.3	53	13	96	84	74	..	..	..
Nepal	23.4	38.0	2.4	4.45	41	11	57.6	57.1	75	..	85	138	104	1,500	..	118,000
Pakistan	152.3	263.0	2.8	5.03	42	35	62.9	65.1	95	25	74	138	136	340	..	1,217,400
Sri Lanka	18.6	23.5	1.0	2.10	27	23	70.9	75.4	17	25	94	23	19	30	110,000	..

TABLE 1: Global Hunger – Life and Death Indicators

	Population Total (millions) 1999	Projected (millions) 2025	Projected growth rate (%) 1995–2000	Projected total fertility rate 1995–2000	% population under age 15 1998	% population urban 1997	Life expectancy at birth 1995-2000 Male	Female	Infant mortality rate per 1,000 live births 1997	% infants with low birth weight 1990-1997	% 1-year-old children immunized (measles) 1995-97	Under-5 mortality rate per 1,000 live births 1960	1997	Maternal mortality rate per 100,000 live births 1980-97	Refugees as of December 31, 1998 Country of origin	Country of asylum
East Asia and the Pacific	..	..	..	..	..	33	..	..	40	10	93	58	52	449	..	..
Cambodia	10.9	16.5	2.3	4.60	41	22	51.5	55.0	106	..	68	193	167	900	51,000	200
China	1,266.8	1,480.4	0.9	1.80	25	32	67.9	72.0	38	9	96	47	47	115	128,000	281,800
Hong Kong[a]	6.8	7.7	2.1	1.32	18	95	75.8	81.4	5x	8x	77x	7	6	7	..	..
Fiji	0.8	1.1	..	2.73	32	41	70.6	74.9	20	12	75	31	24	..	..	..
Indonesia	209.3	273.4	1.4	2.58	31	37	63.3	67.0	45	8	92	95	68	390	8,000	100
Korea, DPR (North)	23.7	29.4	1.6	2.05	28	62	68.9	75.1	23	..	100	35	30	..	..	..
Korea, Rep. (South)	46.5	52.5	0.8	1.65	22	83	68.8	76.0	6	9	85	9	6	30	..	..
Lao, PDR	5.3	9.7	2.6	5.75	44	22	52.0	54.5	99	18	67	163	122	650	12,100	..
Malaysia	21.8	31.0	2.0	3.18	34	55	69.9	74.3	10	8	89	21	11	43	..	50,600
Mongolia	2.6	3.7	1.7	2.60	36	62	64.4	67.3	105	7	91	150	150	65	..	..
Myanmar (Burma)	45.1	58.1	1.2	2.40	29	27	58.5	61.8	81	24	88	130	114	580	238,000	..
Papua New Guinea	4.7	7.5	2.2	4.60	39	17	57.2	58.7	79	23	41	112	112	930	..	8,000
Philippines	74.5	108.3	2.1	3.62	37	56	66.5	70.2	32	9	72	63	41	208	45,000	300
Singapore	3.5	4.2	1.4	1.68	22	100	74.9	79.3	4	7	89	8	4	10	..	..
Solomon Islands	0.4	0.8	..	4.85	43	18	69.7	73.9	23	20	68	36	28	..	..	..
Thailand	60.9	72.7	0.9	1.74	26	21	65.8	72.0	31	6	91	41	38	200	..	187,700
Vietnam	78.7	108.0	1.6	2.60	34	20	64.9	69.6	32	17	96	55	43	105	281,000	15,000
Latin America and the Caribbean	511.3	696.7	1.6	2.70	..	74	66.4	72.9	33	9	89	53	41	191	..	..
Argentina	36.6	47.2	1.3	2.62	28	89	69.7	76.8	21	7	92	28	24	100	..	1,100
Belize	0.2	0.4	2.4	3.66	40	46	73.4	76.1	35	4	98	49	43	..	..	3,500
Bolivia	8.1	13.1	2.3	4.36	40	62	59.8	63.2	69	12	98	124	96	370	..	350
Brazil	168.0	217.9	1.3	2.27	29	80	63.1	71.0	37	8	100	60	44	160	..	2,400
Chile	15.0	19.5	1.4	2.44	29	84	72.3	78.3	11	5	92	20	13	180	..	100
Colombia	41.6	59.8	1.9	2.80	33	74	67.3	74.3	25	9	76	40	30	100	600	200
Costa Rica	3.9	5.9	2.5	2.83	33	50	74.3	78.9	12	7	99	16	14	55	..	23,100
Cuba	11.2	11.8	0.4	1.55	22	77	74.2	78.0	7	7	100	13	8	36	300	1,100
Dominican Republic	8.4	11.2	1.7	2.80	34	63	69.0	73.1	44	13	80	65	53	110	..	600
Ecuador	12.4	17.8	2.0	3.10	34	60	67.3	72.5	30	13	75	50	39	150	..	250
El Salvador	6.2	9.7	2.0	3.17	36	46	66.5	72.5	31	11	97	54	0	300	250,150	100
Guatemala	11.1	19.8	2.6	4.93	44	40	61.4	67.2	43	15	74	81	55	190	151,300	800
Guyana	0.9	1.0	..	2.32	30	36	61.1	67.9	59	15	82	90	82	..	..	..
Haiti	8.1	12.0	1.7	4.38	41	33	51.4	56.2	92	15	30	148	132	600	600	..
Honduras	6.3	10.7	2.8	4.30	42	45	67.5	72.3	36	9	89	61	45	220	..	100
Jamaica	2.6	3.2	0.9	2.50	31	55	72.9	76.8	10	10	88	16	11	120	..	50
Mexico	97.4	130.2	1.6	2.75	34	74	69.5	75.5	29	7	91	46	35	110	..	7,500
Nicaragua	4.9	8.7	2.7	4.42	43	63	65.8	70.6	42	9	94	75	57	160	18,000	150
Panama	2.8	3.8	1.6	2.63	32	56	71.8	76.4	18	8	92	21	20	55	..	1,300
Paraguay	5.4	9.4	2.6	4.17	40	54	67.5	72.0	27	5	61	37	33	190	..	..
Peru	25.2	35.5	1.7	2.98	34	72	65.9	70.9	44	11	94	75	56	280	350	..
Suriname	0.4	0.5	..	2.21	31	50	67.5	72.7	24	13	78	38	30	..	..	..
Trinidad and Tobago	1.3	1.5	0.5	1.65	26	73	71.5	76.2	15	10	88	24	17	90	..	..
Uruguay	3.3	3.9	0.7	2.40	40	91	70.5	78.0	18	8	80	24	21	85	..	..
Venezuela	23.7	34.8	2.0	2.98	35	86	70.0	75.7	21	9	68	27	25	200	..	150
Middle East and North Africa	..	..	..	..	..	58	..	..	48	11	86	74	62	..	..	..
Algeria	30.8	46.6	2.3	3.81	37	57	67.5	70.3	34	9	74	48	39	140	3,000	84,000
Bahrain	0.6	0.9	..	2.90	30	91	71.1	75.3	18	6	95	23	22	..	..	..
Cyprus	0.8	0.9	..	2.03	24	55	75.5	80.0	8	..	90	12	9	..	..	..
Egypt	67.2	95.6	1.9	3.40	36	45	64.7	67.9	54	10	92	106	73	170	..	46,000
Iran	66.8	94.5	1.7	2.80	37	60	68.5	70.0	32	10	96	59	35	120	1,800	1,931,000
Iraq	22.5	41.0	2.8	5.25	42	75	60.9	63.9	94	15	98	48	122	310	584,800	104,000
Jordan	6.5	12.1	3.0	4.86	42	73	68.9	71.5	20	7	90	37	24	150	..	1,413,800
Kuwait	1.9	3.0	3.1	2.89	35	97	74.1	78.2	12	7	95	16	13	18	..	52,000
Lebanon	3.2	4.4	1.7	2.69	33	88	68.1	71.7	30	10	89	40	37	300	..	368,300
Libya	5.5	8.6	2.4	3.80	38	86	68.3	72.2	22	7	92	42	25	220	..	28,000

TABLE 1: Global Hunger – Life and Death Indicators

	Population						Life expectancy at birth 1995-2000		Infant mortality rate per 1,000 live births 1997	% infants with low birth weight 1990-1997	% 1-year-old children immunized (measles) 1995-97	Under-5 mortality rate per 1,000 live births		Maternal mortality rate per 100,000 live births 1980-97	Refugees as of December 31, 1998	
	Total (millions) 1999	Projected (millions) 2025	Projected growth rate (%) 1995–2000	Projected total fertility rate 1995-2000	% population under age 15 1998	% population urban 1997	Male	Female				1960	1997		Country of origin	Country of asylum
Morocco	27.9	38.7	1.8	3.10	33	53	64.8	68.5	58	9	92	83	72	372	..	..
Oman	2.5	5.4	3.3	5.85	45	79	68.9	73.3	15	8	98	30	18	190	..	..
Qatar	0.6	0.8		3.74	26	92	70.0	75.4	16	..	87	36	20	..	..	..
Saudi Arabia	20.9	40.0	3.4	5.80	41	84	69.9	73.4	24	7	87	45	28	18	..	128,300
Syria	15.7	26.3	2.5	4.00	42	53	66.7	71.2	27	7	93	44	33	179	..	369,800
Tunisia	9.5	12.8	1.4	2.55	31	63	68.4	70.7	27	8	92	52	33	170	..	
Turkey	65.5	87.9	1.7	2.50	29	72	66.5	71.7	40	8	76	70	45	180	11,300	12,000
United Arab Emirates	2.4	3.3	2.0	3.42	29	85	73.9	76.5	9	6	35	14	10	26	..	200
West Bank and Gaza[a]	..	..	..	..	52d	..	..	..	..	..	..	..	..	..	3,816,500	1,328,000
Yemen	17.5	39.0	3.7	7.60	48	35	57.4	58.4	76	19	43	129	100	1,400	..	68,700
Countries in Transition[b]	..	..	..	..	..	67	..	..	29	7	89	42	35	62	..	..
Albania	3.1	3.8	−0.4	2.50	30	38	69.9	75.9	34	7	95	41	40	28	..	25,000
Armenia	3.5	3.9	−0.3	1.70	25	69	67.2	73.6	25	7	92	31	30	21	180,000	229,000
Azerbaijan	7.7	9.4	0.5	1.99	29	56	65.5	74.1	34	6	97	44	45	44	218,000	235,300
Belarus	10.3	9.5	−0.3	1.36	19	72	62.2	73.9	14	..	74	20	18	22	..	16,500
Bosnia and Herzegovina	3.8	4.3	3.0	1.35	19	42	70.5	75.9	14	..	85	20	16	..	342,600	40,000
Bulgaria	8.3	7.0	−0.7	1.23	17	69	67.6	74.7	16	6	93	18	19	20	..	2,800
Croatia	4.5	4.2	−0.1	1.56	17	57	68.8	76.5	8	..	91	13	9	12	309,000	27,300
Czech Republic	10.3	9.5	−0.2	1.19	17	66	70.3	77.4	6	6	97	11	7	7	..	2,400
Estonia	1.4	1.1	−1.2	1.29	18	74	63.0	74.5	13	..	88	21	14	52	..	
Georgia	5.0	5.2	−1.1	1.92	22	59	68.5	76.8	23	..	95	31	29	19	23,000	300
Hungary	10.1	8.9	−0.4	1.37	17	66	66.8	74.9	10	9	100	16	11	14	..	3,200
Kazakhstan	16.3	17.7	−0.4	2.30	28	60	62.8	72.5	37	..	92	48	44	53	..	4,100
Kyrgyzstan	4.7	6.1	0.6	3.21	35	39	63.3	71.9	38	..	85	55	48	32	..	15,000
Latvia	2.4	1.9	−1.5	1.25	18	73	62.5	74.4	16	..	97	20	20	15	..	..
Lithuania	3.7	3.4	−0.3	1.43	20	73	64.3	75.6	13	..	96	17	15	13	..	100
Macedonia, FYR	2.0	2.3	0.6	2.06	23	61	70.9	75.3	20	..	98	41	23	22	..	7,300
Moldova	4.4	4.5	0.0	1.76	24	53	63.5	71.5	25	4	99	37	31	33	..	..
Poland	38.7	39.1	0.1	1.53	20	64	68.2	76.9	10	..	91	19	11	10	..	1,300
Romania	22.4	19.9	−0.4	1.17	18	57	66.2	73.9	22	7	97	32	26	41	..	900
Russian Federation	147.2	137.9	−0.2	1.35	19	77	60.6	72.8	20	6	91	30	25	53	500	161,900
Slovakia	5.4	5.4	0.1	1.39	20	60	69.2	76.7	10	..	98	15	11	8	..	300
Slovenia	2.0	1.8	−0.1	1.26	16	52	70.6	78.2	5	..	92	9	6	5	..	7,300
Tajikistan	6.1	8.9	1.5	4.15	41	32	64.2	70.2	56	..	95	78	76	74	15,100	5,500
Turkmenistan	4.4	6.3	1.8	3.60	38	45	61.9	68.9	57	5	100	80	78	44	..	500
Ukraine	50.7	45.7	−0.4	1.38	18	71	63.8	73.7	18	..	97	24	24	30	..	8,600
Uzbekistan	23.9	33.4	1.6	3.45	38	42	64.3	70.7	46	..	88	63	60	24	45,000	..
Yugoslavia, FR	10.6	10.8	0.1	1.84	20	58	70.2	75.5	18	..	94	30	21	12	132,600	480,000
Industrial Countries	..	..	..	..	..	76	70.6	78.4	6	6	90	9	7	13	..	..
Australia	18.7	27.8	1.0	1.83	21	85	75.5	81.1	5	6	87	10	6	9	..	15,000
Austria	8.2	8.2	0.5	1.41	17	64	73.7	80.1	5	6	90	9	5	10	..	16,500
Belgium	10.2	9.9	0.1	1.55	17	97	73.8	80.6	6	6	64	9	7	10	..	25,800
Canada	30.9	37.9	1.0	1.55	19	77	76.1	81.8	6	6	98x	9	7	6	..	46,000
Denmark	5.3	5.2	0.3	1.72	18	85	73.0	78.3	6	6	84	9	6	9	..	6,100
Finland	5.2	5.3	0.3	1.73	18	64	73.0	80.6	4	4	98	7	4	11	..	2,300
France	58.9	61.7	0.4	1.71	19	75	74.2	82.0	5	5	97	9	5	15	..	17,400
Germany	82.2	80.2	0.1	1.30	16	87	73.9	80.2	5	..	75	9	5	22	..	198,000
Greece	10.6	9.9	0.3	1.28	15	60	75.6	80.7	7	6	90	11	8	10	..	2,800
Ireland	3.7	4.4	0.7	1.90	22	58	73.6	79.2	6	4	..	9	7	10	..	5,900
Israel	6.1	8.3	2.2	2.68	28	91	75.7	79.7	6	7	94	12	6	7	..	..
Italy	57.3	51.3	0.0	1.20	14	67	75.0	81.2	5	5	94	10	6	12	..	6,800
Japan	126.5	121.2	0.2	1.43	15	78	76.8	82.9	4	7	94	6	6	8	..	500
Luxembourg	0.4	0.5	..	1.67	18	90	73.3	79.9	5	..	91	9	7	..	..	..
Netherlands	15.7	15.8	0.4	1.50	18	89	75.0	80.7	5	..	96	8	6	12	..	47,000

TABLE 1: Global Hunger – Life and Death Indicators

	Population						Life expectancy at birth 1995-2000		Infant mortality rate per 1,000 live births 1997	% infants with low birth weight 1990-1997	% 1-year-old children immunized (measles) 1995-97	Under-5 mortality rate per 1,000 live births		Maternal mortality rate per 100,000 live births 1980-97	Refugees as of December 31, 1998	
	Total (millions) 1999	Projected (millions) 2025	Projected growth rate (%) 1995–2000	Projected total fertility rate 1995-2000	% population under age 15 1998	% population urban 1997	Male	Female				1960	1997		Country of origin	Country of asylum
New Zealand	3.8	4.7	1.0	2.01	23	86	74.1	79.7	7	6	100	11	7	25	..	..
Norway	4.4	4.8	0.5	1.85	20	74	75.2	80.6	4	4	93x	9	4	6	..	2,500
Portugal	9.9	9.3	0.0	1.37	17	37	71.8	78.9	7	5	94	15	8	15	..	1,400
Spain	39.6	36.7	0.0	1.15	15	77	74.5	81.5	5	4	90x	9	5	7	..	2,500
Sweden	8.9	9.1	0.3	1.57	18	83	76.3	80.8	4	5	96	6	4	7	..	16,700
Switzerland	7.3	7.6	0.7	1.47	18	62	75.4	81.8	5	5	..	8	5	6	..	40,000
United Kingdom	58.7	60.0	0.2	1.72	19	89	74.5	79.8	6	7	95	9	7	9	..	74,000
United States	276.2	325.6	0.8	1.99	22	77	73.4	80.1	7	7	89x	10	8	12	..	651,000
World	**5,978.4**	**7,823.7**	**1.3**	**2.71**	**..**	**46**	**63.3**	**67.6**	**59**	**17**	**80**	**94**	**87**	**437**	**..**	**13,469,000**

.. Data not available.

a Territory.

b Central and Eastern European countries and the newly independent states of the former Soviet Union.

c Special Administrative Region; data is exclusive of China.

d Palestinian refugees from various sources.

x Data refer to a period other than specified in the column heading.

TABLE 2: Global Food, Nutrition and Education

	Food supply				Adult literacy rate 1997			Educational enrollment (% of relevant age group)				
	Per capita dietary energy supply (DES) (calories/day) 1997	Food production per capita 1980=100 1998	Food expenditures (% of household consumption) 1997	Iodine deficiency: total goiter rate (6-11 yrs.) % 1985-97	Total	Female	Male	Total primary school (net) 1997	Primary school (net) 1996 Female	Male	Combined primary, secondary, tertiary (net) 1997 Female	Male
Developing Countries	**2,650.0x**	..	..	**18**	**71.4**	**62.9**	**80.0**	..	**76**	**83**	**52**	**60**
Africa (Sub-Saharan)	**2,182.8**	..	..	**19**	**58.5**	**49.6**	**65.9**	**85.7**	**55**	**61**	..	**49**
Angola	1,902.8	106.8	..	7	45.0	..	..	34.7	..	..	25	29
Benin	2,486.6	113.2	45	24	33.9	20.9	47.8	67.6	43	74	30	54
Botswana	2,182.9	74.1	25	8	74.4	76.9	71.7	80.1	99	94	72	69
Burkina Faso	2,120.8	95.6	..	16	20.7	11.2	30.4	32.3	24	37	15	24
Burundi	1,684.8	76.3	..	42	44.6	36.1	53.8	35.6	48x	56x	20	25
Cameroon	2,111.1	98.4	38	26	71.7	64.6	79.0	61.7	60y	69y	39	48
Cape Verde	3,015.1	107.4	..	26	71.0	62.5	82.1	99.9	100	100	76	79
Central African Republic	2,015.6	107.3	..	63	42.4	30.1	56.0	46.2	55y	70y	20	33
Chad	2,031.8	126.3	..	15	50.3	37.1	64.0	47.9	..	..	19	38
Comoros	1,858.2	88.7	..	..	55.4	48.2	62.9	50.1	48	58	35	42
Congo, Dem. Rep	1,754.7	73.1	..	9	77.0	87.0x	..	58.2	..	..	31	47
Congo, Republic	2,143.5	88.3	36	8	76.9	68.8	84.6	78.3	50	71	62	76
Côte d'Ivoire	2,610.1	101.6	35	6	42.6	33.7	51.4	58.3	46y	59y	32	48
Djibouti	2,084.3	64.9	..	..	48.3	35.0	62.2	31.9	28	37	17	24
Equatorial Guinea	..	77.1	..	..	79.9	70.1	90.5	79.3	..	..	59x	70x
Eritrea	1,621.6	82.7	..	..	25.0	..	..	29.3	30	33	24	30
Ethiopia	1,858.3	89.4	49x	31	35.4	29.2	41.5	35.2	19	28	18	31
Gabon	2,555.6	85.8	37	5	66.2	56.8	76.1	..	86y	87y	60x	60x
Gambia	2,349.6	71.1	..	..	33.1	26.4	40.1	65.9	43y	51y	35	48
Ghana	2,611.0	122.8	50x	10	66.4	56.5	76.5	43.4	69y	70y	37	47
Guinea	2,231.5	107.8	32x	55	37.9	23.9	52.0	45.6	26y	39y	19	36
Guinea-Bissau	2,429.9	100.4	..	19	33.6	18.3	49.7	52.3	33x	60x	24	43
Kenya	1,976.5	88.7	38	7	79.3	71.8	86.9	65.0	83y	85y	49	50
Lesotho	2,243.5	81.5	..	43	82.3	92.5	71.5	68.6	71	60	62	53
Liberia	2,043.7	93.3	..	6	38.0x	..	..	..	53y	59y	..	..
Madagascar	2,021.5	84.2	59x	15	47.0	..	..	58.7	61y	62y	39	39
Malawi	2,043.2	103.6	45	13	57.7	43.4	72.8	98.5	100	100	70	79
Mali	2,029.5	90.1	48	29	35.5	28.3	43.1	38.1	19	30	20	31
Mauritania	2,621.9	83.0	..	..	38.4	27.8	49.4	62.9	55	64	36	45
Mauritius	2,917.0	107.4	24	0	83.0	79.2	86.9	96.5	96	96	63	62
Mozambique	1,832.0	106.0	..	20	40.5	25.0	56.7	39.6	35	45	20	29
Namibia	2,183.3	101.4	..	35	79.8	78.5	81.2	91.4	..	..	84	80
Niger	2,096.9	94.8	..	9	14.3	7.2	21.7	24.4	19y	34y	11	19
Nigeria	2,734.9	108.6	48	20	59.5	50.8	68.5	..	58y	60y	48	61
Rwanda	2,056.5	86.5	29x	26	63.0	55.6	70.7	78.3	76x	76x	42	44
Senegal	2,418.3	79.9	52	12	34.6	24.8	44.5	59.5	48	60	31	40
Sierra Leone	2,034.5	87.8	48	7	33.3	20.0	47.5	44.0	..	..	22x	34x
Somalia	1,565.8	80.3	..	7	24x	..	..	..	..	..	..	..
South Africa	2,989.9	84.6	34x	2	84.0	83.2	84.7	99.9	96	95	94	93
Sudan	2,395.1	136.1	60x	20	53.3	41.3	65.4	..	52y	59y	31	37
Swaziland	2,483.3	75.6	27	..	77.5	76.3	78.9	94.6	96	95	71	74
Tanzania	1,994.7	80.9	64x	37	71.6	62.0	81.7	47.4	48	47	32	33
Togo	2,468.8	104.1	..	22	53.2	38.3	68.7	82.3	72	98	47	75
Uganda	2,085.3	82.9	..	7	64.0	53.0	75.2	..	63y	65y	36	44
Zambia	1,970.4	83.8	47	51x	75.1	67.5	83.3	72.4	75	76	46	53
Zimbabwe	2,145.2	76.4	28	42	90.9	87.6	94.3	93.1	90y	91y	66	71
South Asia	**2,448.8**	..	**51x**	**17**	**52.2**	**38.6**	**65.0**	**78.0**	**63**	**75**	**44**	**60**
Afghanistan	1,744.6	72.0	..	20	32.0x	..	..	..	11y	36y	..	..
Bangladesh	2,085.5	99.3	41x	50	38.9	27.4	49.9	75.1	82y	82y	30	40
Bhutan	..	91.9	..	14	44.2	30.3	58.1	13.2	..	..	10	14
India	2,495.6	104.9	52x	9	53.5	39.4	66.7	77.2	61y	75y	47	62
Maldives	2,484.7	85.9	..	24	95.7	95.6	95.7	..	..	..	75	74
Nepal	2,365.7	95.0	37	44	38.1	20.7	55.7	78.4	60y	80y	49	69
Pakistan	2,475.6	114.9	40	32	40.9	25.0	55.2	..	62y	71y	28	56
Sri Lanka	2,302.1	105.6	38	14	90.7	87.6	94.0	99.1	..	..	67	65

TABLE 2: Global Food, Nutrition and Education

	Food supply		Food expenditures (% of household consumption) 1997	Iodine deficiency: total goiter rate (6-11 yrs.) % 1985-97	Adult literacy rate 1997			Total primary school (net) 1997	Educational enrollment (% of relevant age group)			
	Per capita dietary energy supply (DES) (calories/day) 1997	Food production per capita 1980=100 1998							Primary school (net) 1996		Combined primary, secondary, tertiary (net) 1997	
					Total	Female	Male		Female	Male	Female	Male
East Asia and the Pacific	**2,669.6d**	..	**45x**	**20**	**83.4**	**75.4**	**91.2**	**71.0**	**96**	**98**	..	..
Brunei	2,856.6	97.7	..	..	90.1	86.0	93.7	87.9	91	91	73	71
Cambodia	2,048.4	107.4	..	12	66.0	..	..	99.9	..	..	54	68
China	2,897.1	144.8	61x	20	82.9	74.5	90.8	99.9	98	99	67	71
Hong Kong[a]	3,206.2	17.3	10	..	92.4	88.4	96.1	91.3	..	..	67	64
Fiji	2,864.6	87.4	30	..	91.8	89.4	94.1	99.9	100x	99x	79	81
Indonesia	2,886.0	106.4	45	28	85.0	79.5	90.6	99.2	95	99	61	68
Korea, DPR (North)	1,837.3	61.2	..	..	..	..	..	..	..	..	..	..
Korea, Rep. (South)	3,154.7	118.0	21	..	97.2	95.5	98.9	99.9	99	98	84	94
Lao, PDR	2,107.9	105.1	..	25	58.6	46.8	71.1	73.0	67y	70y	48	62
Malaysia	2,976.7	103.2	23x	20	85.7	81.0	90.2	99.9	92	91	66	64
Mongolia	1,916.5	76.2	..	31	84.0	78.6	89.3	85.1	81	78	61	49
Myanmar (Burma)	2,862.4	118.6	..	18	83.6	78.8	88.5	99.3	85y	85y	54	55
Papua New Guinea	2,223.6	83.8	..	30	73.7	64.7	82.0	78.9	..	..	33	40
Philippines	2,365.9	99.5	33	7	94.6	94.3	94.8	99.9	91y	89y	85	80
Singapore	..	25.3	14	..	91.4	87.0	95.9	91.4	..	..	71	74
Solomon Islands	2,122.1	91.1	..	..	62.0	..	..	..	..	..	44	48
Thailand	2,359.9	103.2	23	4	94.7	92.8	96.7	88.0	..	..	59	58
Vietnam	2,483.9	124.1	40	20	91.9	89.0	95.1	99.0	..	..	59	64
Latin America and Caribbean	**2,798.1**	..	**34x**	**11**	**87.2**	**86.2**	**88.3**	**93.3**	**90**	**89**	**71**	**73**
Argentina	3,093.1	118.1	35x	8	96.5	96.5	96.6	99.9	..	..	82	77
Belize	2,906.8	130.9	28	0	75.0	..	..	99.9	98	100	72	72
Bolivia	2,174.3	112.8	33x	5	83.6	76.8	90.7	97.4	89y	90y	64	75
Brazil	2,974.3	115.3	35x	14x	84.0	83.9	84.1	97.1	94y	93y	77	82
Chile	2,795.9	117.0	29x	1	95.2	94.9	95.4	90.4	85	87	76	78
Colombia	2,596.9	94.1	29x	7	90.9	90.8	91.0	89.4	91y	90y	71	70
Costa Rica	2,648.8	106.4	33x	4	95.1	95.1	95.0	91.8	87x	86x	65	66
Cuba	2,479.7	58.6	..	10	95.9	95.9	95.9	99.9	99	99	73	70
Dominican Republic	2,287.6	89.8	46x	5	82.6	82.3	82.8	91.3	83	79	69	63
Ecuador	2,679.4	127.9	30x	10	90.7	88.8	92.7	99.9	92	91	67	78
El Salvador	2,561.5	99.0	33x	25	77.0	74.2	80.1	89.1	80	78	63	64
Guatemala	2,339.2	99.2	36x	20	66.6	58.9	74.2	73.8	55y	61y	43	51
Guyana	2,529.8	163.6	..	..	98.1	97.5	98.7	92.8	89	90	64	64
Haiti	1,868.7	81.4	..	4x	45.8	43.4	48.3	19.4	69y	68y	24	25
Honduras	2,403.2	91.1	39x	9	70.7	70.2	71.1	87.5	91	89	59	57
Jamaica	2,553.2	110.4	26	..	85.5	89.6	81.2	95.6	100x	100x	63	62
Mexico	3,096.6	109.4	35x	3	90.1	87.9	92.3	99.9	..	..	69	71
Nicaragua	2,186.1	98.5	..	4	63.4	63.4	63.3	78.6	85	82	65	61
Panama	2,430.3	79.6	38x	13	91.1	90.4	91.7	89.9	92x	91x	74	72
Paraguay	2,566.2	100.1	30x	49	92.4	91.1	93.8	96.3	89	89	64	65
Peru	2,301.6	122.3	35x	36	88.7	83.7	93.9	93.8	90	91	77	80
Suriname	2,664.7	78.9	..	..	93.5	91.6	95.4	99.9	..	..	..	..
Trinidad and Tobago	2,661.4	91.7	20	..	97.8	97.0	98.7	99.9	94	83	66	67
Uruguay	2,815.9	124.2	31x	..	97.5	97.8	97.0	94.3	95	95	81	74
Venezuela	2,321.2	98.2	23x	11	92.0	91.6	92.5	82.5	90x	87x	68	66
Middle East and North Africa	**2,990.0**	..	**39x**	**20**	..	..	..	..	**76**	**85**	..	..
Algeria	2,853.2	105.6	..	9	60.3	47.7	72.7	96.0	91	99	64	71
Bahrain	..	67.9	..	..	86.2	80.7	89.9	98.2	100	99	84	79
Cyprus	3,429.2	97.8	..	..	95.9	93.5	98.4	..	96	96	75x	75x
Egypt	3,286.9	123.2	44	5	52.7	40.5	64.7	95.2	72y	83y	66	77
Iran	2,835.9	121.2	23	30	73.3	65.8	80.7	90.0	93y	99y	68	76
Iraq	2,618.8	81.2	..	7	58.0	..	..	74.6	74x	83x	44	57
Jordan	3,014.2	116.4	35x	..	87.2	81.8	92.2	..	89x	89x	..	..
Kuwait	3,096.2	184.6	..	..	80.4	77.5	83.1	65.2	65	65	56	56
Lebanon	3,276.6	117.1	..	15	84.4	78.3	91.2	76.1	..	..	77	76
Libya	3,288.8	98.6	..	6	76.5	62.9	88.7	99.9	96x	98x	92	92

TABLE 2: Global Food, Nutrition and Education

	Food supply		Food expenditures (% of household consumption) 1997	Iodine deficiency: total goiter rate (6-11 yrs.) % 1985-97	Adult literacy rate 1997			Educational enrollment (% of relevant age group)				
	Per capita dietary energy supply (DES) (calories/day) 1997	Food production per capita 1980=100 1998						Total primary school (net) 1997	Primary school (net) 1996		Combined primary, secondary, tertiary (net) 1997	
					Total	Female	Male		Female	Male	Female	Male
Morocco	3,077.9	94.3	45	20	45.9	32.7	59.3	76.6	62	81	42	55
Oman	..	79.1	..	10	67.1	55.0	76.9	67.7	70	72	57	60
Qatar	..	131.3	..	..	80.0	81.2	79.6	83.3	80	81	74	69
Saudi Arabia	2,783.2	68.0	..	..	73.4	62.5	81.0	60.1	61	63	53	58
Syria	3,351.5	124.7	..	73	71.6	56.5	86.5	94.7	87	95	56	63
Tunisia	3,282.6	105.6	35	4x	67.0	55.8	78.1	99.9	95	98	68	72
Turkey	3,524.7	101.5	23	36	83.2	73.9	92.4	99.9	94	98	54	67
United Arab Emirates	3,389.8	174.7	..	..	74.8	76.8	73.9	82.0	82	84	72	66
Yemen	2,050.7	88.5	..	32	42.5	21.0	64.2	..	39y	73y	27	70
Countries in Transition[b]	**2,904.1**	**..**	**..**	**22**	**98.7**	**98.4**	**98.8**	**..**	**94**	**95**	**77**	**74**
Albania	2,961.1	122.4	..	41	85.0	85.0	85.0	..	97	95	68	67
Armenia	2,370.8	72.4	..	40	98.8	98.8	98.8	..	..	..	68	75
Azerbaijan	2,236.3	54.7	..	20	96.3	96.3	96.3	..	..	..	73	69
Belarus	3,225.5	66.6	16	22	99.0	98.5	99.0	..	94	97	82	78
Bosnia and Herzegovina	2,265.5	36.8	..	..	..	..	..	..	..	..	..	..
Bulgaria	2,685.9	69.2	15	20	98.2	97.6	98.8	97.9	96	98	73	68
Croatia	..	60.1	17	..	97.7	96.4	99.0	99.9	82	83	68	67
Czech Republic	3,244.4	83.0	15	..	99.0	99.0	99.0	99.9	98	98	74	74
Estonia	2,849.0	49.4	..	..	99.0	99.0	99.0	99.9	94	93	83	80
Georgia	2,614.1	73.1	..	64	99.0	..	..	89.0	82	81	71	70
Hungary	3,312.8	80.6	14	..	99.0	99.0	99.0	97.5	94	92	75	73
Kazakhstan	3,084.9	48.2	..	20	99.0	99.0	99.0	..	..	..	79	74
Kyrgyzstan	2,447.2	100.4	..	20	97.0	..	..	..	87y	86y	71	68
Latvia	2,863.8	42.4	..	..	99.0	99.0	99.0	99.9	82	86	72	69
Lithuania	3,260.6	69.4	..	..	99.0	99.0	99.0	..	..	..	77	73
Macedonia, FYR	2,664.2	93.4	..	19	94.0	94.0	94.0	..	84	86	70	70
Moldova	2,567.1	54.9	28	..	98.3	97.4	99.0	..	..	..	71	69
Poland	3,365.9	87.1	20	10	99.0	99.0	99.0	99.4	96	97	78	77
Romania	3,252.8	94.8	24	10	97.8	96.7	98.9	99.9	92	92	68	68
Russian Federation	2,903.8	56.6	18	..	99.0	98.8	99.0	99.9	100	100	80	74
Slovakia	2,984.2	71.9	17	..	99.0	99.0	99.0	..	..	..	76	74
Slovenia	3,100.9	96.5	13	..	99.0	99.0	99.0	..	99	100	78	74
Tajikistan	2,001.4	52.6	..	20	98.9	98.3	99.0	..	..	..	65	73
Turkmenistan	2,306.4	85.1	..	20	98.0	..	..	..	80y	81y	90x	90x
Ukraine	2,795.3	52.5	21x	10	99.0	..	..	..	..	..	80	74
Uzbekistan	2,433.4	96.5	..	18	99.0	..	..	..	83y	83y	74	78
Yugoslavia, FR	3,031.1	100.8	..	..	98.0x	..	..	..	70x	69x	..	..
Industrial Countries	**3,340.0**	**..**	**14x**	**..**	**98.7**	**98.6**	**98.9**	**99.9**	**98**	**98**	**93**	**90**
Australia	3,224.0	124.5	14	..	99.0	99.0	99.0	99.9	98	98	100d	100d
Austria	3,535.8	95.8	13	..	99.0	99.0	99.0	99.9	100	100	85	86
Belgium	3619.2c	108.1c	15	5	99.0	99.0	99.0	99.9	98	98	100d	100d
Canada	3,119.4	108.9	9	..	99.0	99.0	99.0	99.9	94	96	100d	96
Denmark	3,407.3	101.1	10	5	99.0	99.0	99.0	99.9	99	98	91	87
Finland	3,100.1	92.0	11	..	99.0	99.0	99.0	99.9	99	99	100d	94
France	3,518.4	102.3	12	5x	99.0	99.0	99.0	99.9	99	99	94	91
Germany	3,381.7	89.9	11x	10	99.0	99.0	99.0	99.9	100	100	87	89
Greece	3,648.6	95.0	28x	10	99.0	94.9	96.6	99.9	98x	98x	79	79
Ireland	3,565.1	108.8	14	..	96.6	99.0	98.3	99.9	100	100	90	86
Israel	3,277.6	81.6	21x	..	95.4	93.4	97.5	..	..	..	81	79
Italy	3,506.9	100.9	14	20	98.3	97.8	98.8	99.9	..	..	83	80
Japan	2,932.2	91.7	11	..	99.0	99.0	99.0	99.9	100	100	83	86
Luxembourg	..	..	10x	..	99.0	99.0	99.0	..	..	..	69	69
Netherlands	3,283.8	91.6	11	3	99.0	99.0	99.0	99.9	99	99	97	100

TABLE 2: Global Food, Nutrition and Education

	Food supply		Food expenditures (% of household consumption) 1997	Iodine deficiency: total goiter rate (6-11 yrs.) % 1985-97	Adult literacy rate 1997			Total primary school (net) 1997	Educational enrollment (% of relevant age group)			
	Per capita dietary energy supply (DES) (calories/day) 1997	Food production per capita 1980=100 1998							Primary school (net) 1996		Combined primary, secondary, tertiary (net) 1997	
					Total	Female	Male		Female	Male	Female	Male
New Zealand	3,394.6	113.2	12	..	99.0	99.0	99.0	99.9	100	100	99	92
Norway	3,356.5	98.8	13	..	99.0	99.0	99.0	99.9	99	99	98	93
Portugal	3,667.0	96.2	20	15	90.8	88.3	93.7	99.9	100	100	93	88
Spain	3,310.0	104.7	17	10	97.2	96.2	98.4	99.9	100	100	94	89
Sweden	3,193.9	96.7	10	..	99.0	99.0	99.0	99.9	100	100	100d	95
Switzerland	3,223.4	89.7	12	..	99.0	99.0	99.0	99.9	100	100	76	83
United Kingdom	3,276.0	97.0	11	10	99.0	99.0	99.0	99.9	100	100	100d	99
United States	3,699.1	111.4	8	..	99.0	99.0	99.0	99.9	97	96	97	91
World	**2,720.0**	**104.2**	**..**	**18**	**78.0**	**71.1**	**84.3**	**87.6**	**79**	**85**	**60**	**67**

.. Data not available.

a Special Administrative Region, data is exclusive of China.

b Central and Eastern European countries and the newly independent states of the former Soviet Union.

c Luxembourg included.

d Data does not include Papua New Guinea.

x Data refer to a period other than specified in the column heading.

y Indicates net primary school data derived from household surveys.

The number '0' (zero) means zero or less than half the unit shown.

TABLE 3: Hunger, Malnutrition and Poverty

| | Undernourished population | | % under-5 (1990-1997) suffering from: | | | | % population with access to safe water 1990-1997 | | | Population in Poverty (%) | | | |
| | Percent of the population undernourished 1995-1997 | Number of undernourished people (millions) 1995-1997 | Underweight | | Wasting | Stunting | | | | Below national poverty line 1984-1996 | | | Population below $1 a day[h] 1981-1996 |
			moderate & severe	severe	moderate & severe	moderate & severe	Total	Urban	Rural	National	Urban	Rural	
Developing Countries	**17.87**	**791.36**	**32.0**	**10.0**	**9.0**	**39.0**	..	..	..	..	..	..	**32.0**
Africa (Sub-Saharan)	**33.32**	**179.58**	**30.0**	**9.0**	**8.0**	**41.0**	50	75		..	..	..	**39.0g**
Angola	43.10	4.89	42.0	14.0	6.0	53.0	31	46	22	..	..	..	..
Benin	15.43	0.85	29.2	7.4	14.3	25.0	56	46	71	33.0	..	..	..
Botswana	24.95	0.38	15.0x	..	..	44.0x	90	100	88	..	..	..	33.0
Burkina Faso	30.00	3.21	32.7	9.3	13.2	33.3	42	66	37	..	..	..	..
Burundi	63.44	3.97	37.5	10.0	5.7	47.4	52	92	49	36.2	..	..	..
Cameroon	31.61	4.28	15.1	3.8	2.9	26.0	50	57	43	40.0	44.4	32.4	..
Cape Verde	..	..	18.8	..	3.3	25.8	51	70	34	44.0	..	..	..
Central African Republic	41.96	1.41	23.2	6.0	6.4	28.4	38	55	21	..	..	..	..
Chad	45.58	3.14	31.0	..	..	..	24	48	17	..	..	..	..
Comoros	..	..	25.8	7.9	8.3	33.8	53	76	45	..	..	..	..
Congo, Dem. Rep.	55.20	25.79	34.4	10.2	9.6	45.2	42	89	26	..	..	..	..
Congo, Rep.	34.19	0.90	23.9	4.7	5.5	27.5	34	53	7	..	..	..	..
Côte d'Ivoire	14.55	2.01	23.8	6.3	8.3	24.4	42	56	32	..	..	..	17.7
Djibouti	..	..	22.9	8.8	10.7	22.2	90	77	100	..	..	..	..
Equatorial Guinea	..	..	..	..	..	..	95	88	100	..	..	..	..
Eritrea	66.75	2.21	41.0	..	10.0	66.0	22	60	8	..	..	..	..
Ethiopia	50.51	28.68	47.7	16.0	8.0	64.2	25	91	19	..	..	..	46.0
Gabon	8.34	0.09	..	..	..	..	67	80	30	..	..	..	..
Gambia	24.95	0.29	..	..	..	..	69	80	65	64.0	..	..	..
Ghana	11.27	2.05	27.3	7.9	11.3	25.9	65	88	52	31.4	26.7	34.3	..
Guinea	31.35	2.27	26.0	9.0	12.0	32.0	46	69	36	..	..	..	26.3
Guinea-Bissau	..	..	23.0x	..	..	..	43	32	67	48.8	24.1	60.9	88.2
Kenya	41.02	11.42	22.5	5.6	7.8	33.6	53	67	49	42.0	29.3	46.4	<2.0
Lesotho	28.20	0.56	21.4	2.0x	15.8	32.9	62	91	57	49.2	27.8	53.9	48.8
Liberia	41.84	0.93	..	..	..	..	46	79	13	..	..	..	..
Madagascar	39.19	5.56	34.1	9.9	7.4	49.8	26	68	12	59.0	..	..	72.3
Malawi	37.25	3.67	29.9	8.7	7.0	48.3	47	95	40	..	..	..	..
Mali	28.95	2.95	40.0	16.5	23.3	30.1	66	87	55	..	..	..	..
Mauritania	13.23	0.32	23.0	9.2	7.2	44.0	74	88	59	57.0	..	..	31.4
Mauritius	5.72	0.06	14.9	2.0	13.7	9.7	98	95	100	10.6	..	..	..
Mozambique	62.89	11.27	27.0	11.0	8.0	55.0	63	44x	17x	..	..	..	..
Namibia	29.76	0.47	26.2	5.8	8.6	28.5	83	100	71	..	..	..	..
Niger	38.58	3.65	42.6	15.0	15.0	39.5	48	76	44	..	..	..	61.5
Nigeria	8.15	8.26	35.3	11.8	8.9	42.7	49	58	40	34.1	30.4	36.4	28.9
Rwanda	36.91	2.05	29.4	6.0	3.8	48.7	..	..	79	51.2	..	..	45.7
Senegal	17.30	1.48	22.2	5.6	8.4	24.7	63	90	44	..	..	..	54.0
Sierra Leone	42.82	1.84	28.7	..	8.5	34.7	34	58	21	75.0	..	..	..
Somalia	73.20	6.22	..	..	..	..	26	..	28x	..	..	..	..
South Africa	..	..	9.2	1.4	2.5	22.8	87	99	70	..	..	..	23.7
Sudan	20.16	5.48	33.9	11.0	13.1	34.3	73	84x	41x	..	..	..	..
Swaziland	13.54	0.12	9.7	..	0.9	30.3	50	80x	42x	..	..	..	..
Tanzania	40.07	12.29	28.9	7.2	6.0	43.2	66	92	58	51.1	..	..	16.4
Togo	22.88	0.95	24.5	5.9	5.3	29.2	55	82	41	32.3	..	..	..
Uganda	28.47	5.54	25.5	6.7	5.3	38.3	46	77	41	55.0	..	..	69.3
Zambia	44.54	3.74	25.2	5.7	5.1	39.8	38	84	10	86.0	..	..	84.6
Zimbabwe	39.05	4.31	15.5	3.0	5.5	21.4	79	99	69	25.5	..	..	41.0
South Asia	**23.34**	**296.56**	**52.0**	**20.0**	**16.0**	**53.0**	80	86	78	..	..	..	**43.0**
Afghanistan	62.32	12.66	..	..	..	..	12	39	5	..	..	..	..
Bangladesh	36.51	44.04	68.3	24.9	16.7	64.2	95	99	95	35.6	14.3	39.8	29.0
Bhutan	..	..	37.9	..	4.1	56.1	58	75	54	..	..	..	..
India	21.51	204.35	53.4	20.6	17.5	52.0	81	85	79	35.0	30.5	36.7	47.0
Maldives	..	..	39.0	8.3	16.0	30.1	60	98	50	..	..	..	..
Nepal	21.29	4.64	46.9	16.1	11.2	48.4	71	93	68	42.0	23.0	44.0	50.3
Pakistan	18.78	26.31	38.2	12.8	9.0	50.0	79	89	73	34.0	28.0	36.9	11.6
Sri Lanka	25.20	4.56	37.7	7.0	15.5	23.8	57	88	52	35.3	28.4	38.1	4.0

TABLE 3: Hunger, Malnutrition and Poverty

	Undernourished population		% under-5 (1990-1997) suffering from:				% population with access to safe water 1990-1997			Population in Poverty (%)			
	Percent of the population undernourished 1995-1997	Number of undernourished people (millions) 1995-1997	Underweight		Wasting	Stunting				Below national poverty line 1984-1996			Population below $1 a day[h] 1981-1996
			moderate & severe	severe	moderate & severe	moderate & severe	Total	Urban	Rural	National	Urban	Rural	
East Asia and the Pacific	**13.44**	**241.55**	**23.0**	**4.0**	**5.0**	**34.0**	**68**	**95**	**57**	..	..	..	**26.0**
Brunei	..	..	..	..	..	..	..	..	..	..	..	..	..
Cambodia	33.41	3.42	40.0	7.0	8.0	38.0	30	..	25	36.1	21.1	40.1	..
China	13.27	164.40	17.4	2.9	3.4	31.4	67	97	56	8.6	0.4	11.5	22.2
Hong Kong[a]	d	d	0.3	..	2.0	3.0	..	100x	96x	..	..	..	..
Fiji	..	..	7.9	0.8	8.2	2.7	77	..	..	..	..	..	..
Indonesia	5.73	11.48	39.9	7.5	..	..	75	91	66	15.1	16.8	14.3	7.7
Korea, DPR (North)	47.64	10.77	..	..	..	..	81	..	..	..	..	..	..
Korea, Rep. (South)	<2.50	0.44	..	..	..	..	93	100	76	..	..	..	..
Lao, PDR	32.61	1.60	40.0	11.7	10.5	47.3	44	..	..	46.1	24.0	53.0	..
Malaysia	<2.50	0.37	20.1	0.6	..	..	78	96	66	15.5	..	..	4.3
Mongolia	47.54	1.19	12.3	2.4	1.7	26.4	40	73	3	36.3	38.5	33.1	..
Myanmar (Burma)	6.52	2.83	42.9	15.8	8.0	45.0	60	78	50	..	..	..	..
Papua New Guinea	24.01	1.06	29.9	6.4	5.5	43.2	32	78	23	..	..	..	..
Philippines	22.31	15.59	29.6	5.0	7.5	32.7	84	93	80	37.5	22.5	51.2	26.9
Singapore	..	..	..	..	..	..	100x	100x	..	..	..	..	..
Solomon Islands	..	..	21.3	3.6	6.6	27.3	..	80	62	..	..	..	..
Thailand	24.20	14.32	25.3	4.0	5.3	21.5	81	88	73	13.1	10.2	15.5	0.1
Vietnam	18.74	14.08	44.9	11.0	11.6	46.9	43	47	42	50.9	25.9	57.2	..
Latin America and the Caribbean	**11.10**	**53.41**	**11.0**	**2.0**	**3.0**	**20.0**	**77**	**87**	**42**	..	..	..	**24.0**
Argentina	<2.50	0.48	1.9	0.0	1.1	4.7	71	77	29	25.5	..	..	..
Belize	..	..	6.2	1.3	..	..	83	100	69	35.0	..	..	..
Bolivia	23.15	1.76	14.9	3.4	4.2	26.8	63	86	32	..	..	..	7.1
Brazil	10.00	16.16	5.7	0.6	2.3	10.5	76	88	25	17.4	13.1	32.6	23.6
Chile	4.85	0.70	0.9	..	0.3	2.4	91	99	41	20.5	..	..	15.0
Colombia	12.38	4.86	8.4	0.9	1.4	15.0	85	97	56	17.7	8.0	31.2	7.4
Costa Rica	6.68	0.24	2.2	0.2	2.0	8.0	96	100	92	11.0	..	..	18.9
Cuba	18.84	2.08	1.5	0.1	0.4	3.1	93	96	85	..	..	..	..
Dominican Republic	26.26	2.09	10.3	1.7	1.4	16.5	65	80	40x	20.6	10.9	29.8	19.9
Ecuador	5.29	0.62	16.5	0.0x	1.7	34.0	68	80	49	35.0	25.0	47.0	30.4
El Salvador	10.41	0.60	11.2	1.2	1.3	23.1	66	84	40	48.3	43.1	55.7	..
Guatemala	16.53	1.69	26.6	5.9	3.3	49.7	77	76	78	58.0	..	..	53.3
Guyana	16.02	0.13	18.3	2.2	..	..	91	96	85	43.0	..	..	..
Haiti	61.42	4.72	27.5	8.1	7.8	31.9	37	50	28	65.0	..	81.0	..
Honduras	20.92	1.22	18.3	3.2	2.0	39.6	76	90x	62	50.0	56.0	46.0	46.9
Jamaica	11.26	0.28	10.2	2.7	3.5	9.6	86	92x	48x	34.2	..	..	4.3
Mexico	5.53	5.12	14.2	2.9	6.0	22.8	85	90x	66x	10.1	..	..	14.9
Nicaragua	31.07	1.41	11.9	1.0	1.9	23.7	62	88	32	50.3	31.9	76.1	43.8
Panama	17.02	0.46	7.0	1.0	1.0	9.0	93	..	..	..	..	..	25.6
Paraguay	12.58	0.62	3.7	0.5	0.3	13.9	60	70x	10x	21.8	19.7	28.5	..
Peru	19.03	4.56	10.7	1.7	1.7	31.8	67	84	33	49.0	4.0	64.7	49.4
Suriname	9.04	<0.10	..	..	..	..	72x	78x	54x	..	..	..	..
Trinidad and Tobago	11.36	0.14	6.5	0.4	3.8	4.8	97	99	91	21.0	..	..	..
Uruguay	3.92	0.13	4.4	0.7	1.4	9.5	83x	95	5x	..	..	..	..
Venezuela	14.74	3.29	4.5	0.7	2.9	13.2	79	80	75	31.3	..	..	11.8
Middle East and North Africa	**5.96**	**20.26**	**16.0**	**4.0**	**7.0**	**24.0**	**83**	**97**	**70**	..	..	..	**4.0[h]**
Algeria	5.10	1.46	12.8	3.4	8.9	18.3	78	91	64	22.6	14.7	30.3	1.6
Bahrain	..	..	7.2	0.8	5.5	9.9	94	94	100x	..	..	..	..
Cyprus	..	..	..	..	..	..	100	100	100	..	..	..	..
Egypt	3.89	2.47	12.4	2.6	4.6	29.8	87	97	79	..	..	..	7.6
Iran	5.88	3.73	15.7	..	6.6	18.9	90	98	82	..	..	..	..
Iraq	15.33	3.16	11.9	2.3	3.4	21.8	81	96	48	..	..	..	..
Jordan	3.00	0.14	6.4	0.8	3.1	15.8	98	98x	94x	15.0	..	..	2.5
Kuwait	3.27	0.06	6.4	..	2.6	12.2	..	..	..	..	..	..	..
Lebanon	<2.50	0.05	3.0	..	2.9	12.2	94	96	88	..	..	..	..
Libya	<2.50	<0.10	4.7	..	2.8	15.1	97	97	97	..	..	..	..

TABLE 3: Hunger, Malnutrition and Poverty

| | Undernourished population | | % under-5 (1990-1997) suffering from: | | | | % population with access to safe water 1990-1997 | | | Population in Poverty (%) | | | |
| | Percent of the population undernourished 1995-1997 | Number of undernourished people (millions) 1995-1997 | Underweight | | Wasting | Stunting | | | | Below national poverty line 1984-1996 | | | Population below $1 a day[h] 1981-1996 |
			moderate & severe	severe	moderate & severe	moderate & severe	Total	Urban	Rural	National	Urban	Rural	
Morocco	5.13	1.35	9.5	2.0	2.2	24.2	65	98	34	13.1	7.6	18.0	1.1
Oman	..	..	14.1	0.9	9.1	15.7	85	98x	56x	..	..	..	..
Qatar	..	..	5.5	..	1.5	8.1	..	100	100x	..	..	..	..
Saudi Arabia	3.97	0.75	..	..	..	..	95x	95x	74x	..	..	..	..
Syria	<2.50	0.21	12.1	3.0	8.1	26.6	86	95	77	..	..	..	..
Tunisia	<2.50	0.06	9.0	2.0x	3.9	22.5	98	100	95	14.1	8.9	21.6	3.9
Turkey	<2.50	1.04	10.3	3.4	3.0	21.0	49	66	25	..	..	..	..
United Arab Emirates	<2.50	<0.10	..	..	..	..	97	98x	98x	..	..	..	..
Yemen	36.56	5.73	30.0	4.3	12.7	44.1	61	88	55	19.1	18.6	19.2	..
Countries in Transition[b]	**6.32**	**25.09**	..	..	..	..	..	..	..	..	..	..	..
Albania	..	..	..	..	..	..	..	..	..	..	19.6	..	..
Armenia	..	..	..	..	..	..	..	..	..	..	..	..	..
Azerbaijan	..	..	10.1	2.3	2.9	22.2	..	..	..	..	..	..	..
Belarus	..	..	..	..	..	..	..	..	..	37.0	..	..	<2
Bosnia and Herzegovina	..	..	..	..	..	..	..	..	..	..	..	..	..
Bulgaria	..	..	..	..	..	..	..	..	..	..	..	..	2.6
Croatia	..	..	1.0	..	1.0	1.0	..	98x	74x	..	..	..	..
Czech Republic	..	..	1.0	0.0	2.1	1.9	..	..	..	..	..	..	3.1
Estonia	..	..	..	..	..	..	..	..	..	8.9	6.8	14.7	6.0
Georgia	..	..	..	..	..	..	..	..	..	30.0	..	..	..
Hungary	..	..	2.2	0.2	1.6	2.9	..	..	..	25.3	..	..	0.7
Kazakhstan	..	..	8.3	1.5	3.3	15.8	93	99	84	..	..	..	<2.0
Kyrgyzstan	..	..	..	..	7.0	..	71	84x	..	45.4	32.0	52.2	18.9
Latvia	..	..	..	..	..	..	..	..	..	..	..	..	<2.0
Lithuania	..	..	..	..	..	..	..	..	..	..	..	..	<2.0
Macedonia, FYR	..	..	..	..	..	..	..	..	..	..	24.0	28.0	..
Moldova	..	..	..	..	..	..	55	98	18	..	..	..	6.8
Poland	..	..	..	..	..	..	..	..	..	23.8	..	..	6.8
Romania	..	..	5.7	0.6	2.5	7.8	..	..	..	21.5	15.6	28.0	17.7
Russian Federation	..	..	3.0	0.5	3.9	12.7	..	..	..	30.9	..	..	1.1
Slovakia	..	..	..	..	..	..	..	..	..	..	..	..	12.8
Slovenia	..	..	..	..	..	..	..	..	..	..	..	..	1.0d
Tajikistan	..	..	..	..	..	30.0	60	82	49	..	..	..	..
Turkmenistan	..	..	..	..	..	..	74	..	..	..	..	..	4.9
Ukraine	..	..	..	..	..	..	97x	..	..	31.7	..	..	<2.0
Uzbekistan	..	..	..	..	..	..	90	99	88	..	..	..	29.0d
Yugoslavia, FR	..	..	..	..	..	..	76	98	57	..	..	..	..
Industrial Countries	**<2.50**	**7.96**	..	..	..	..	..	..	..	..	..	..	..
Australia	..	..	..	..	..	..	..	..	..	..	..	..	8.0c
Austria	..	..	..	..	..	..	..	..	..	..	..	..	..
Belgium	..	..	..	..	..	..	..	..	..	..	..	..	12.0c
Canada	..	..	..	..	..	..	..	..	..	..	..	..	6.0c
Denmark	..	..	..	..	..	..	..	..	..	..	..	..	8.0c
Finland	..	..	..	..	..	..	..	..	..	..	..	..	4.0c
France	..	..	..	..	..	..	..	..	..	..	..	..	12.0c
Germany	..	..	..	..	..	..	..	..	..	..	..	..	12.0c
Greece	..	..	..	..	..	..	..	..	..	..	..	..	..
Ireland	..	..	..	..	..	..	..	..	..	..	..	..	37.0c
Israel	..	..	..	..	..	..	..	..	..	..	..	..	..
Italy	..	..	..	..	..	..	..	..	..	..	..	..	2.0c
Japan	..	..	..	..	..	..	..	..	..	..	..	..	5.0c
Luxembourg	..	..	..	..	..	..	..	..	..	..	..	..	4.0c
Netherlands	..	..	..	..	..	..	..	..	..	..	..	..	14.0c

TABLE 3: Hunger, Malnutrition and Poverty

| | Undernourished population | | % under-5 (1990-1997) suffering from: | | | | % population with access to safe water 1990-1997 | | | Population in Poverty (%) | | | |
| | Percent of the population undernourished 1995-1997 | Number of undernourished people (millions) 1995-1997 | Underweight | | Wasting | Stunting | | | | Below national poverty line 1984-1996 | | | Population below $1 a day[h] 1981-1996 |
			moderate & severe	severe	moderate & severe	moderate & severe	Total	Urban	Rural	National	Urban	Rural	
New Zealand	..	..	..	..	..	..	97	100	82	..	..	..	..
Norway	..	..	..	..	..	..	..	..	..	..	..	..	3.0c
Portugal	..	..	..	..	..	..	..	..	..	..	..	..	..
Spain	..	..	..	..	..	..	..	..	..	..	..	..	21.0c
Sweden	..	..	..	..	..	..	..	..	..	..	..	..	5.0c
Switzerland	..	..	..	..	..	..	..	..	..	..	..	..	..
United Kingdom	..	..	..	..	..	..	..	..	..	..	..	..	13.0c
United States	..	..	..	..	..	..	..	..	..	..	..	..	14.0c
World	..	..	**28.7**	**9.0**	**8.5**	**35.3**	**72**	**90**	**62**	..	..	..	..

.. Data not available.

a Special Administrative Region, data exclusive of China.

b Central and Eastern European countries and the newly independent states of the former Soviet Union.

c Poverty line is $14.40 (1985 PPP$) per person per day.

d Poverty line is $4.00 (1990 PPP$) per person per day.

e Bread for the World Institute estimate.

f Data included as part of China.

g Djibouti, Somalia and Sudan are included in Middle East and North Africa.

h Measured in 1985 international prices and adjusted to local currency using purchasing power parities.

The number '0' (zero) means zero or less than half the unit of measure.

x Indicates data that refer to years or periods other than those specified in the column heading, differ from the standard definition or refer to only part of a country.

TABLE 4: Economic and Development Indicators

	GNP per capita US$ (billions) 1997	GNP per capita Purchasing Power Parity (PPP), $ 1997	GNP per capita Average annual growth % 1996-97	Human Development Index (HDI) rank[c] 1999	Distribution of income or consumption by quintiles[k] 1986-1996 Lowest 20%	Second quintile	Third quintile	Fourth quintile	Highest 20%	Ratio of highest 20% to lowest 20%[#]	Central government expenditure (% of GDP) 1996	Public education expenditure (% of central government expenditure) 1993-1996	Military expenditure (% of central government expenditure) 1995	Per capita energy consumption (kg. of oil equivalent) 1996	Annual deforestation[m] (% of total forest) 1990-1995
Developing Countries	..	..	..	..	..	..	..	..	..	..	**19.5x**	**14.8**	**63.0x**	**973**	..
Africa (Sub-Saharan)	**510**	**1,460**	**0.2**		..	..	..	..	..	..	..	..	..	**670**	**0.7e**
Angola	260	820i	−2.5	160	..	..	..	..	..	..	..	..	..	532	1.0
Benin	380	1,260	2.7	155	..	..	..	..	..	..	..	15.2	8.6x	341	1.2
Botswana	3,310	7,430	3.0	122	..	..	..	..	..	..	39.4	20.2	12.7	..	0.5
Burkina Faso	250	1,000i	3.2	171	5.5	8.7	12.0	18.7	55.0	10.00	..	11.1	12.0x	..	0.7
Burundi	140	620i	−1.5	170	..	..	..	..	..	..	27.7	18.3	24.8	..	0.4
Cameroon	620	1,770	1.7	134	..	..	..	..	..	..	12.7x	..	10.2x	369	0.6
Cape Verde	1,090	2,950	1.9	106	..	..	..	..	..	..	..	..	..	..	−24.0
Central African Republic	320	1,310i	3.6	165	..	..	..	..	..	..	..	..	..	..	0.4
Chad	230	950i	3.5	162	..	..	..	..	..	..	..	..	..	..	0.8
Comoros	400	1,530	−2.4	139	..	..	..	..	..	..	..	..	..	..	5.6
Congo, Dem. Rep.	110	760i	−8.6	141	..	..	..	..	..	..	8.3x	..	3.7	305	0.7
Congo, Republic	670	1,290	−2.7	135	..	..	..	..	..	..	..	14.7	..	457	0.2
Côte d'Ivoire	710	1,690	4.3	154	6.8	11.2	15.8	22.2	44.1	6.49	..	..	..	382	0.6
Djibouti	g	..	..	157	..	..	..	..	..	..	..	..	..	..	0.0
Equatorial Guinea	1,060	..	125.5	131	..	..	..	..	..	..	..	5.6	..	..	0.5
Eritrea	230	1,040	10.4	167	..	..	..	..	..	..	..	..	..	..	0.0
Ethiopia	110	500	3.0	172	7.1	10.9	14.5	19.8	47.7	6.72	18.1x	13.7	9.2x	284	0.5
Gabon	4,120	6,560	3.3	124	..	..	..	..	..	..	..	..	9.6x	1,403	0.5
Gambia	340	1,440i	2.1	163	4.4	9.0	13.5	20.4	52.8	12.00	21.5x	21.2	16.2	..	0.9
Ghana	390	1,610i	1.7	133	8.4	12.2	15.8	21.9	41.7	4.96	22.1x	..	5.8x	380	1.3
Guinea	550	1,790	1.9	161	6.4	10.4	14.8	21.2	47.2	7.38	..	..	..	..	1.1
Guinea-Bissau	230	..	4.4	168	2.1	6.5	12.0	20.6	58.9	28.05	..	..	..	37	0.4
Kenya	340	1,160	0.4	136	5.0	9.7	14.2	20.9	50.2	10.04	28.9	16.7	6.2	476	0.3
Lesotho	680	2,490i	2.1	127	2.8	6.5	11.2	19.4	60.1	21.46	55.2	..	2.5	..	0.0
Liberia	..	..	..	..	..	..	..	..	..	..	..	..	..	..	0.6
Madagascar	250	900	1.5	147	5.1	9.4	13.3	20.1	52.1	10.22	17.3	13.6	5.0	..	0.8
Malawi	210	700	2.5	159	..	..	..	..	..	..	..	..	3.5x	..	1.6
Mali	260	720	3.5	166	4.6	8.0	11.9	19.3	56.2	12.22	..	..	..	..	1.0
Mauritania	440	1,650i	2.1	149	6.2	10.8	15.4	22.0	45.6	7.35	..	..	9.3x	..	0.0
Mauritius	3,870	9,230	3.9	59	..	..	..	..	..	..	22.4	..	1.6	..	0.0
Mozambique	140	690i	10.5	169	..	..	..	..	..	..	38.5x	..	5.5x	481	0.7
Namibia	2,110	5,100i	−1.3	115	..	..	..	..	..	..	..	25.6	..	..	0.3
Niger	200	830i	0.0	173	2.6	7.1	13.9	23.1	53.3	20.50	..	..	7.9x	..	0.0
Nigeria	280	860	2.1	146	4.0	8.9	14.4	23.4	49.4	12.35	..	11.5	3.5x	722	0.9
Rwanda	210	650	−5.6	164	9.7	13.2	16.5	21.6	39.1	4.03	25.8x	..	23.3x	..	0.2
Senegal	540	1,690	2.5	153	3.1	7.4	12.1	19.5	57.9	18.68	..	..	..	302	0.7
Sierra Leone	160	410	−20.6	174	1.1	2.0	9.8	23.7	63.4	57.64	14.8	..	28.9	..	3.0
Somalia	f	..	..	..	..	..	..	..	..	..	..	..	..	..	0.2
South Africa	3,210	7,190	−0.4	101	2.9	5.5	9.2	17.7	64.8	22.34	34.7	23.9	6.7	2,482	0.2
Sudan	290	1,370i	4.2	142	..	..	..	..	..	..	..	9.0	37.6x	397	0.8
Swaziland	1,520	3,690	3.4	113	..	..	..	..	..	..	..	18.1	..	..	0.0
Tanzania	210j	620	1.2	156	6.8	11.0	15.1	21.6	45.5	6.69	..	..	8.4	453	1.0
Togo	340	1,460	2.0	143	..	..	..	..	..	..	..	24.7	10.2	..	1.4
Uganda	330	1,160i	3.0	158	6.6	10.9	15.2	21.3	46.1	6.98	..	21.4	13.3	..	0.9
Zambia	370	910	1.8	151	4.2	8.2	12.8	20.1	54.8	13.05	21.4	7.1	12.6	628	0.8
Zimbabwe	720	2,240	0.1	130	4.0	6.3	10.0	17.4	62.3	15.58	34.1x	..	10.5x	929	0.6
South Asia	**380**	**1,590**	**3.4**		..	..	..	..	..	..	**17.4**	**11.2**	**61.0**	**441**	**0.3e**
Afghanistan	f	..	..	..	..	..	..	..	..	..	..	..	..	..	6.8
Bangladesh	360	1,090	4.6	150	9.4	13.5	17.2	22.0	37.9	4.03	..	..	9.9x	197	0.8
Bhutan	430	..	4.9	145	..	..	..	..	..	..	..	..	..	..	0.3
India	1,180	1,660	4.3	132	9.2	13.0	16.8	21.7	39.3	4.27	15.8	11.6	12.7	476	0.0
Maldives	220	1,180	6.3	93	..	..	..	..	..	..	..	..	..	..	..
Nepal	220	3,340	1.7	144	7.6	11.5	15.1	21.0	44.8	5.89	17.5	13.5	5.8	320	1.1
Pakistan	500	1,580	−2.4	138	9.4	13.0	16.0	20.3	41.2	4.38	23.8	8.1	25.3	446	2.9
Sri Lanka	800	2,460	5.9	90	8.9	13.1	16.9	21.7	39.3	4.42	27.7	8.9	15.7	371	1.1

TABLE 4: Economic and Development Indicators

	GNP per capita US$ (billions) 1997	GNP per capita Purchasing Power Parity (PPP), $ 1997	GNP per capita Average annual growth % 1996-97	Human Development Index (HDI) rank[c] 1999	Distribution of income or consumption by quintiles[k] 1986-1996 Lowest 20%	Second quintile	Third quintile	Fourth quintile	Highest 20%	Ratio of highest 20% to lowest 20%[e]	Central government expenditure (% of GDP) 1996	Public education expenditure (% of central government expenditure) 1993-1996	Military expenditure (% of central government expenditure) 1995	Per capita energy consumption (kg. of oil equivalent) 1996	Annual deforestation[m] (% of total forest) 1990-1995
East Asia and the Pacific	**970**	**3,170**	**4.9**	..	..	..	..	..	..	..	**11.6**	..	..	**855**	**0.5e**
Brunei	h	..	..	25	..	..	..	..	..	..	..	..	..	..	0.6
Cambodia	300	1,290i	–1.4	137	..	..	..	..	..	..	..	..	..	..	1.6
China	860	3,070	7.4	98	5.5	9.8	14.9	22.3	47.5	8.64	8.0	11.9	18.5	902	0.1
Hong Kong[a]	25,200	24,350	2.1	24	..	..	..	..	..	..	..	..	..	1,931	..
Fiji	2,460	3,860	–2.0	61	..	..	..	..	..	..	27.5x	..	..	..	0.4
Indonesia	1,110	3,390	2.6	105	8.0	11.3	15.1	20.8	44.9	5.61	14.6	7.9	8.9	672	1.0
Korea, DPR (North)	g	..	..	..	..	..	..	..	..	..	..	..	..	1,063	0.0
Korea, Rep. (South)	10,550	13,430	3.9	30	..	..	..	..	..	..	18.6	17.5	13.6	3,576	0.2
Lao, PDR	400	1,300	3.8	140	9.6	12.9	16.3	21.0	40.2	4.19	..	..	22.3x	..	1.2
Malaysia	4,530	7,730	4.8	56	4.6	8.3	13.0	20.4	53.7	11.67	21.9	..	12.4	1,950	2.4
Mongolia	390	1,490	1.5	119	7.3	12.2	16.6	23.0	40.9	5.60	21.6	19.3	7.0	..	0.0
Myanmar (Burma)	f	..	..	128	..	..	..	..	..	..	10.1	14.4	..	294	1.4
Papua New Guinea	930	..	–15.9	129	4.5	7.9	11.9	19.2	56.5	12.56	29.4	..	5.6	..	0.4
Philippines	1,200	3,670	3.0	77	5.9	9.6	13.9	21.1	49.6	8.41	18.5	..	8.5	528	3.5
Singapore	32,810	29,230	6.7	22	..	..	..	..	..	..	21.0	23.4	24.0	7,835	0.0
Solomon Islands	870	2,270	0.0	118	..	..	..	..	..	..	..	..	..	..	0.2
Thailand	2,740	6,490	–2.1	67	5.6	8.7	13.0	20.0	52.7	9.41	16.5	20.1	15.2	1,333	2.6
Vietnam	310	1,590	3.8	110	7.8	11.4	15.4	21.4	44.0	5.64	..	7.4	10.9	448	1.4
Latin America and the Caribbean	**3,940**	**6,730**	**3.9**		..	..	..	..	..	..	**25.6x**	**17.9**	**29.0**	**1,163**	**0.6e**
Argentina	8,950	10,100	6.7	39	..	..	..	..	..	..	14.0	12.6	27.0x	1,673	0.3
Belize	2,670	2,670	–0.7	83	..	..	..	..	..	..	31.1x	19.5	..	..	0.3
Bolivia	970	2,810	1.4	112	5.6	9.7	14.5	22.0	48.2	8.61	22.8	11.1	9.5	479	1.2
Brazil	4,790	6,350	1.9	79	2.5	5.7	9.9	17.7	64.2	25.68	33.8x	..	3.9	1,012	0.5
Chile	4,820	12,240	5.7	34	3.5	6.6	10.9	18.1	61.0	17.43	21.0	14.8	17.5	1,419	0.4
Colombia	2,180	6,570	1.2	57	3.1	6.8	10.9	17.6	61.5	19.84	14.4x	19.0	16.2	799	0.5
Costa Rica	2,680	6,510	1.7	45	4.0	8.8	13.7	21.7	51.8	12.95	30.6	22.8	2.7	657	3.0
Cuba	g	..	..	58	..	..	..	..	..	..	..	12.6	..	1,448	1.2
Dominican Republic	1,750	4,690	6.4	88	4.2	7.9	12.5	19.7	55.7	13.26	15.6	13.4	9.1	652	1.6
Ecuador	1,570	4,700	3.9	72	5.4	8.9	13.2	19.9	52.6	9.74	15.7	13.0	18.3	731	1.6
El Salvador	1,810	2,860	1.8	107	3.7	8.3	13.1	20.5	54.4	14.70	13.7x	..	7.4	700	3.3
Guatemala	1,580	4,060	1.8	117	2.1	5.8	10.5	18.6	63.0	30.00	8.9x	18.2	14.2	510	2.0
Guyana	800	2,800	6.7	99	6.3	10.7	15.0	21.2	46.9	7.44	..	10.0	..	..	0.0
Haiti	380	1,260	–1.1	152	..	..	..	..	..	..	..	..	21.6	268	3.4
Honduras	740	2,260	3.5	114	3.4	7.1	11.7	19.7	58.0	17.06	..	16.5	8.7	503	2.3
Jamaica	1,550	3,330	–2.9	82	5.8	10.2	14.9	21.6	47.5	8.19	..	12.9	1.4	1,465	7.2
Mexico	3,700	8,110	6.3	50	3.6	7.2	11.8	19.2	58.2	16.17	15.5	23.0	5.1	1,525	0.9
Nicaragua	410	1,820	10.4	121	4.2	8.0	12.6	20.0	55.2	13.14	33.2x	..	5.3	525	2.5
Panama	3,080	6,890	2.5	49	2.3	6.2	11.3	19.8	60.4	26.26	27.4	20.9	5.3x	853	2.1
Paraguay	2,000	3,860	7.4	84	2.3	5.9	10.7	18.7	62.4	27.13	13.0x	18.6	7.3	865	2.6
Peru	2,610	4,580	5.4	80	4.4	9.1	14.1	21.3	51.2	11.64	16.5	19.2	9.3	582	0.3
Suriname	1,320	..	25.7	64	..	..	..	..	..	..	..	..	..	..	0.1
Trinidad and Tobago	4,250	6,460	7.0	46	..	..	..	..	..	..	28.3x	11.6	4.0x	6,081	1.5
Uruguay	6,130	9,110	4.2	40	..	..	..	..	..	..	31.4	15.5	7.3	912	0.0
Venezuela	3,480	8,660	5.2	48	4.3	8.8	13.8	21.3	51.8	12.05	16.9	..	6.3	2,463	1.1
Middle East and North Africa	**2,070**	**4,630**	**0.8**		..	..	..	..	..	..	..	..	..	**1,246**	**0.4e**
Algeria	1,500	4,250	–0.5	109	7.0	11.6	16.1	22.7	42.6	6.09	29.7	16.4	6.9	842	1.2
Bahrain	g	..	..	37	..	..	..	..	..	..	..	12.8	..	..	0.0
Cyprus	h	..	..	26	..	..	..	..	..	..	..	13.2	..	..	0.0
Egypt	1,200	3,080	4.5	120	8.7	12.5	16.3	21.4	41.1	4.72	34.3x	..	13.7	638	0.0
Iran	1,780	5,690	1.5	95	..	..	..	..	..	..	23.2x	..	13.6x	1,491	1.7
Iraq	g	..	..	125	..	..	..	..	..	..	..	..	..	1,174	0.0
Jordan	1,520	3,350	–1.8	94	5.9	9.8	13.9	20.3	50.1	8.49	35.0	19.8	21.7	1,040	2.5
Kuwait	h	..	..	35	..	..	..	..	..	..	45.2	8.9	25.5	8,167	0.0
Lebanon	3,350	6,090	..	69	..	..	..	..	..	..	37.9	8.2	9.7x	1,164	7.8
Libya	..	..	..	65	..	..	..	..	..	..	..	..	..	2,935	0.0

TABLE 4: Economic and Development Indicators

	GNP per capita			Human Development Index (HDI) rank[c] 1999	Distribution of income or consumption by quintiles[k] 1986-1996						Central government expenditure (% of GDP) 1996	Public education expenditure (% of central government expenditure) 1993-1996	Military expenditure (% of central government expenditure) 1995	Per capita energy consumption (kg. of oil equivalent) 1996	Annual deforestation[m] (% of total forest) 1990-1995
	US$ (billions) 1997	Purchasing Power Parity (PPP), $ 1997	Average annual growth % 1996-97		Lowest 20%	Second quintile	Third quintile	Fourth quintile	Highest 20%	Ratio of highest 20% to lowest 20%[e]					
Morocco	1,260	3,210	−3.9	126	6.6	10.5	15.0	21.7	46.3	7.02	33.3x	24.9	13.8x	329	0.3
Oman	..	..	..	89	..	..	..	..	..	..	42.4x	17.8	33.9	2,231	0.0
Qatar	h	..	..	41	..	..	..	..	..	..	..	..	..	..	0.0
Saudi Arabia	7,150	10,540i	−1.4	78	..	..	..	..	..	..	..	17.0	41.0x	4,753	0.8
Syria	1,120	3,000	0.9	111	..	..	..	..	..	..	23.8	13.6	..	1,002	2.2
Tunisia	2,110	5,050	9.2	102	5.9	10.4	15.3	22.1	46.3	7.85	32.6	17.4	6.3x	735	0.5
Turkey	3,130	6,470	6.8	86	..	..	..	..	..	..	26.9	17.6	17.6	1,045	0.0
United Arab Emirates	h	..	..	43	..	..	..	..	..	..	11.8x	16.7	38.4	13,155	0.0
Yemen	270	720	−0.5	148	6.1	10.9	15.3	21.6	46.1	7.56	32.8	20.8	29.4x	187	0.0
Countries in Transition[b]	..	..	..		..	..	..	..	..	..	**29.9x**	..	..	**2,732**	**−0.1e**
Albania	760	2,170i	−8.2	100	..	..	..	..	..	..	31.0x	..	3.2	362	0.0
Armenia	560	2,540	8.2	87	..	..	..	..	..	..	..	10.3	..	474	−2.7
Azerbaijan	510	1,520	2.5	103	..	..	..	..	..	..	..	21.3	..	1,570	0.0
Belarus	2,150	4,820	11.4	60	8.5	13.5	17.7	23.1	37.2	4.38	33.9	17.8	..	2,386	−1.0
Bosnia and Herzegovina	f	..	..		..	..	..	..	..	..	..	..	..	777	0.0
Bulgaria	1,170	3,870	−6.0	63	8.3	13.0	17.0	22.3	39.3	4.73	48.1	7.0	6.3	2,705	0.0
Croatia	4,060	4,930	3.8	55	..	..	..	..	..	..	46.7	..	32.0	1,418	0.0
Czech Republic	5,240	10,380	1.2	36	10.5	13.9	16.9	21.3	37.4	3.56	36.4	..	6.6	3,917	0.0
Estonia	3,360	5,090	8.6	54	6.2	12.0	17.0	23.1	41.8	6.74	33.8	22.3	2.9x	3,834	−1.0
Georgia	860	1,980	13.1	85	..	..	..	..	..	..	9.7	..	..	291	0.0
Hungary	4,510	6,970	5.1	47	9.7	13.9	16.9	21.4	38.1	3.93	43.2	..	4.6	2,499	−0.5
Kazakhstan	1,350	3,530	2.4	76	7.5	12.3	16.9	22.9	40.4	5.39	..	..	..	2,724	−1.9
Kyrgyzstan	480	2,180	7.2	97	6.7	11.5	16.4	23.1	42.3	6.31	..	23.5	..	645	0.0
Latvia	2,430	3,970	7.7	74	8.3	13.8	18.0	22.9	37.0	4.46	31.0	14.1	..	1,674	−0.9
Lithuania	2,260	4,140	4.1	62	8.1	12.3	16.2	21.3	42.1	5.20	25.0	22.8	2.1	2,414	−0.6
Macedonia, FYR	1,100	3,180i	0.4	73	..	..	..	..	..	..	..	20.0	..	..	0.0
Moldova	460	1,450	0.0	104	6.9	11.9	16.7	23.1	41.5	6.01	..	28.1	..	1,064	0.0
Poland	3,590	6,510	6.7	44	9.3	13.8	17.7	22.6	36.6	3.94	42.2	..	5.4	2,807	−0.1
Romania	1,410	4,270	−6.5	68	8.9	13.6	17.6	22.6	37.3	4.19	31.4	10.5	11.2	2,027	0.0
Russian Federation	2,680	4,280	0.6	71	4.2	8.8	13.6	20.7	52.8	12.57	24.7	9.6	38.1x	4,169	..
Slovakia	3,680	7,860	6.7	42	11.9	15.8	18.8	22.2	31.4	2.64	..	..	6.8	3,266	−0.1
Slovenia	9,840	11,880	5.3	33	9.3	13.3	16.9	21.9	38.6	4.15	..	12.6	3.5	3,098	0.0
Tajikistan	330	1,100	0.5	108	..	..	..	..	..	..	..	11.5	..	594	0.0
Turkmenistan	640	1,410	−25.0	96	6.7	11.4	16.3	22.8	42.8	6.39	..	..	..	2,646	0.0
Ukraine	1,040	2,170	−2.4	91	4.3	9.0	13.8	20.8	52.2	12.14	..	..	7.8	3,012	−0.1
Uzbekistan	1,020	..	..	92	..	..	..	..	..	..	..	21.1	..	1,826	−2.7
Yugoslavia, FR	g	..	..		..	..	..	..	..	..	..	..	..	1,364	0.0
Industrial Countries	**25,890**	**22,930**	**2.3**		..	..	..	..	..	..	**32.1x**	**12.3**	..	**5,259**	**−0.2e**
Australia[l]	20,650	19,510	−0.6	7	7.0	12.2	16.6	23.3	40.9	5.84	26.3	12.9	8.8	5,494	0.0
Austria	27,920	22,010	0.7	16	10.4	14.8	18.5	22.9	33.3	3.20	41.7	10.6	2.2x	3,373	0.0
Belgium[l]	26,730	23,090	2.1	5	9.5	14.6	18.4	23.0	34.5	3.63	48.2	..	3.5x	5,552	0.0
Canada[l]	19,640	21,750	2.9	1	7.5	12.9	17.2	23.0	39.3	5.24	24.2x	13.5	7.1x	7,880	−0.1
Denmark[l]	34,890	23,450	3.6	15	9.6	14.9	18.3	22.7	34.5	3.59	41.4x	13.1	4.1	4,346	0.0
Finland[l]	24,790	19,660	5.9	13	10.0	14.2	17.6	22.3	35.8	3.58	40.1	12.2	5.1	6,143	0.1
France[l]	26,300	22,210	3.2	11	7.2	12.7	17.1	22.8	40.1	5.57	46.9	11.1	6.6	4,355	−1.1
Germany[l]	28,280	21,170	1.7	14	9.0	13.5	17.5	22.9	37.1	4.12	33.7	9.5	..	4,267	0.0
Greece	11,640	12,540	0.7	27	..	..	..	..	..	..	32.8	..	10.8	2,328	−2.3
Ireland	17,790	17,420	7.3	20	6.7	11.6	16.4	22.4	42.9	6.40	38.1x	..	3.4	3,293	−2.7
Israel[l]	16,180	17,680	−0.6	23	6.9	11.4	16.3	22.9	42.5	6.16	48.7	..	21.1	2,843	0.0
Italy[l]	20,170	20,100	1.4	19	7.6	12.9	17.3	23.2	38.9	5.12	49.5	9.0	3.9x	2,808	−0.1
Japan[l]	38,160	24,400	1.5	4	..	..	..	..	..	..	23.7x	9.9	4.2x	4,058	0.1
Luxembourg	..	..	..	17	9.5	13.6	17.7	22.4	36.7	3.86	..	15.1	..	..	0.0
Netherlands[l]	25,380	21,300	2.8	8	8.0	13.0	16.7	22.5	39.9	4.99	48.0	8.7	4.4	4,885	0.0

TABLE 4: Economic and Development Indicators

	GNP per capita				Distribution of income or consumption by quintiles[k] 1986-1996						Central government expenditure (% of GDP) 1996	Public education expenditure (% of central government expenditure) 1993-1996	Military expenditure (% of central government expenditure) 1995	Per capita energy consumption (kg. of oil equivalent) 1996	Annual deforestation[m] (% of total forest) 1990-1995
	US$ (billions) 1997	Purchasing Power Parity (PPP), $ 1997	Average annual growth % 1996-97	Human Development Index (HDI) rank[c] 1999	Lowest 20%	Second quintile	Third quintile	Fourth quintile	Highest 20%	Ratio of highest 20% to lowest 20%[e]					
New Zealand[l]	15,830	15,780	−0.4	18	..	..	..	..	..	..	31.9	..	3.3	4,388	−0.6
Norway[l]	36,100	24,260	2.8	2	10.0	14.3	17.9	22.4	35.3	3.53	36.8	..	6.5x	5,284	−0.3
Portugal[l]	11,010	14,180	4.3	28	..	..	..	..	..	..	41.6	..	5.9x	1,928	−0.9
Spain[l]	14,490	15,690	2.8	21	7.5	12.6	17.0	22.6	40.3	5.37	36.8x	12.8	5.6	2,583	0.0
Sweden[l]	26,210	19,010	1.3	6	9.6	14.5	18.1	23.2	34.5	3.59	46.1	..	5.8	5,944	0.0
Switzerland[l]	43,060	26,580	2.5	12	7.4	11.6	15.6	21.9	43.5	5.88	26.3	14.7	6.0x	3,622	0.0
United Kingdom[l]	20,870	20,170	3.7	10	7.1	12.8	17.2	23.1	39.8	5.61	41.7x	..	7.2	3,992	−0.5
United States[l]	29,080	29,080	2.8	3	4.8	10.5	16.0	23.5	45.2	9.42	22.2	14.4	17.4	8,051	−0.3
World	..	**6,260**	**1.8**	..	..	..	..	..	..	..	**29.8x**	**12.7**	**9.9**	**1,684**	**0.3e**

.. Data not available.

a Special Administrative Region, data is exclusive of China.

b Central and Eastern European countries and the newly independent states of former Soviet Union.

e Bread for the World Institute estimate.

f Estimated to be low income ($785 or less).

g Estimated to be lower middle income ($785 to $3,115).

h Estimated to be high income($9386 or more).

i Estimate based on regression; others are extrapolated from the latest International Comparison Programme benchmark estimates.

j GDP data.

k Income shares by percentiles of population; ranked by per capita income, excepted as noted.

l Income shares by percentiles of households; ranked by household income.

m Positive data indicate loss of forest; negative data indicate gain in forest.

x Data refer to a period other than specified in the column heading.

The number '0' (zero) means zero or less than half the unit of measure.

TABLE 5: Economic Globalization

| | Trade | | | | | | Investment 1997 | | | | | | Debt | | |
| | Exports of goods and services (% of GDP) | | Manufactured exports (% of merchandise exports) 1997 | Food Trade | | Imports of goods and services (% of GDP) 1997 | Gross domestic investment (GDI) (% of GDP) 1997 | Net private capital flows ($ millions) | Foreign direct investment ($ million) 1997 | Aid (% of GDI) | Foreign direct investment net inflows (% of GDI) | Foreign direct investment net inflows (% of GDP) | Total External debt (US $ billions) 1997 | Debt service (% of exports of goods and services) 1997 | Workers' remittances, receipts (US $ millions) 1996 |
	1980	1997		Food exports (% of merchandise exports)[e] 1997	Food imports (% of merchandise imports)[e] 1997										
Developing Countries	**18**	**24**	**58**	..	..	**25**	**25**	**285,885**	**160,579**	..	**10.3**	**1.3**	**2,173.23**	**17.0**	..
Africa (Sub-Saharan)	**33**	**32**	..	..	..	**32**	**18**	**6,674**	**5,222**	**27.7**	**7.7**	**1.3**	**219.45**	**12.8**	..
Angola	..	68	..	0.14	16.86	65	25	−24	350	23.0	18.5	4.6	10.16	15.9	..
Benin	23	25	..	49.53	18.35	33	18	3	3	56.9	0.8	0.1	1.62	9.1	84.00
Botswana	50	56	..	4.12	18.35	38	26	95	100	9.5	7.6	2.0	0.56	4.9x	..
Burkina Faso	10	14	..	36.36	12.14	30	25	0	0	60.8	0.0	0.0	1.30	11.8	76.00
Burundi	9	10	..	98.59	22.67	14	7	1	1	182.7	1.5	0.1	1.07	29.0	0.00
Cameroon	27	27	8	28.15	9.56	22	16	16	45	34.0	3.1	0.5	9.29	20.4	67.00
Cape Verde	..	25	..	0.88	25.10	..	..	..	..	..	..	..	3.28	5.5	92.00
Central African Republic	25	21	43	19.29	24.22	23	9	6	6	100.4	6.0	0.5	0.89	6.2	6.00
Chad	17	17	..	66.90	20.50	35	19	15	15	72.4	4.8	0.9	1.03	12.5	1.00
Comoros	..	16	..	42.98	35.48	..	..	..	..	..	..	..	0.20	3.9	17.00
Congo, Dem. Rep.	16	24	..	20.01	41.13	22	7	1	1	38.7	0.2	0.0	12.33	0.9	..
Congo, Republic	60	77	3	1.00	25.36	68	26	9	9	44.8	1.5	0.4	5.07	6.2	..
Côte d'Ivoire	35	47	5	49.68	14.68	40	16	−91	327	27.1	20.0	3.2	15.61	27.4	0.00
Djibouti	..	41	..	20.96	29.26	..	..	..	..	..	..	..	0.28	3.1	1.00
Equatorial Guinea	..	101	..	6.11	13.25	..	..	..	..	..	..	..	0.28	1.4	..
Eritrea	..	31	..	2.59	15.72	89	41	0	0	46.0	0.0	0.0	0.08	0.1	122.70
Ethiopia	11	16	11	87.61	13.26	26	19	28	5	52.3	0.4	0.1	10.08	9.5	0.00
Gabon	65	64	2	0.43	14.22	42	26	−105	−100	2.9	−7.4	−1.9	4.28	13.1	0.00
Gambia	43	47	..	28.24	33.84	61	18	12	12	57.3	16.6	2.9	0.43	11.6	..
Ghana	8	24	..	39.75	13.77	38	24	203	130	30.0	7.8	1.9	5.98	29.5	27.50
Guinea	..	18	..	6.58	19.46	21	22	−23	1	45.2	0.1	0.0	3.52	21.5	1.07
Guinea-Bissau	13	21	..	44.53	50.87	40	24	2	2	197.6	3.1	0.8	0.92	17.3	0.00
Kenya	28	29	25	50.29	16.80	37	19	−87	20	23.4	1.0	0.2	6.49	21.5	..
Lesotho	20	33	..	5.47	15.48	128	86	42	29	11.5	3.6	3.1	0.66	6.4	0.00
Liberia	..	..	..	9.04	18.83	..	..	..	..	..	..	..	1.70y	..	..
Madagascar	13	22	28	32.99	15.36	30	12	13	14	200.8	3.4	0.4	4.11	27.0	6.10
Malawi	25	24	7	64.20	9.09	35	12	1	2	112.7	0.6	0.1	2.21	12.4	0.00
Mali	16	25	..	48.56	9.52	35	23	15	15	77.2	2.5	0.6	2.95	10.5	105.00
Mauritania	37	40	..	9.01	65.58	49	18	2	3	130.3	1.6	0.3	2.45	24.2	6.00
Mauritius	51	62	71	21.18	14.14	65	28	771	53	3.4	4.4	1.2	2.47	10.9	0.00
Mozambique	15	18	17	23.65	19.93	34	30	37	35	118.5	4.3	1.3	5.99	18.6	0.00
Namibia	76	53	..	14.34	6.26	58	20	..	187	25.6	28.8	5.7	0.84y	..	7.68
Niger	25	16	..	17.84	22.24	24	11	−12	2	170.2	1.0	0.1	1.58	19.5	6.00
Nigeria	29	41	..	2.71	8.52	34	15	1,285	1,539	3.3	25.2	3.9	28.46	7.8	826.00
Rwanda	14	6	..	32.20	27.13	24	11	1	1	293.9	0.5	0.1	1.11	13.3	..
Senegal	27	33	50	9.52	32.64	38	19	44	30	50.3	3.5	0.7	3.67	15.3	86.00
Sierra Leone	18	14	..	13.76	91.71	17	−5	4	4	−310.7	−9.5	0.5	1.15	21.5	0.00
Somalia	..	..	..	50.49	48.85	..	..	..	..	..	..	..	2.10	..	..
South Africa	36	28	55	7.95	6.73	27	16	3,610	1,725	2.4	8.4	1.3	25.22	12.8	0.00
Sudan	11	..	3	93.55	20.62	..	..	0	0	..	..	0.0	16.33	9.2	251.40
Swaziland	..	82	..	31.24	8.30	..	..	..	..	..	..	..	0.37	2.5	..
Tanzania	..	22	..	56.05	16.94	36	20	143	158	68.4	11.2	2.3	7.18	12.9	0.00h
Togo	51	31	..	57.34	16.99	37	16	−6	0	53.6	0.0	0.0	1.34	8.1	20.00
Uganda	19	13	..	74.10	9.38	20	15	179	180	83.6	17.9	2.7	3.71	22.1	0.00
Zambia	41	33	..	4.28	8.49	38	15	79	70	107.4	12.2	1.8	6.76	19.9	0.00
Zimbabwe	23	36	32	46.30	7.24	43	19	32	70	19.7	4.2	0.8	4.96	22.0	0.00
South Asia	**8**	**13**	**76**	..	..	**18**	**23**	**11,110**	**4,662**	**3.6**	**3.8**	**0.9**	**154.95**	**20.3**	..
Afghanistan	..	..	..	57.76	33.76	..	..	..	..	..	..	..	5.49y	..	..
Bangladesh	4	12	87	2.87	12.47	18	21	118	135	11.7	1.6	0.3	15.13	10.6	1,217.00
Bhutan	..	31	..	14.29	11.68	..	..	..	..	..	..	..	0.09	5.1	0.00
India	7	12	72	15.02	7.43	16	24	8,306	3,351	1.8	3.7	0.9	94.40	19.6	7,840.00
Maldives	..	..	..	..	15.94	..	..	..	..	..	..	..	0.16	6.7	0.00
Nepal	12	26	95	17.16	11.97	38	21	12	23	25.6	2.2	0.5	2.40	6.9	77.60
Pakistan	12	16	86	10.35	15.90	21	15	2,097	713	6.4	7.6	1.2	29.67	35.2	1.46
Sri Lanka	32	36	73x	23.32	13.00	44	24	574	430	9.4	11.7	2.8	7.64	6.4	832.21

TABLE 5: Economic Globalization

| | Trade | | | | | | Investment 1997 | | | | | | Debt | | |
| | Exports of goods and services (% of GDP) | | Manufactured exports (% of merchandise exports) 1997 | Food Trade | | Imports of goods and services (% of GDP) 1997 | Gross domestic investment (GDI) (% of GDP) 1997 | Net private capital flows ($ millions) 1997 | Foreign direct investment ($ million) 1997 | Aid (% of GDI) | Foreign direct investment net inflows (% of GDI) 1997 | Foreign direct investment net inflows (% of GDP) 1997 | Total External debt (US $ billions) 1997 | Debt service (% of exports of goods and services) 1997 | Workers' remittances, receipts (US $ millions) 1996 |
	1980	1997		Food exports (% of merchandise exports)e 1997	Food imports (% of merchandise imports)e 1997										
East Asia and the Pacific	**17**	**33**	**72**	..	..	**31**	**36**	**91,188**	**61,440**	..	**11.1**	**1.0**	**511.18**	**11.3**	..
Brunei	..	..	..	0.67	9.94	..	..	..	..	..	..	..	0.22y	..	..
Cambodia	..	30	..	14.72	17.72	42	16	200	203	76.3	41.4	6.7	2.13	1.1	10.00
China	6	23	85	4.40	6.22	18	38	60,828	44,236	0.6	12.8	4.9	146.70	8.6	1,672.00
Hong Konga	90	132	89	3.01	5.28	135	34	..	..	0.0	..	..	40.73y	..	..
Fiji	..	57	..	31.66	13.25	..	..	..	..	..	24.0x	..	0.21	3.0	..
Indonesia	34	28	42	11.28	10.72	28	31	10,863	4,677	1.3	7.0	2.2	136.17	30.0	810.00
Korea, DPR (North)	..	..	..	9.26	27.71	..	..	..	..	..	..	..	7.69y	..	..
Korea, Rep. (South)	34	38	92	1.33	6.71	39	35	13,069	2,844	−0.1	1.8	0.6	143.37	8.6	466.00
Lao, PDR	..	24	..	18.59	5.52	41	29	90	90	68.1	17.9	5.1	2.32	6.5	0.00
Malaysia	58	94	76	9.10	5.47	93	43	9,312	5,106	−0.6	12.1	5.2	47.23	7.5	0.00
Mongolia	21	55	10	14.85	14.96	59	22	16	7	130.7	3.6	0.8	0.72	11.7	0.00
Myanmar (Burma)	9	1	..	39.15	5.21	1	13	180	80	..	..	..	5.07	8.0	..
Papua New Guinea	43	56	..	22.43	20.94	60	37	143	200	20.3	11.6	4.3	2.27	15.0	..
Philippines	24	49	45	7.84	7.74	59	25	4,164	1,222	3.4	6.0	1.5	45.43	9.2	569.00
Singapore	215	187	84	3.30	3.99	170	37	..	8,631	0.0	24.0	9.0	10.10y	..	..
Solomon Islands	..	..	..	12.25	12.01	..	..	..	..	..	..	..	0.14	2.4	..
Thailand	24	47	71	9.31	2.95	46	35	3,444	158	1.2	7.0	2.4	93.42	15.4	..
Vietnam	..	46	..	19.14	8.73	54	29	1,994	1,800	14.0	25.0	7.2	21.63	7.8	..
Latin America and the Caribbean	**13**	**15**	**46**	..	..	**16**	**22**	**118,918**	**61,573**	..	**13.1**	**1.4**	**703.67**	**35.5**	..
Argentina	5	9	34	46.64	5.66	11	20	19,834	6,645	0.3	10.2	2.0	123.22	58.7	41.00
Belize	..	49	..	72.10	19.50	..	..	..	..	..	..	..	0.38	9.2	14.00
Bolivia	25	21	16	36.26	8.81	29	19	812	601	48.1	40.3	7.5	5.25	32.5	2.10
Brazil	9	8	54	31.00	10.73	10	21	43,377	19,652	0.3	11.3	2.4	193.66	57.4	2.16
Chile	23	27	16	14.92	6.84	29	27	9,637	5,417	0.7	26.1	7.0	31.44	20.4	..
Colombia	16	15	31	34.94	11.49	18	19	10,151	5,982	1.5	33.2	6.2	31.78	26.6	140.20
Costa Rica	26	46	25	54.48	7.95	48	27	104	57	−0.1	2.2	0.6	3.55	11.8	0.00
Cuba	..	..	..	53.40	17.98	..	..	..	..	..	..	..	35.34y	..	..
Dominican Republic	19	48	78	44.85	16.64	51	25	401	405	2.1	11.0	2.7	4.24	6.2	847.00
Ecuador	25	30	9	36.92	9.83	29	20	829	577	4.4	14.5	2.9	14.92	31.0	0.00
El Salvador	34	24	39	29.91	14.50	35	15	61	11	17.7	0.7	0.1	3.28	7.0	1.06
Guatemala	22	18	30	62.29	14.64	24	14	166	90	12.4	3.7	0.5	4.09	9.9	375.40
Guyana	..	100	..	38.16	10.24	..	..	..	..	..	..	..	1.61	17.6	..
Haiti	22	8	..	21.49	46.53	23	10	3	3	115.7	1.0	0.1	1.06	15.9	..
Honduras	36	37	27	35.60	19.54	47	32	124	122	21.4	8.5	2.7	4.70	20.9	150.00
Jamaica	51	51	69	21.11	11.67	64	35	377	137	5.0	9.6	3.3	3.91	16.2	410.00
Mexico	11	30	81	9.64	10.57	30	26	20,533	12,477	0.1	11.7	3.1	149.69	32.4	4,223.70
Nicaragua	24	41	25	49.65	15.06	66	28	157	173	..	15.6	4.3	5.68	31.7	95.00
Panama	98	94	17	51.97	10.36	91	29	1,443	1,030	3.7x	9.9	2.9	6.34	16.4	15.80
Paraguay	15	22	15	66.89	21.50	24	23	273	250	5.3	10.8	2.5	2.05	5.0	..
Peru	22	13	17	10.84	15.28	17	25	3,094	2,030	3.1	12.9	3.2	30.50	30.9	404.00
Suriname	..	..	..	10.78	25.06	..	..	..	..	..	..	..	0.19y	..	..
Trinidad and Tobago	50	49	44	9.00	10.19	56	22	96	340	2.6	26.5	5.8	2.16	19.6	30.00
Uruguay	15	23	37	63.73	16.01	23	13	632	160	2.2	6.3	1.2	6.65	15.4	0.00
Venezuela	29	29	12	2.33	11.32	20	18	6,281	5,087	0.2	32.9	5.8	35.54	31.3	..
Middle East and North Africa	**43**	**33**	**19**	..	..	**32**	**24**	**8,120**	**5,368**	..	**0.9**	**0.5**	**193.41**	**13.2**	..
Algeria	34	31	3	0.33	32.85	22	26	−543	7	2.0	0.1	0.0	30.92	27.2	1,045.00
Bahrain	..	104	..	0.28	8.30	..	..	..	..	..	..	..	7.08y	..	..
Cyprus	..	..	..	59.33	26.35	..	..	..	..	..	..	..	35.40y	..	..
Egypt	31	20	40	11.28	26.02	25	18	2,595	891	14.6	6.7	1.2	29.85	9.0	2,798.00
Iran	13	21	..	4.39	19.94	16	29	−303	50	..	0.1	0.0	11.82	32.2	..
Iraq	..	..	..	4.05	64.67	..	..	..	0	..	..	..	21.91y	..	..
Jordan	40	51	49	7.59	20.19	74	29	61	22	23.1	1.1	0.1	8.23	11.1	1,544.00
Kuwait	78	53	14	0.35	15.33	41	13	..	16	0.1	0.4	0.1	7.69y	..	..

TABLE 5: Economic Globalization

	Exports of goods and services (% of GDP) 1980	Exports of goods and services (% of GDP) 1997	Manufactured exports (% of merchandise exports) 1997	Food exports (% of merchandise exports)[e] 1997	Food imports (% of merchandise imports)[e] 1997	Imports of goods and services (% of GDP) 1997	Gross domestic investment (GDI) (% of GDP) 1997	Net private capital flows ($ millions)	Foreign direct investment ($ million) 1997	Aid (% of GDI)	Foreign direct investment net inflows (% of GDI)	Foreign direct investment net inflows (% of GDP)	Total External debt (US $ billions) 1997	Debt service (% of exports of goods and services) 1997	Workers' remittances, receipts (US $ millions) 1996
Lebanon	..	10	..	20.14	14.96	54	27	1,070	150	6.0	3.8	1.0	5.04	14.4	2,503.00
Libya	66	..	..	0.51	22.24	..	..	..	..	..	..	..	3.36y	..	..
Morocco	17	28	49	18.14	18.23	32	21	1,303	1,200	6.7	17.4	3.6	19.32	26.6	2,009.70
Oman	63	..	17	3.54	17.16	..	..	118	90	..	4.0	0.4	3.60	5.9	39.01
Qatar	..	..	..	0.34	9.09	..	..	..	..	..	..	..	6.53y	..	..
Saudi Arabia	71	45	9	0.73	17.65	31	20	..	..	0.1	−4.4	−0.8	17.69y	..	0.00
Syria	18	30	17	26.47	21.03	40	29	69	80	3.8	1.5	0.4	20.87	9.3	0.00
Tunisia	40	44	78	9.53	11.43	46	27	903	316	3.9	6.3	1.7	11.32	16.0	735.56
Turkey	5	25	75	19.84	8.41	30	25	12,221	805	0.0	1.7	0.4	91.21	18.4	3,542.00
United Arab Emirates	78	..	..	1.91	7.26	..	..	..	..	..	..	..	12.34y	..	..
Yemen	..	44	1	1.72	61.75	52	21	−138	−138	30.6	−11.5	−2.4	3.86	2.4x	1,134.50
Countries in Transition[b]	..	31	53	..	13.65	33	23	49,875	22,314	2.2	8.3	1.9	390.58	11.5	..
Albania	23	12	65	18.23	28.93	37	12	47	48	56.5	16.0	2.0	0.71	7.1	499.60
Armenia	..	20	..	6.76	31.83	58	9	51	51	110.9	33.3	3.1	0.67	5.8	11.12
Azerbaijan	..	19	..	12.55	33.33	37	28	658	650	14.8	52.6	14.8	0.50	6.8	..
Belarus	..	60	..	5.70	11.86	64	26	169	200	0.7	3.4	0.9	1.16	1.8	29.90
Bosnia and Herzegovina	..	..	..	..	..	..	..	..	..	..	..	..	0.95y	..	..
Bulgaria	36	61	..	14.15	9.56	56	12	569	498	17.6	41.7	4.9	9.86	14.4	..
Croatia	..	42	69	10.84	9.12	53	15	2,397	388	4.7x	12.4	1.8	6.84	11.9	..
Czech Republic	..	58	85	5.45	7.45	63	34	1,818	1,286	0.6	7.3	2.5	21.46	14.1	..
Estonia	..	77	66	20.72	17.67	89	30	347	266	4.6	19.1	5.7	0.66	1.4	0.05
Georgia	..	12	..	12.60	25.34	23	7	50	50	65.9	13.3	1.0	1.45	6.4	..
Hungary	39	45	77	15.10	56.72	46	27	2,605	2,079	1.3	16.6	4.5	24.37	29.7	10.51
Kazakhstan	..	35	..	14.48	14.10	37	16	2,158	1,321	3.8	38.2	6.0	4.28	6.5	..
Kyrgyzstan	..	38	38	32.78	15.24	46	22	50	50	62.9	13.1	2.8	0.93	6.3	..
Latvia	..	50	58	5.12	8.26	61	20	559	521	7.4	47.8	9.4	0.50	4.4	..
Lithuania	..	55	70	15.32	11.26	65	27	637	355	4.0	13.9	3.7	1.54	6.0	1.85
Macedonia, FYR	..	40	..	40.78	24.17	56	19	8	15	34.9	3.5	0.7	1.54	8.8	..
Moldova	..	53	23	79.84	7.79	76	24	257	60	13.9	13.3	3.2	1.04	10.9	..
Poland	28	26	73	12.15	9.02	30	22	6,787	4,908	2.1	16.3	3.6	39.89	6.1	723.00
Romania	35	30	79	7.35	7.58	37	21	2,274	1,215	2.7	16.2	3.5	10.44	15.7	10.00
Russian Federation	..	23	23	1.42	23.46	20	22	12,453	6,241	0.7	6.4	1.4	125.65	6.5	0.00
Slovakia	..	56	79	5.01	8.03	64	35	1,074	165	1.0	2.4	0.8	9.99	12.2	4.11
Slovenia	..	57	89	4.16	8.45	58	24	1,219x	321	2.2	7.3	1.8	2.99y	8.7x	41.60
Tajikistan	..	114	..	25.50	23.59	114	17	20	20	..	5.1	0.8	0.90	4.6	..
Turkmenistan	..	..	..	47.99	19.83	..	..	847	85	..	..	2.5	1.77	34.7	0.00
Ukraine	..	41	..	13.72	6.44	44	20	1,419	623	1.8	6.2	1.3	10.90	6.6	0.00
Uzbekistan	..	38	..	52.77	17.78	38	19	435	285	2.8	6.0	1.1	2.76	12.9	..
Yugoslavia, FR	..	..	61	16.37	14.66	..	..	..	0	..	..	..	0.06y	..	..
Industrial Countries	20	21	81	..	..	20	21	..	233,897	..	3.9	1.1	..	..	..
Australia	16	20	29	28.87	4.82	20	20	..	9,146	n/a	6.9	2.3	..	..	..
Austria	36	41	88	4.68	6.78	41	24	..	2,466	n/a	8.2	1.2	..	..	321.84
Belgium	57	68	77x	10.52	10.36	64	18	..	..	n/a	..	..	..	..	120.41
Canada	28	40	63	7.03	5.35	36	18	..	7,132	n/a	6.5	1.2	..	..	..
Denmark	33	35	63	20.89	10.76	31	19	..	2,792	n/a	2.2	1.7	..	..	..
Finland	33	38	83	3.57	7.08	21	17	..	2,128	n/a	5.4	1.8	..	..	..
France	22	24	78	12.76	9.10	21	17	..	23,045	n/a	8.4	1.7	..	..	1.72
Germany	..	24	83	4.80	9.47	23	21	..	−344	n/a	−0.5	0.0	..	..	..
Greece	16	15	52	27.15	14.49	24	19	..	984	n/a	6.4	0.9	..	..	2.89
Ireland	48	76	81	11.80	8.31	61	18	..	2,727	n/a	20.7	3.6	..	..	..
Israel	44	32	92	6.07	6.63	45	22	..	2,706	5.6	12.7	2.8	..	..	0.00
Italy	22	27	89	6.60	11.59	21	17	..	3,700	n/a	1.7	0.3	..	..	337.21
Japan	14	10	95	0.39	11.27	9	30	..	3,200	n/a	0.0	0.1	..	..	256.53
Luxembourg	..	91	..	..	..	..	..	..	..	n/a	..	..	..	..	..
Netherlands	51	54	71	15.80	9.63	47	20	..	8,725	n/a	9.9	2.4	..	..	..

TABLE 5: Economic Globalization

| | Trade | | | | | | | Investment 1997 | | | | | | Debt | | |
| | Exports of goods and services (% of GDP) | | Manufactured exports (% of merchandise exports) 1997 | Food Trade | | Imports of goods and services (% of GDP) 1997 | Gross domestic investment (GDI) (% of GDP) | Net private capital flows ($ millions) | Foreign direct investment ($ million) 1997 | Aid (% of GDI) | Foreign direct investment net inflows (% of GDI) | Foreign direct investment net inflows (% of GDP) | Total External debt (US $ billions) 1997 | Debt service (% of exports of goods and services) 1997 | Workers' remittances, receipts (US $ millions) 1996 |
	1980	1997		Food exports (% of merchandise exports)[e] 1997	Food imports (% of merchandise imports)[e] 1997										
New Zealand	30	29	29	50.44	8.37	28	22	..	933	n/a	11.1	1.4	..	..	0.00
Norway	43	41	24	1.10	5.44	32	23	..	3,545	n/a	8.7	2.3	..	..	..
Portugal	25	31	86	6.32	11.74	38	24	..	1,713	n/a	2.7	1.7	..	..	3,712.39
Spain	16	26	78	15.08	10.35	25	21	..	5,556	n/a	5.4	1.0	..	..	2.79
Sweden	29	40	80	2.36	6.39	33	15	..	9,867	n/a	15.0	4.3	..	..	135.71
Switzerland	35	36	93	2.98	6.59	32	20	..	3,512x	n/a	5.9	1.2	..	..	169.90
United Kingdom	27	30	83	6.21	8.85	30	16	..	38,081	n/a	14.1	3.0	..	..	..
United States	10	12	81	9.08	4.57	13	18	..	93,448	n/a	6.0	1.2	..	..	..
World	**20**	**21**	**77**	..	..	**21**	**22**	..	**394,476**	..	**5.1**	**1.1**	..	..	

.. Data not available.

a Special Administrative Region, data exclusive of China.

b Central and Eastern European countries and the newly independent states of the former Soviet Union.

c Net private capital flows consist of private debt flows (commercial bank lending, bonds and other private credits) and nondebt private flows (foreign direct investment and portfolio equity investment).

e Bread for the World Institute estimate.

x Data refer to year other than specified.

y OECD data from 1996.

The number '0' (zero) means zero or less than half the unit of measure.

n/a Not applicable

TABLE 6: United States – National Hunger and Poverty Trends

	1970	1980	1985	1986	1987	1988	1989	1990	1991	1992	1993	1994	1995	1996	1997	1998
Total population (millions)	205.1	227.8	239.3	241.6	243.9	246.3	248.3	249.4	252.1	255.0	257.8	260.4	262.9	265.3	267.6	270.3
Food Insecurity Prevelance Estimates																
All U.S. Households																
Food Insecure	..	..	..	..	..	..	..	..	..	..	..	..	10.3	10.4	8.7	10.2
Without Hunger	..	..	..	..	..	..	..	..	..	..	..	..	6.4	6.3	5.6	6.6
With Hunger	..	..	..	..	..	..	..	..	..	..	..	..	3.9	4.1	3.1	3.6
Adult Members (total)																
Food Insecure	..	..	..	..	..	..	..	..	..	..	..	..	9.5	9.6	8.1	11.3
Without Hunger	..	..	..	..	..	..	..	..	..	..	..	..	6.1	6.0	5.4	7.9
With Hunger	..	..	..	..	..	..	..	..	..	..	..	..	3.4	3.6	2.6	3.3
Child Members (total)																
Food Insecure	..	..	..	..	..	..	..	..	..	..	..	..	17.4	18.2	14.6	19.7
Without Hunger	..	..	..	..	..	..	..	..	..	..	..	..	11.6	12.0	10.5	14.9
With Hunger	..	..	..	..	..	..	..	..	..	..	..	..	5.8	6.2	4.1	4.8
Percent of federal budget spent on food assistance[a]	0.5	2.4	2.0	1.9	1.9	1.9	1.9	1.9	2.0	2.3	2.5	2.47	2.48	2.43	1.94	..
Total infant mortality rate (per 1,000 live births)	20.0	12.6	10.6	10.4	10.1	10.0	9.7	9.1	8.9	8.5	8.4	8.0	7.6	7.3	7.2	..
White infant mortality rate	17.8	11.0	9.3	8.9	8.6	8.5	8.5	7.7	7.3	6.9	6.8	6.6	6.3	6.1	6.0	..
African American infant mortality rate	32.6	21.4	18.2	18.0	17.9	17.6	17.6	17.0	17.6	16.8	16.5	15.8	15.1	14.7	14.2	..
Hispanic infant mortality rate	..	..	..	..	7.9	8.1	8.5	7.8	7.5	6.8	..	..	..	5.9	..	..
Total poverty rate (%)	12.6	13.0	14.0	13.6	13.4	13.1	12.8	13.5	14.2	14.8	15.1	14.5	13.8	13.7	13.3	12.7
Northeastern region poverty rate	..	..	..	..	..	..	10.2	10.2	11.3	12.6	13.3	12.9	12.5	12.7	12.6	12.3
Midwestern region poverty rate	..	..	..	..	..	..	12.0	11.9	12.8	13.3	13.4	13.0	11.0	10.7	10.4	10.3
Southern region poverty rate	..	..	..	..	..	..	15.6	15.9	16.2	17.1	17.1	16.1	15.7	15.1	15.7	13.7
Western region poverty rate	..	..	..	..	..	..	12.8	11.6	12.4	14.8	15.6	15.3	14.9	15.4	14.6	14.0
White poverty rate	9.9	10.2	11.4	11.0	10.4	10.1	10.0	10.7	11.3	11.9	12.2	11.7	11.2	11.2	11.0	10.5
African American poverty rate	33.5	32.5	31.1	31.1	32.6	31.6	30.7	31.9	32.7	33.4	33.1	30.6	29.3	28.4	26.5	26.1
Hispanic poverty rate	..	25.7	29.0	27.3	28.1	26.8	26.2	28.1	28.7	29.6	30.6	30.7	30.3	29.4	27.1	25.6
Elderly poverty rate	24.6	15.7	12.6	12.4	12.5	12.0	11.4	12.2	12.4	12.9	12.2	11.7	10.5	11.5	10.5	10.5
Female-headed households poverty rate	38.1	36.7	37.6	38.3	38.3	37.2	32.2	33.4	39.7	39.0	38.7	34.6	32.4	32.6	31.6	29.9
Total child poverty rate (%)	15.1	18.3	20.7	20.5	20.5	19.7	19.6	20.6	21.1	22.3	22.7	21.8	20.8	20.5	19.9	18.9
White child poverty rate	..	13.9	16.2	16.1	15.4	14.6	14.8	15.9	16.1	17.4	17.8	16.9	16.2	16.3	16.1	15.1
African American child poverty rate	..	42.3	43.6	43.1	45.6	44.2	43.7	44.8	45.6	46.6	46.1	43.8	41.9	39.9	37.2	36.7
Hispanic child poverty rate	..	33.2	40.3	37.7	39.6	37.9	36.2	38.4	39.8	40.0	40.9	41.5	40.0	40.3	36.8	34.4
Unemployment rate (%)	4.9	7.1	7.2	7.0	6.2	5.5	5.3	5.6	6.8	7.5	6.9	6.1	5.6	5.4	4.9	4.5
White unemployment rate	4.5	6.3	6.2	6.0	5.3	4.7	4.5	4.8	6.1	6.6	6.1	5.3	4.9	4.7	4.2	3.9
African American unemployment rate	..	14.3	15.1	14.5	13.0	11.7	11.4	11.4	12.5	14.2	13.0	11.5	10.4	10.5	10.0	8.9
Hispanic unemployment rate	..	10.1	10.5	10.6	8.8	8.2	8.0	8.2	10.0	11.6	10.8	9.9	9.3	8.9	7.7	7.2

TABLE 6: United States – National Hunger and Poverty Trends

	1970	1980	1985	1986	1987	1988	1989	1990	1991	1992	1993	1994	1995	1996	1997	1998
Household income distribution (per quintile in %)																
All races																
Lowest 20 percent	4.1	4.2	3.9	3.8	3.8	3.8	3.8	3.9	3.8	3.8	3.6	3.6	3.7	3.7	3.6	3.6
Second quintile	10.8	10.2	9.8	9.7	9.6	9.6	9.5	9.6	9.6	9.4	9.0	8.9	9.1	9.0	8.9	9.0
Third quintile	17.4	16.8	16.2	16.2	16.1	16.0	15.8	15.9	15.9	15.8	15.1	15.0	15.2	15.1	15.0	15.0
Fourth quintile	24.5	24.8	24.4	24.3	24.3	24.3	24.0	24.0	24.2	24.2	23.5	23.4	23.3	23.3	23.2	23.2
Highest 20 percent	43.3	44.1	45.6	46.1	46.2	46.3	46.8	46.6	46.5	46.9	48.9	49.1	48.7	49.0	49.4	49.2
Ratio of highest 20 percent to lowest 20 percent[e]	10.6	10.5	11.7	12.1	12.2	12.2	12.3	11.9	12.2	12.3	13.6	13.6	13.2	13.2	13.7	13.7
White																
Lowest 20 percent	4.2	4.4	4.1	4.1	4.1	4.1	4.1	4.2	4.1	4.1	3.9	3.8	4.0	3.9	3.8	3.8
Second quintile	11.1	10.5	10.1	10.0	10.0	10.0	9.8	10.0	9.9	9.7	9.3	9.2	9.3	9.2	9.1	9.2
Third quintile	17.5	17.0	16.4	16.3	16.3	16.2	16.0	16.0	16.0	15.9	15.3	15.1	15.3	15.2	15.0	15.1
Fourth quintile	24.3	24.6	24.3	24.2	24.2	24.1	23.8	23.9	24.1	24.1	23.3	23.2	23.3	23.2	23.0	23.1
Highest 20 percent	42.9	43.5	45.1	45.4	45.5	45.6	46.3	46.0	45.8	46.2	48.2	48.6	48.1	48.4	49.1	48.8
Ratio of highest 20 percent to lowest 20 percent[e]	10.2	9.9	11.0	11.1	11.1	11.1	11.3	11.0	11.2	11.3	12.4	12.8	12.0	12.4	12.9	12.8
African American																
Lowest 20 percent	3.7	3.7	3.5	3.1	3.3	3.3	3.2	3.1	3.1	3.1	3.0	3.0	3.2	3.1	3.2	3.1
Second quintile	9.3	8.7	8.3	8.0	7.9	7.7	8.0	7.9	7.8	7.8	7.7	7.9	8.2	8.0	8.5	8.2
Third quintile	16.3	15.3	15.2	14.9	14.8	14.6	15.0	15.0	15.0	14.7	14.3	14.3	14.8	14.5	15.1	14.8
Fourth quintile	25.2	25.2	25.0	25.0	24.4	24.7	24.9	25.1	25.2	24.8	23.7	24.3	24.2	23.7	24.5	24.4
Highest 20 percent	45.5	47.1	48.0	49.0	49.7	49.7	48.9	49.0	48.9	49.7	51.3	50.5	49.6	50.7	48.7	49.5
Ratio of highest 20 percent to lowest 20 percent[e]	12.3	12.7	13.7	15.8	15.1	15.1	15.3	15.8	15.8	16.0	17.1	16.8	15.5	16.4	15.2	16.0
Hispanic origin																
Lowest 20 percent	..	4.3	4.1	3.9	3.7	3.7	3.8	4.0	4.0	4.0	3.9	3.7	3.8	3.8	3.6	3.6
Second quintile	..	10.1	9.4	9.5	9.1	9.3	9.5	9.5	9.4	9.4	9.1	8.7	8.9	9.0	8.9	8.9
Third quintile	..	16.4	16.1	15.8	15.5	15.6	15.7	15.9	15.8	15.7	15.1	14.8	14.8	14.7	14.9	15.0
Fourth quintile	..	24.8	24.8	24.8	24.1	24.2	24.4	24.3	24.3	24.1	23.1	23.3	23.3	23.1	23.1	23.2
Highest 20 percent	..	44.5	45.6	46.1	47.6	47.2	46.6	46.3	46.5	46.9	48.7	49.6	49.3	49.5	49.5	49.4
Ratio of highest 20 percent to lowest 20 percent[e]	..	10.3	11.1	11.8	12.9	12.8	12.3	11.6	11.6	11.7	12.5	13.4	13.0	13.0	13.8	13.7

.. Data not available.

a Data refer to fiscal year.

e Bread for the World Institute estimate.

TABLE 7: United States – State Hunger and Poverty Statistics

| | Total population (millions) July 1998 | Food insecure (% of households) 1996-98 average | Food insecure with hunger (% of households) 1996-98 average | Infant mortality rate per 1,000 live births 1997 | | | % population in poverty 1998 | Unemployment rate (%) (seasonally adjusted) 1998 |
				All Races	White	African American		
Alabama	4.35	11.3	3.2	9.5	7.5	13.9	14.5	4.2
Alaska	0.61	7.6	3.5	7.5	6.8	..	9.4	5.8
Arizona	4.67	12.8	4.2	7.1	6.8	14.4	16.6	4.1
Arkansas	2.54	12.6	4.6	8.7	7.4	13.8	14.7	5.5
California	32.67	11.4	4.1	5.9	5.6	13.1	15.4	5.9
Colorado	3.97	8.8	3.4	7.0	6.7	16.3	9.2	3.8
Connecticut	3.27	8.8	3.8	7.2	6.3	14.3	9.5	3.4
Delaware	0.74	6.8	2.6	7.8	5.7	14.5	10.3	3.8
District of Columbia	0.52	11.1	4.6	13.2	..	16.7	22.3	8.8
Florida	14.92	11.5	4.2	7.1	5.7	12.3	13.1	4.3
Georgia	7.64	9.7	3.2	8.6	6.1	13.8	13.5	4.2
Hawaii	1.19	10.4	2.8	6.6	..	..	10.9	6.2
Idaho	1.23	10.1	3.3	6.8	6.9	..	13.0	5.0
Illinois	12.05	8.2	3.1	8.4	6.4	17.1	10.1	4.5
Indiana	5.90	7.8	2.8	8.2	7.3	15.8	9.4	3.1
Iowa	2.86	7.0	2.5	6.2	5.9	18.2	9.1	2.8
Kansas	2.63	9.9	4.0	7.4	6.6	17.1	9.6	3.8
Kentucky	3.94	8.4	3.2	7.3	7.0	11.0	13.5	4.6
Louisiana	4.37	12.8	4.4	9.5	6.6	13.8	19.1	5.7
Maine	1.24	8.7	3.7	5.1	5.3	..	10.4	4.4
Maryland	5.13	7.1	3.0	8.8	5.1	16.2	7.2	4.6
Massachusetts	6.15	6.3	2.0	5.2	5.0	8.8	8.7	3.3
Michigan	9.82	8.1	2.9	8.2	6.1	17.5	11.0	3.9
Minnesota	4.73	6.9	2.9	5.9	5.1	16.5	10.3	2.5
Mississippi	2.75	14.0	4.2	10.6	7.1	14.9	17.6	5.4
Missouri	5.44	8.6	2.9	7.6	6.1	16.3	9.8	4.2
Montana	0.88	10.2	3.0	6.9	6.0	..	16.6	5.6
Nebraska	1.66	7.5	2.4	7.4	6.8	19.2	12.3	2.7
Nevada	1.75	8.6	3.7	6.5	6.2	13.6	10.6	4.3
New Hampshire	1.19	7.4	2.9	4.3	4.3	..	9.8	2.9
New Jersey	8.12	7.3	2.8	6.3	4.9	13.4	8.6	4.6
New Mexico	1.74	15.1	4.7	6.1	5.6	..	20.4	6.2
New York	18.18	10.0	3.9	6.7	5.7	10.9	16.7	5.6
North Carolina	7.55	8.8	2.6	9.2	6.9	15.7	14.0	3.5
North Dakota	0.64	4.6	1.4	7.7	5.3	..	15.1	3.2
Ohio	11.21	8.5	3.4	7.8	6.5	15.6	11.2	4.3
Oklahoma	3.35	11.9	4.2	7.5	6.7	15.0	14.1	4.5
Oregon	3.28	12.6	5.8	5.8	5.7	..	15.0	5.6
Pennsylvania	12.00	7.1	2.3	7.6	6.0	17.6	11.3	4.6
Rhode Island	0.99	8.7	2.6	7.0	7.0	..	11.6	4.9
South Carolina	3.84	10.2	3.4	9.6	6.4	15.4	13.7	3.8
South Dakota	0.74	6.4	2.1	7.7	5.3	..	10.8	2.9
Tennessee	5.43	10.9	4.3	8.6	6.5	16.3	13.4	4.2
Texas	19.76	12.9	5.0	6.4	5.9	10.9	15.1	4.8
Utah	2.10	8.8	3.1	5.8	5.8	..	9.0	3.8
Vermont	0.59	7.7	2.6	6.1	6.1	..	9.9	3.4
Virginia	6.79	8.3	2.9	7.8	6.0	14.2	8.8	2.9
Washington	5.69	11.9	4.6	5.6	5.3	15.4	8.9	4.8
West Virginia	1.81	9.0	3.1	9.6	9.1	..	17.8	6.6
Wisconsin	5.22	7.2	2.3	6.5	5.7	13.9	8.8	3.4
Wyoming	0.48	9.0	3.3	5.8	5.6	..	10.6	4.8
Puerto Rico	..	..	..	11.3	11.9	..	..	13.3
United States	**270.30**	**9.7**	**3.5**	**7.2**	**6.0**	**14.2**	**12.7**	**4.5**

.. Data not available.

Table 8: United States – Nutrition and Assistance Programs

	Food Stamp Participation: Monthly Average by State Number of Individuals				
	1995	1996	1997	1998	1999[c]
Alabama	524,522	509,214	469,268	426,819	408,334
Alaska	45,448	46,233	45,234	42,451	41,100
Arizona	480,195	427,481	363,779	295,703	255,546
Arkansas	272,174	273,900	265,854	255,710	254,609
California	3,174,651	3,143,390	2,814,761	2,259,069	2,057,877
Colorado	251,880	243,692	216,748	191,015	177,137
Connecticut	226,061	222,758	209,529	195,866	180,868
Delaware	57,090	57,836	53,655	45,581	38,725
District of Columbia	93,993	92,751	90,391	85,396	84,476
Florida	1,395,296	1,371,352	1,191,664	990,571	942,869
Georgia	815,920	792,502	698,323	631,720	630,594
Hawaii	124,575	130,344	126,901	122,027	125,688
Idaho	80,255	79,855	70,413	62,393	58,021
Illinois	1,151,035	1,105,160	1,019,600	922,927	828,871
Indiana	469,647	389,537	347,772	313,116	299,922
Iowa	184,025	177,283	161,184	141,067	130,316
Kansas	184,241	171,831	148,734	119,218	114,890
Kentucky	520,088	485,628	444,422	412,028	397,347
Louisiana	710,597	670,034	575,411	536,834	519,470
Maine	131,955	130,872	123,767	115,099	110,272
Maryland	398,727	374,512	354,436	322,653	276,789
Massachusetts	409,870	373,599	339,505	292,997	265,660
Michigan	970,760	935,416	838,917	771,580	701,999
Minnesota	308,206	294,825	260,476	219,744	210,092
Mississippi	479,934	457,106	399,062	329,058	292,299
Missouri	575,882	553,930	477,703	410,966	406,846
Montana	70,873	70,754	66,605	62,328	61,311
Nebraska	105,133	101,625	97,176	94,944	94,354
Nevada	98,538	96,712	82,419	71,531	62,929
New Hampshire	58,353	52,809	46,000	39,578	37,444
New Jersey	550,628	540,452	491,337	424,738	390,410
New Mexico	238,854	235,060	204,644	174,699	180,043
New York	2,183,101	2,098,561	1,913,548	1,627,170	1,559,684
North Carolina	613,502	631,061	586,415	527,790	492,102
North Dakota	41,401	39,825	37,688	33,801	33,677
Ohio	1,155,490	1,045,066	873,562	733,565	649,166
Oklahoma	374,893	353,790	321,894	287,577	274,858
Oregon	288,687	287,607	258,615	238,446	224,906
Pennsylvania	1,173,420	1,123,541	1,008,864	906,735	849,782
Rhode Island	93,434	90,873	84,627	72,301	76,566
South Carolina	363,822	358,341	349,137	333,017	313,109
South Dakota	50,158	48,843	46,901	45,173	44,449
Tennessee	662,014	637,773	585,889	538,467	515,509
Texas	2,557,693	2,371,958	2,033,750	1,636,175	1,426,984
Utah	118,836	110,011	98,338	91,764	89,445
Vermont	59,292	56,459	53,005	45,702	44,827
Virginia	545,829	537,531	476,088	396,581	367,304
Washington	476,019	476,391	444,800	364,418	315,331
West Virginia	308,505	299,719	287,035	269,140	251,419
Wisconsin	320,142	283,255	232,103	192,887	183,403
Wyoming	33,579	33,013	28,584	25,452	24,070
Puerto Rico[d]	n/a	n/a	n/a	n/a	n/a
United States	**26,618,773**	**25,540,331**	**22,854,273**	**19,788,115**	**18,409,685**

Table 8: United States – Nutrition and Assistance Programs

	WIC[a] Participation: Monthly Average by State Number of Individuals				
	1995	1996	1997	1998	1999[c]
Alabama	121,979	118,163	118,899	117,319	116,306
Alaska	19,235	22,410	23,537	23,829	25,409
Arizona	122,179	141,466	145,849	142,000	142,635
Arkansas	87,362	90,662	87,310	82,939	82,534
California	1,003,611	1,141,598	1,224,224	1,216,253	1,239,490
Colorado	70,617	70,523	75,068	74,679	74,911
Connecticut	63,625	62,520	59,368	60,267	58,219
Delaware	15,444	15,831	15,581	15,635	15,174
District of Columbia	17,368	16,116	16,747	16,593	16,453
Florida	317,095	332,130	354,971	345,150	339,721
Georgia	217,207	223,746	230,153	232,258	229,094
Hawaii	25,410	27,466	30,807	34,098	35,432
Idaho	31,120	31,085	31,475	31,678	31,674
Illinois	244,661	244,223	236,068	237,262	239,365
Indiana	132,621	132,532	132,700	131,099	128,708
Iowa	65,260	66,020	66,293	65,885	64,844
Kansas	55,890	54,377	54,754	52,896	52,512
Kentucky	118,198	119,457	122,948	122,910	121,793
Louisiana	133,992	139,603	139,223	136,866	138,598
Maine	26,905	26,300	26,663	25,786	24,962
Maryland	86,349	87,961	91,412	92,744	93,240
Massachusetts	113,605	115,942	118,818	117,681	115,464
Michigan	209,272	212,270	218,371	217,924	214,652
Minnesota	90,979	93,971	94,807	95,101	90,202
Mississippi	102,718	102,532	100,124	99,097	97,863
Missouri	127,005	129,245	131,638	128,176	126,203
Montana	20,889	22,155	21,679	21,428	21,407
Nebraska	35,715	36,101	33,041	31,770	33,139
Nevada	31,053	36,310	37,324	37,972	37,259
New Hampshire	19,423	19,342	19,179	18,678	18,235
New Jersey	141,962	137,988	141,514	140,732	129,046
New Mexico	53,816	56,131	54,040	56,183	56,255
New York	452,997	466,185	478,980	482,882	477,617
North Carolina	182,264	188,828	194,566	197,954	199,720
North Dakota	17,754	17,484	16,898	15,810	15,128
Ohio	259,121	258,400	254,668	250,815	245,648
Oklahoma	95,964	103,373	108,348	109,581	109,246
Oregon	82,212	86,048	89,299	91,341	93,955
Pennsylvania	260,544	262,111	257,018	246,337	234,941
Rhode Island	21,450	22,382	22,596	22,768	22,229
South Carolina	124,252	123,669	118,966	118,556	111,936
South Dakota	22,397	22,439	21,945	20,507	20,453
Tennessee	137,280	144,174	150,289	148,692	148,005
Texas	637,229	641,150	683,583	691,292	701,781
Utah	53,287	54,893	57,511	57,391	59,719
Vermont	16,140	16,061	16,133	16,308	16,075
Virginia	126,882	126,760	129,520	132,317	132,329
Washington	112,915	129,256	145,147	144,052	141,062
West Virginia	51,890	54,173	55,065	53,962	52,108
Wisconsin	109,151	109,712	108,886	108,352	104,559
Wyoming	11,745	11,965	12,447	11,789	11,688
Puerto Rico	182,795	204,717	211,454	206,968	200,947
United States	**6,894,413**	**7,187,831**	**7,406,866**	**7,367,397**	**7,329,285**

Table 8: United States – Nutrition and Assistance Programs

	TANF[b] Participation: Monthly Average by State Number of Individuals				
	1995	1996	1997	1998	1999[c]
Alabama	121,837	108,269	91,723	61,809	46,934
Alaska	37,264	35,432	36,189	31,689	28,020
Arizona	195,082	171,617	151,526	113,209	92,467
Arkansas	65,325	59,223	54,879	36,704	29,340
California	2,692,202	2,648,772	2,476,564	2,144,495	1,818,197
Colorado	110,742	99,739	87,434	55,352	39,346
Connecticut	170,719	161,736	155,701	138,666	90,799
Delaware	26,314	23,153	23,141	18,504	16,581
District of Columbia	72,330	70,082	67,871	56,128	52,140
Florida	657,313	575,553	478,329	320,886	198,101
Georgia	388,913	367,656	306,625	220,070	137,976
Hawaii	65,207	66,690	65,312	75,817	45,515
Idaho	24,050	23,547	19,812	4,446	2,897
Illinois	710,032	663,212	601,854	526,851	382,937
Indiana	197,225	147,083	121,974	95,665	109,675
Iowa	103,108	91,727	78,275	69,504	60,151
Kansas	81,504	70,758	57,528	38,462	32,873
Kentucky	193,722	176,601	162,730	132,388	99,560
Louisiana	258,180	239,247	206,582	118,404	111,074
Maine	60,973	56,319	51,178	41,265	3,408
Maryland	227,887	207,800	169,723	130,196	89,003
Massachusetts	286,175	242,572	214,014	181,729	151,592
Michigan	612,224	535,704	462,291	376,985	263,583
Minnesota	180,490	171,916	160,167	141,064	140,128
Mississippi	146,319	133,029	109,097	66,030	38,426
Missouri	259,595	238,052	208,132	162,950	135,383
Montana	34,313	32,557	28,138	20,137	15,508
Nebraska	42,038	38,653	36,535	38,090	34,662
Nevada	41,846	40,491	28,973	29,262	20,283
New Hampshire	28,671	24,519	20,627	15,947	16,090
New Jersey	321,151	293,833	256,064	217,320	175,223
New Mexico	105,114	102,648	89,814	64,759	80,686
New York	1,266,350	1,200,847	1,074,189	941,714	828,302
North Carolina	317,836	282,086	253,286	192,172	138,570
North Dakota	14,920	13,652	11,964	8,884	8,355
Ohio	629,719	552,304	518,595	386,239	282,444
Oklahoma	127,336	110,498	87,312	69,630	56,640
Oregon	107,610	92,182	66,919	48,561	45,450
Pennsylvania	611,215	553,148	484,321	395,107	312,364
Rhode Island	62,407	60,654	54,809	54,537	53,859
South Carolina	133,567	121,703	98,077	73,179	42,504
South Dakota	17,652	16,821	14,091	10,514	8,445
Tennessee	281,982	265,620	195,891	139,022	152,695
Texas	765,460	714,523	626,617	439,824	313,823
Utah	47,472	41,145	35,493	29,868	26,428
Vermont	27,716	25,865	236,570	21,013	18,230
Virginia	189,493	166,012	136,053	107,192	88,910
Washington	290,940	276,018	263,792	228,723	174,033
West Virginia	107,668	98,439	98,690	51,348	44,367
Wisconsin	214,404	184,209	132,383	44,630	28,863
Wyoming	15,434	13,531	10,322	2,903	1,770
Puerto Rico	171,932	156,805	145,749	130,283	107,447
United States	**13,930,953**	**12,876,661**	**11,423,007**	**9,131,716**	**7,334,976**

a Special Supplemental Nutrition Program for Women, Infants and Children.

b Temporary Assistance for Needy Families.

c Data as of Sept. 31, 1999.

d Puerto Rico receives block grants for their food stamp program.

n/a Not applicable.

Sources for Tables

Table 1: Global Hunger – Life and Death Indicators

Total population, projected population, projected growth rate, projected fertility rate, life expectancy: United Nations Population Fund (UNFPA) *The State of the World's Population 1999* (New York: UNFPA, 1999).

Population under age 15: Statistics and Population Division of the United Nations Secretariat, "Indicators of Youth and Elderly Populations," data posted at: www.un.org/Depts/unsd/social/main.htm.

Infant mortality, low birth-weight infants, children immunized, under-5 mortality rate, maternal mortality rate: United Nations Children's Fund, *The State of the World's Children, 1999* (*SWC*) (New York: UNICEF, 1999).

Refugees: U.S. Committee for Refugees, *World Refugees Survey, 1999* (Washington, DC: Immigration and Refugee Services of America, 1999). Data posted at: www.refugees.org.

Population urban: United Nations Development Programme, *Human Development Report, 1999* (*HDR*) (New York: Oxford University Press, 1999).

Table 2: Global Food, Nutrition and Education

Daily energy supply, food production: Food and Agriculture Organization of the United Nations (FAO), data posted at: apps.fao.org.

Food expenditures, gender-related primary school enrollment: The World Bank, *1999 World Development Indicators (WDI)* (Washington, DC: The World Bank, 1999).

Iodine deficiency: *SWC*, 1999.

Adult literacy rate, total primary school enrollment, gender-related combined school enrollment: *HDR*, 1999.

Table 3: Hunger, Malnutrition and Poverty

Undernourished population: FAO, *The State of Food Insecurity in the World, 1999* (Rome: FAO, 1999).

Underweight, wasting, stunting, safe water: *SWC*, 1999.

Population in poverty: *WDI*, 1999.

Table 4: Economic and Development Indicators

GNP per capita, distribution of income or consumption, military expenditures, energy consumption: *WDI*, 1999.

HDI rank, central government expenditures, education expenditures: *HDR*, 1999.

Annual deforestation: FAO, *State of the World's Forests, 1997* (Rome: FAO, 1997).

Table 5: Economic Globalization

Exports of goods and services, manufactured exports, imports of goods and services, investment, aid, debt: *WDI*, 1999.

Food exports, food imports: FAO, data posted at: apps.fao.org.

Workers' remittances: *WDI*, 1997.

Table 6: United States – National Hunger and Poverty Trends

Total population: U.S. Bureau of the Census, data posted at: www.census.gov/population/www/estimates/popest.html.

Poverty: U.S. Bureau of the Census, data posted at: www.census.gov/hhes/www/poverty.html.

Income: U.S. Bureau of the Census, data posted at: www.census.gov/hhes/www.income.html.

Food insecurity prevalence: USDA, *Prevalence of Food Insecurity and Hunger by State, 1996-1998,* Food Assistance and Research Nutrition Service, Report No. 2 (FANRR-2). Report posted at: www.ers.usda.gov.

Percent of federal budget spent on food assistance: Congressional Budget Office.

Infant mortality: Centers for Disease Control and Prevention, National Center for Health Statistics, "Deaths: Final Data for 1997" *National Vital Statistics Reports*, Vol.47, No. 19:108, (PHS) 99-1120. Report posted at: www.cdc.gov/nchswww.

Unemployment: *Handbook of U.S. Labor Statistics, 3rd Edition,* Eva E. Jacobs, ed. (Lanham, MD: Bernan Press, 1999).

Table 7: United States – State Hunger and Poverty Trends

Total population: U.S. Bureau of the Census, data posted at: www.census.gov/population/www/estimates/popest.html.

Poverty: U.S. Bureau of the Census, data posted at: www.census.gov/hhes/www/poverty.html.

Food insecurity prevalence: USDA, *Prevalence of Food Insecurity and Hunger by State, 1996-1998.* Food Assistance and Research Nutrition Service, Report No. 2 (FANRR-2). Report posted at: www.ers.usda.gov.

Infant Mortality: Centers for Disease Control and Prevention, National Center for Health Statistics, "Deaths: Final Data for 1997" *National Vital Statistics Reports*, Vol.47, No. 19:108, (PHS) 99-1120. Report posted at: www.cdc.gov/nchswww.

Unemployment Rate: U.S. Bureau of Labor Statistics, data posted at: www.bls.gov/datahome.htm.

Table 8: United States – Nutrition and Assistance Programs

Food Stamp participation, WIC participation: USDA, Food and Nutrition Service national databank, unpublished data.

TANF: U.S. Department of Health and Human Services Administration for Children and Families, data posted at: www.acf.dhhs.gov/news/tables.htm.

Abbreviations

AFDC – Aid to Families with Dependent Children
AIDS – Acquired Immune Deficiency Syndrome
BFW – Bread for the World
BFWI – Bread for the World Institute
CAS – Country Assistance Strategy
CBPP – Center on Budget and Policy Priorities
CDF – Children's Defense Fund
CFED – Corporation for Economic Development
CGIAR – Consultative Group on International Agricultural Research
CHIP – Children's Health Insurance Program
CIS – Commonwealth of Independent States (former Soviet Union)
COASAD – Coalition of African Organizations for Food Security and Sustainable Development
CPI – Consumer Price Index
CSO – Civil Society Organization
DAC – OECD Development Assistance Committee
EBT – Electronic Benefits Transfer
EDF – Environmental Defense Fund
EITC – Earned Income Tax Credit
ESAF – Enhanced Structural Adjustment Facility
EU – European Union
FAO – Food and Agriculture Organization of the United Nations
FRAC – Food Research and Action Center
G-7/G-8 – Group of Seven/Group of Eight (United States, Great Britain, Germany, France, Canada, Japan, Italy and Russia)
GAO – U.S. General Accounting Office
GATT – General Agreement on Tariffs and Trade
GDP – Gross Domestic Product
GNP – Gross National Product
HIPC – Highly Indebted Poor Country
HHS – U.S. Department of Health and Human Services
HUD – U.S. Department of Housing and Urban Development
ICESCR – International Covenant on Economic, Social and Cultural Rights, 1966
IDA – Individual Development Accounts
IDB – Inter-American Development Bank
IFAD – International Fund for Agricultural Development
IFPRI – International Food Policy Research Institute
IFST – International Food Security Treaty

ILO – International Labour Organization
IMF – International Monetary Fund
J2000 – Jubilee 2000
LIFDC – Low-Income Food Deficit Country
MAI – Multilateral Agreement on Investment
MEA – Multilateral Environmental Agreements
NATO – North Atlantic Treaty Organization
NGO – Nongovernmental Organization
ODA – Official Development Assistance
OECD – Organization for Economic Cooperation and Development
OL – Offering of Letters
OPEC – Organization of Petroleum Exporting Countries
PIPA – Program on International Policy Attitudes, University of Maryland
PRWORA – Personal Responsibility and Work Opportunity Reconciliation Act, 1996
PTO – U.S. Patent and Trademark Office
SAP – Structural Adjustment Program
SSI – Supplemental Security Income
TAHL – Transforming Anti-Hunger Leadership Program, BFW Institute
TANF – Temporary Assistance for Needy Families
TRIM – Trade-Related Investment Measure
TRIP – Trade in Intellectual Property Rights
UDN – Uganda Debt Network
U.N. – United Nations
UNCTAD – U.N. Conference on Trade and Development
UNDAF – U.N. Donor Assistance Framework
UNDP – U.N. Development Programme
UNEP – U. N. Environment Programme
UNHCR – U.N. High Commissioner for Refugees
UNICEF – U.N. Children's Fund
UNRISD – U.N. Research Institute for Social Development
U.S. – United States
USAID – U.S. Agency for International Development
USDA – U.S. Department of Agriculture
VAD – Vitamin-A Deficiency
WFP – World Food Programme
WHO – World Health Organization
WIC – Special Supplemental Nutrition Program for Women, Infants and Children
WTO – World Trade Organization

Glossary

Absolute poverty – The income level below which a minimally nutritionally adequate diet plus essential non-food requirements are not affordable.

Block grants – Federal government lump-sum payments to the states, which then have wide discretion over the use of these funds.

Campaign finance reform – Reform of the laws governing the kinds and amounts of donations that may be made to political campaigns.

Civil society – The sphere of civic action outside government, comprised of citizens' groups, nongovernmental organizations, religious congregations, labor unions and foundations.

Coalition – A set of actors (e.g., NGOs, public interest groups, foundations) that coordinate shared strategies and tactics to influence public policy and social change broadly.

Cold War – The global state of tension and military rivalry that existed from 1945 to 1990 between the United States and the former Soviet Union and their respective allies.

Daily calorie requirement – The average number of calories needed to sustain normal levels of activity and health, taking into account age, sex, body weight and climate; on average, about 2,350 calories per person per day.

Debt relief – Measures to reduce the debt owed by developing country governments to either private lenders (commercial banks like Citibank), governments (like the United States or Germany), or international financial institutions (like the World Bank or IMF).

Democratization – The process by which political systems move toward democratic principles and practices, such as open multi-party regime with regular and fair elections, universal suffrage, freedom of the press and other civil liberties (freedom of expression, freedom of organization).

Developed countries – Countries in which most people have a high economic standard of living (though there are often significant populations living in poverty). Also called the "**industrial countries**" or the "**North**."

Developing countries – Countries in which most people have a low economic standard of living. Also known as the "**Third World**," the "**South**" and the "**less-developed countries**."

Dietary energy supply (DES) – The total daily food supply, expressed in calories, available within a country for human consumption.

Earned income tax credit (EITC) – A U.S. federal government program that reduces or eliminates taxes for many low-income working people and, in some cases of very low incomes, provides funds.

Empowerment – The process by which people gain greater economic and political voice and power over the decisions affecting their lives.

Famine – A situation of extreme scarcity of food, potentially leading to widespread starvation.

Food security – Assured access for every person, primarily by production or purchase, to enough nutritious food to sustain an active and healthy life with dignity. It includes food availability, food access and appropriate food utilization.

Food self-reliance – A strategy where countries boost yields, employing sustainable and efficient farming practices, and diversify their agricultural production, some for export and some for domestic consumption.

Food self-sufficiency – A strategy whereby countries, communities or regions rely exclusively on their own food production.

Food stamps – Cash assistance for low-income people to buy food in retail stores, either in the form of coupons or electronic transfers.

Foreign direct investment (FDI) – Investment from abroad in ownership and control of productive activities, as opposed to more passive stock and bond investment.

Free trade agreements – Agreements between two countries (bilateral), or among several (multilateral), to eliminate or reduce practices that distort trade. These may include tariffs (taxes on traded goods and services) and/or non-tariff barriers such as quotas (limits on the amount traded).

General Agreement on Tariffs and Trade (GATT) – An agreement established in 1948 providing the ground rules for multilateral trade policy by its member nations. Successive negotiating rounds of the GATT culminated in the Uruguay Round (1986-1994). In 1995, the GATT was replaced by the **World Trade Organization** (WTO).

Global communications revolution – The growing interconnection of people around the world through communications technologies such as television, satellites, cellular phones, computers and the Internet.

Globalization – In economic terms, the process of increasing integration of national economies at the global level.

Gross domestic product (GDP) – The value of all goods and services produced within a nation during a specified period, usually a year.

Gross national product (GNP) – The value of all goods and services produced by a country's citizens, wherever they are located.

Human Development Index (HDI) – As used by the United Nations Development Programme, a measure of well-being based on economic growth, educational attainment and health.

Human rights – The basic rights and freedoms due all human beings, including the right to food and other basic necessities, the right to life and liberty, freedom of thought and expression and equality before the law.

Hunger – A condition in which people do not get enough food to provide the nutrients (carbohydrates, fats, proteins, vitamins, minerals and water) for active and healthy lives.

Infant mortality rate (IMR) – The annual number of deaths of infants under 1 year of age per 1,000 live births.

International Monetary Fund (IMF) – An international organization that makes loans to countries with short-term foreign exchange and monetary problems. These loans are conditioned upon the borrowing country's willingness to adopt IMF-approved economic policies.

Internet – The global communication network formed by the interconnection of all the Internet Protocol computer networks linking nearly 200 countries.

Jubilee 2000 – A worldwide movement calling for cancellation of the unpayable foreign debt of heavily indebted poor countries by the year 2000.

Jubilee 2000/USA – A movement in the United States, working in collaboration with Jubilee 2000 (see above), calling for cancellation of poor country debt. That cancellation includes acknowledgment of responsibility by both lenders and borrowers, as well as mechanisms to prevent recurrence of such debts.

Livelihood security – The ability of a household to meet *all* its basic needs – for food, shelter, water, sanitation, health care and education.

Living wage – The wage level necessary for ensuring that a person earns enough to live at an adequate standard of living.

Macroeconomic policies – Policies related to general levels of production and income, and the relationship among economic sectors. **Microeconomics** deals with individual units of activity, such as a firm, household or prices for a specific product.

Malnutrition – A condition resulting from inadequate consumption (**undernutrition**) or excessive consumption (**overnutrition**) of a nutrient that can impair physical and mental health, and cause or be the consequence of infectious diseases.

Market economy – An economy in which prices for goods and services are set primarily by private markets rather than by government planning or regulation.

Microcredit – Small, short-term loans to low-income people, too poor to borrow from commercial banks, to help them start their own businesses, generate income and raise their standard of living.

Minimum caloric requirements – See "Daily calorie requirement."

Minimum wage – The lowest acceptable level of hourly wages set by law.

Multilateral trade negotiations – Trade negotiations among more than two countries, as distinct from **bilateral trade negotiations**, which take place among two countries.

Nongovernmental organizations (NGOs) – Voluntary, nonprofit organizations that support community development, provide social services, protect the environment and promote the public interest.

North-South – Pertaining to relations between the developed or rich countries of the North and the developing or poor developed countries of the South.

Poverty line – An official measure of poverty defined by national governments. In the United States, it is calculated as three times the cost of the U.S. Department of Agriculture's "Thrifty Food Plan," which provides a less-than-adequate diet. In 1998, the poverty line was $13,003 for a family of three, $16,660 for a family of four.

Privatization – The transfer of ownership of companies and delivery of services from government to private firms or agencies.

Public policy advocacy – Citizen political action focused on the policies, programs and practices of governments, international financial institutions and corporations.

Social safety nets – Government and private charitable programs to meet the basic human needs (health, education, nutrition) of low-income, disabled and other vulnerable people.

Starvation – Suffering or death from extreme or prolonged lack of food.

Structural adjustment program (SAP) – Economic policy changes, often negotiated as a condition for loans, intended to stimulate economic growth. These measures generally involve reducing the role of government in the economy and increasing exports.

Stunting – Failure to grow to normal height caused by chronic undernutrition during the formative years of childhood.

Sustainable development – The reduction of hunger and poverty in environmentally sound ways. It includes: meeting basic human needs, expanding economic opportunities, protecting and enhancing the environment, and promoting pluralism and democratic participation.

Trade deficit – The difference between the value of a country's imports and the value of its exports when the former is greater than the latter.

Under-5 mortality rate – The annual number of deaths of children under 5 years of age per 1,000 live births. A high rate correlates closely with hunger and malnutrition.

Undernutrition – A condition resulting from inadequate consumption of calories, protein and nutrients to meet the basic physical requirements for an active and healthy life.

Uruguay Round – See the **General Agreement on Tariffs and Trade (GATT)**.

Vulnerability to hunger – Individuals, households, communities or nations who have enough to eat most of the time, but whose poverty makes them especially susceptible to hunger due to changes in the economy, climate, political conditions or personal circumstances.

Wasting – A condition in which a person is seriously below the normal weight for her or his height due to acute undernutrition or a medical condition.

Welfare – Financial and other assistance provided by government and private charitable organizations to people in need in the areas of nutrition, education, health care and employment.

World Bank – An intergovernmental agency that makes long-term loans to the governments of developing nations.

World Trade Organization (WTO) – An international organization, headquartered in Geneva, established in 1995 to enforce the Uruguay Round global trade agreement.

Notes

Introduction

[1] Summary comment by the moderator of a listserve discussing The World Bank's forthcoming *World Development Report 2001*, at: WDR2001@jazz.worldbank.org.

[2] Amartya Sen, "Public Action to Remedy Hunger," Arturo Tanco Memorial Lecture, London, August 2, 1990, at: www.thp.org/thp/reports/sen/sen890.htm.

[3] Reuters Limited, 8/26/99.

[4] Correspondence with Steve Hansch, Oct. 28, 1999.

[5] Chrisopher Murray and Alan D. Lopez (eds.), *The Global Burden of Disease: Summary.* Geneva: World Health Organization, 1996, 28.

[6] From the introduction and summary of a report adopted by the OECD's Development Assistance Committee meeting on 6-7 May 1996, 1.

[7] Ochoa, Grant, van Hengel are all recipients (along with Nobel Prize winner Amartya Sen) of the Alan Shawn Feinstein World Hunger/Merit Awards, presented at Brown University.

[8] "James P. Grant: achiever of greatness for humanity," Opinion Editorial, *Global Child Health News & Review,* Vol. 3, No. 1, 1995, at: www.edie.cprost.sfu.ca/gcnet/gchnr.html.

Chapter 1

[1] Statement made at the Release of the U.S. Action Plan on Food Security, Woodrow Wilson Center, Washington, DC, March 26, 1999, at: ecsp.si.edu/food-security.

[2] The estimated number of undernourished in the developing world over this period was 959 million people for 1969-1971 and 791 million people for 1995-1997. Food and Agriculture Organization (FAO) of the United Nations, *The State of Food Insecurity in the World 1999*, Rome: FAO, October 1999.

[3] FAO, *The State of Food Insecurity in the World, 1999*, Rome: FAO, October 1999, 7.

[4] *Ibid.*

[5] UNDP, *Overcoming Human Poverty: UNDP Poverty Report 1998*, New York: UNDP, 1998, 47.

[6] Simon Maxwell, "International Targets for Poverty Reduction and Food Security," *IDS Bulletin*, 30(2):92-105, April 1999.

[7] Robert W. Kates, Mid-Course Review of the Bellagio Declaration: Overcoming Hunger in the 1990s. *Food Policy*, 20(6):599, December.

[8] Eradicating polio by 2005 represents savings of $1.5 billion per year as governments "no longer have to immunize infants or treat and rehabilitate people affected by polio." Western Europe saves $200 million annually, the U.S. about $230 million. Cited in: Linda Mastny, "Polio Nearly Eradicated," In: *Vital Signs 1999*, New York: W. W. Norton and Company, 1999, 104.

[9] Remarks by the President to the 1999 Annual Meeting of the International Monetary Fund and World Bank, The White House, Office of the Press Secretary, September 29, 1999.

[10] FAO, *World Agriculture: Towards 2010*, Rome: FAO, 1996.

[11] J. Dirck Stryker and Jeffrey C. Metzel, *Meeting the Food Summit Target: The United States' Contribution – Proposal for a Presidential Initiative*, Agricultural Policy Analysis Project, Phase III Research Report 1038, Prepared for the Office of Economic Growth and Agricultural Development, Global Bureau, U.S. Agency for International Development, Cambridge, MA: Associates for International Resources and Development, September 1998.

[12] U.S. Department of Agriculture, *U.S. Action Plan on Food Security: Solutions to Hunger*, Washington, DC: USDA, March 26, 1999, at: www.fas.usda.gov:80/icd/summit/usactplan.pdf.

[13] Oscar Arias, "...More Weapons, More Danger," *Washington Post*, February 16, 1999, A-17.

[14] UNICEF, *State of the World's Children 1998*, New York: Oxford University Press, 13.

[15] *Ibid.*, 15.

[16] Anthony R. Measham and Meera Chatterjee, *Wasting Away: The Crisis of Malnutrition in India*, Washington, DC: World Bank, May 1999, 47.

[17] U.S. General Accounting Office, *Food Security: Factors that Could Affect Progress Toward Meeting World Food Summit Goals*, Washington, DC: GAO/NSIAD-99-15, March 1999, 16; See also, Per Pinstrup-Andersen, *Food Policy for Developing Countries: Emerging Issues and Unfinished Business*, Washington, DC: IFPRI, April 1999, 16.

[18] J. Dirck Stryker and Jeffrey C. Metzel, *Meeting the Food Summit Target: The United States Contribution – Global Strategy*, Agricultural Policy Analysis Project, Phase III, Research Report No. 1039, Prepared for the Office of Economic Growth and Agricultural Development, Global Bureau, U.S. Agency for International Development, Cambridge, MA: Associates for International Resources and Development, September 1998, 3.

[19] FAO, *The State of Food Insecurity in the World, 1999*, Rome: FAO, October 1999.

[20] Per Pinstrup-Andersen, "Changing Approaches to Development Aid: The Effect on International Stability," *Global Governance*, 4(4):381-394, October-December, 1998, 386.

[21] Per Pinstrup Andersen, Rajul Pandya-Lorch, and Mark W. Rosegrant, *World Food Prospects: Critical Issues for the Early Twenty-First Century*, Food Policy Report, Washington, DC: IFPRI, October 1999, 18.

[22] IMPACT Model Results, July 1999 version, personal communication, Mark W. Rosegrant, IFPRI, Washington, DC.

[23] Shahla Shapouri and Stacey Rosen, *Food Security Assessment: Why Countries Are At Risk*, U.S. Department of Agriculture, Agriculture Information Bulletin Number 754, August 1999, 2, 7.

[24] Alexander McCalla, "Food Security and the Challenge to Agriculture in the 21st Century," *Rural Development Note*, No. 1, Washington, DC: World Bank, March 1999, 1.

[25] FAO, *The State of Food Insecurity in the World, 1999*, Rome: FAO, October 1999.

[26] J. Dirck Stryker and Jeffrey C. Metzel, Research Report 1039, 22.

[27] Henry A. Kissinger, "Address at the World Food Conference," 5-16 November 1974, Rome.

[28] Cited in: "Americans' Awareness and Attitudes about Global Infectious Diseases: Executive Summary," Poll conducted for the Global Health Council by Lake Snell Perry & Associates, Washington, DC, June 16, 1999, 3.

[29] Cited by Barbara Alison Rose, director of operations for Future Harvest, In; "Four Million Killed in Post-Cold War Conflicts," Washington, DC: Future Harvests, February 16, 1999, at: www.futureharvest.org/news.

[30] Ellen Messer, Marc J. Cohen and Jashinta D'Costa, *Food from Peace: Breaking the Links between Conflict and Hunger*. Food, Agriculture, and the Environment Discussion Paper 24, Washington, DC: IFPRI, 1998.

[31] Jimmy Carter, "First Step Toward Peace Is Eradicating Hunger," *International Herald Tribune*, June 17, 1999.

[32] Grahame Russell, "Hurricane Mitch," *Third World Resurgence*, January 1999.

[33] Cited in: "IMF Stressed Concern for the Poor, Backing World Bank," *Bloomberg News*, September 28, 1999.

[34] Jean Drèze and Amartya Sen, *Hunger and Public Action*, Oxford: Clarendon Press, 1989, vii.

Chapter 2

[1] For our purposes, "ending hunger" means reducing household hunger to zero percent (from 1998 level of 3.6 percent) and household food insecurity to 5 percent (from 1998 level of 10.2 percent) of the U.S. population.

[2] Unemployment figure is from Lawrence Mishel et al., *The State of Working America: 1998-1999*, Ithaca, NY: Cornell University Press, 1999, 2. Inflation figure is from Economic Statistics Briefing Room, at: www.whitehouse.gov/fsbr/prices.html.

[3] *Household Food Security in the United States 1995 – 1998 (Advance Report)*, at: www.fns.usda.gov/fsp/Clintoninitiative/default.htm, 1.

[4] *Food Security Institute Bulletin*, Food Security Institute, Center on Hunger & Poverty, School of Nutrition Science & Policy, Tufts University, September 1999,1-3.

[5] *Poverty in the United States: 1998*, Washington, DC: U.S Census Bureau, September 1999, v.

[6] Center on Budget and Policy Priorities, "Low Unemployment, Rising Wages Fuel Poverty Decline," Washington, DC, September 30, 1999.

[7] *Ibid.*

[8] *Poverty in the United States: 1998, op. cit.*, v.

[9] *Ibid.*, viii.

[10] "Extreme Child Poverty Rises by More than 400,000 in One Year, New Analysis Shows," press release, Children's Defense Fund, August 22, 1999.

[11] *Ibid.*

[12] See Bruce Bradbury and Markus Jantti, "Child-Poverty Across the Industrialized World: Evidence from the Luxembourg Income Study," Paper presented at the Conference on "Child Well-Being in Rich and Transition Countries: Are Children in Growing Danger of Social Exclusion?," Dommeldange, Luxembourg, September 30-October 2, 1999, 12-20; Marc J. Cohen, ed., *What Governments Can Do: Hunger 1997*, Silver Spring, MD: Bread for the World Institute, 1996, 12-14.

[13] Mishel, *op. cit.*, 266.

[14] George Hager, "Study Reports Record U.S. Income Gap," *Washington Post*, September 5, 1999, A-8.

[15] David Cay Johnston, "Gap Between the Rich and Poor Substantially Wider," *New York Times*, September 5, 1999, 14.

[16] AFL-CIO, cited in Bread for the World fact sheet, September, 1999.

[17] Mishel, *op. cit.*, 258.

[18] Arloc Sherman, *Wasting America's Families*, Washington, DC: Children's Defense Fund, 1998.

[19] "On Third Anniversary of Welfare Reform, New National Study Looks Beyond Caseload Reduction," August 2, 1999, Urban Institute: Washington, DC, at: www.urbaninstitute.org/news/pressrel/pr990176.html.

[20] Wendell Primus et al., *The Initial Impacts of Welfare Reform on the Incomes of Single-Mother Families*, Center on Budget and Policy Priorities, Washington, DC: 1999, 39.

[21] Mary McGrory, "Hunger, an Issue with Edge," *Washington Post*, March 25, 1999; *U.S. Action Plan on Food Security: Solutions to Hunger*, Washington, DC: U.S. Department of Agriculture, March 1999, at: www.usda.gov.

[22] Robert B. Reich, "The Other Surplus Option," *New York Times*, August 11, 1999.

[23] "About FSP: An Introduction," USDA web site, at: www.fns.usda.gov/fsp/menu/about/about.htm. Figure given by the U.S. Department of Agriculture, Food and Consumer Services Agency.

[24] Laura Castner and Jacquelyn Anderson, "Characteristics of Food Stamp Households: Fiscal Year 1998 (Advance Report)," Princeton, NJ: Mathematica Policy Research, Inc., July 1999.

[25] "Food Expenditure and Consumption Patterns of Food Stamp Households," testimony presented to the U.S. House of Representatives, Committee on Agriculture, Subcommittee on Department Operations and Nutrition, Mathematica Policy Research, Inc., November 16, 1993, 4.

[26] For a discussion of this crucial difference, see Janet Poppendieck, *Sweet Charity? Emergency Food and the End of Entitlement*, New York: Viking Penguin, 1998.

[27] Peter K. Eisinger, *Toward an End to Hunger in America*, Washington, DC: Brookings Institution Press, 1998, 124.

[28] John T. Cook, "The Importance of the Food Stamp Program for Low-Income Legal Immigrants," Tufts University, Center on Hunger and Poverty, May 6, 1998.

[29] Children's Defense Fund, *The State of America's Children: Yearbook 1998*, Washington, DC, 1998, 56.

[30] Gail Vines, "Eating for Two," *New Scientist*, Vol. 155, Issue 2093, August 2, 1997, 4.

[31] Mathematica Policy Research, Inc., "The Savings in Medicaid Costs for Newborns and Their Mothers from Prenatal Participation in the WIC Program," Vol. 1, October 1990.

[32] Center on Hunger, Poverty and Nutrition Policy, Tufts University, "Statement on the Link between Nutrition and Cognitive Development in Children," School of Nutrition Science and Policy, 1998, at: www.tufts.edu/Nutrition/centeronhunger/statement.html.

[33] Bob Herbert, "Senior Citizens on the Breadline," *New York Times*, April 11, 1999.

[34] James V. Riker, ed., *The Changing Politics of Hunger: Hunger 1999*, Silver Spring, MD: Bread for the World Institute, 1998.

35 Michael Massing, "The End of Welfare?" *The New York Review of Books*, October 7, 1999, 25. See also, "How Low the Boom Can Go," *New York Times*, June 13, 1999.

36 Poverty threshold found in *1998 Green Book: Background Material and Data on Programs Within the Jurisdiction of the Committee on Ways and Means*, Washington, DC: U.S. Government Printing Office, 1998,1301.

37 Jared Bernstein, "The Next Step: The New Minimum Wage Proposal and the Old Opposition," *EPI Issue Brief*, No. 130, Washington, DC: Economic Policy Institute, April 27, 1999. The 11.8 million figure represents 10.1 percent of the workforce, and they earn an average $5.65 an hour. An increase in the minimum wage would bring spillover benefits for workers earning near the minimum.

38 White House calculations based on data from Bureau of the Census, September 1999.

39 "Toward a New Generation of Community Jobs Programs," *1997 Entrepreneurial Economy Review*, Washington, DC: Corporation for Enterprise Development, 64.

40 Cited in: Katherine Q. Seelye, "Recipients of Welfare Are Fewest Since 1969," *New York Times*, April 11, 1999, 17.

41 Washington Post/ABC News Poll, "Issues 2000," cited in: Dan Balz, "Fall Signals a Turn to the Issues," *Washington Post*, September 5, 1999, A-22.

42 "Equity Considerations in Funding Urban Schools," *The Future of Children: Financing Schools*, Vol. 7, No. 3, Winter 1997.

43 National Priorities Project, "Choices that Matter: Federal Decisions and Your Hometown," Northhampton, MA, 1999.

44 Robert B. Reich, "The Other Surplus Option," *New York Times*, August 11, 1999.

45 Paul Desruisseaux, "U.S. Trails 22 Nations in High-School Completion," *The Chronicle of Higher Education*, December 4, 1998, A-45.

46 The survey was conducted for the National Center for Public Policy and Higher Education, see: Richard Morin, "Grading the Schools," *Washington Post*, February 7, 1999, B-5.

47 National Priorities Project, "Choices that Matter: Federal Decisions and Your Hometown," Northhampton, MA, 1999.

48 Sandra H. Venner, *State Investments in Work Participation: Making the Promise of Welfare-to-Work,* Tufts University, Center on Hunger and Poverty, August 1998.

49 "Special Report: The State of America's Children," *CDF Reports*, April/May 1999, 5.

50 See: "Number without Insurance Grows," *Washington Post*, September 27, 1998, A-16; Peter Kilborn, "Third of Hispanic Americans Do Without Health Coverage," *New York Times*, April 9, 1999; John C. Baldwin and C. Everett Koop, "Search for the Cure," *Washington Post*, May 6, 1999, A-29.

51 Ronald J. Sider, *Just Generosity: A New Vision for Overcoming Poverty in America*, Grand Rapids, MI: Baker Book House Company, 1999, 141.

52 *Losing Health Insurance: The Unintended Consequences of Welfare Reform*, Washington, DC: Families USA Foundation, 1999, 1.

53 Jocelyn Guyer and Cindy Mann, "Employed But Not Insured: A State-by State Analysis of the Number of Low-Income Working Parents Who Lack Health Insurance," February 9, 1999, Center on Budget and Policy Priorities web site: www.cbpp.org/2-9-99mcaid.htm.

54 Robert Pear, "Many States Slow to Use Children's Insurance Fund," *New York Times*, May 9, 1999, 1, 16.

55 American Academy of Pediatrics (AAP), "The American Academy of Pediatrics' Proposal to Insure America's Children," Washington, DC: AAP, October 11, 1999, at: www.aap.org/advocacy/washing/web101199.htm.

56 E. J. Dionne Jr., "Putting Poor Children Before Politics," *Washington Post*, February 16, 1999, A-17.

57 Katherine Q. Seelye, "Recipients of Welfare Are Fewest Since 1969," *New York Times*, April 11, 1999, 17.

58 Federal Election Commission, at: www.fec.gov/pages/htmlto5.htm.

59 National Legal Aid & Defender Association, "In the News," Washington, DC, August 4, 1999, at: www.nlada.org.

60 "Food Stamp Infractions," *New York Times*, January 23, 1999.

61 World Hunger Year may be contacted at: 505 Eighth Avenue, 21st Floor, New York, New York 10018-6582. Phone: (212) 629-8850, web site: www.worldhungeryear.org.

62 Figures from the Center for Responsive Politics, cited in "Campaign Finance Reform," at: www.epn.org.

63 "The $2 Billion Election," *New York Times*, August 11, 1999; and Ruth Marcus and Juliet Eilperin, "Battle for House Fuels Cash Race," *Washington Post*, August 11, 1999, A-1, A-8.

64 Robert Dreyfuss, "Reform Gets Rolling: Campaign Finance at the Grass Roots," *The American Prospect*, No. 45, July-August 1999, 39-43.

Chapter 3

1 Kofi Annan, interviewed by Djibril Diallo, *Choices: The Human Development Magazine*, Vol. 8, No. 3, New York: UNDP, 1999, 7.

2 Linda Mastny, "Third World Debt Still Rising," In: *Vital Signs 1999*, New York: W.W. Norton Company, 1999, 66.

3 Sara Grusky, "Debt Relief From the IMF and the World Bank: What are the Conditions?," in *Debt and Development Dossier*, September, 1999, 3.

4 See also "IMF Executive Board Review HIPC Initiative Modifications," August 13, 1999, IMF website, at www.imf.org/external/np/sec/pn/1999/pn9976.htm.

5 "Dealing with the Devil: The Hell of Corruption," *Impact*, Spring 1999, Vol. 3, No. 2, International Finance Corporation, The World Bank Group, Washington, DC, 4.

6 Vito Tanzi and Hamid Davoodi, "Roads to Nowhere: How Corruption in Public Investment Hurts Growth," Washington, DC: International Monetary Fund, 1998, 11.

7 InterAction, at: www.interaction.org.

8 Development Assistance Committee (DAC) of the Organization for Economic Cooperation and Development (OECD), at: www.oecd.org/dac/htm/agusa98.htm.

9 Source: *Global Development Finance*, Washington: The World Bank, 1999, 24.

10 Christopher Wren, "U.S. Told It Must Pay $550 Million or Risk Losing U.N. Vote," *New York Times*, October 6, 1999.

11 Jeffrey Sachs, "Helping the World's Poorest," in *The Economist*, August 14, 1999, 17.

12 Steven Kull, "U.N. Dues and IMF Funding," PIPA web site at: www.pipa.org/imf.html.

13 Madeleine K. Albright, "Investing in Our Interests," *Washington Post*, September 9, 1999, A-21.

14 *The Foreign Policy Gap: Executive Summary*, Program on International Policy Attitudes, University of Maryland, Washington, DC: 1999, on PIPA website at: www.pipa.org/exec-sum.html.

15 Steven Kull, *The Foreign Policy Gap: How Policymakers Misread the Public*, Program on International Policy Attitudes, University of Maryland, Washington, DC: 1997, 111.

16 *Ibid.*

17 *Ibid.*

18 Carol Lancaster, in *The Reality of Aid: An Independent Review of Development Cooperation, 1997-1998*, Oxford: Earthscan, 1997, 153.

19 John Hoddinott, "The Shift from Development to Emergency Assistance and its Impact on Poverty and Nutrition: A Conceptual Framework," paper presented at Inter-American Development Bank Conference on Social Protection and Poverty, February 4, 1999, 4.

20 Per Pinstrup-Andersen, "Changing Approaches to Development Aid: The Effect on International Stability, *Global Governance*, 4(4):381-394, October-December, 1998.

21 John Hoddinott, *op. cit.*, 5.

22 Marc J. Cohen, ed., *Countries in Crisis: Hunger 1996*, Silver Spring, MD: Bread for the World Institute, 36.

23 Deborah Eade, *Capacity-Building: An Approach to People-Centred Development*, Oxfam, Oxford, UK: 1997, 172.

24 "US Food Aid Jumps Fivefold in 1999," *Bloomberg News*, Washington, DC: September 10, 1999.

25 See for example Jindra Čekan and Kimberly Miller, "Food Aid and Food Security in an Era of Downsizing," In: *What Governments Can Do*, Marc J. Cohen, ed., Bread for the World Institute, Silver Spring: 1997, 87- 89.

26 Steven Kull, *op. cit.*, 1997.

27 UNDP Programming Manual, 8, on UNDP web site at: www.undp.org

28 "Foreign Operations, Export Financing and Related Programs, Appropriations Act, 1999," which amended the International Financial Institutions Act, Title XVII, Sec. 614, to, among other things, require the release of documents such as Letters of Intent, Policy Framework Papers, and Article IV consultations. Cited in *News & Notices 22*, March, 1999.

29 *Heavily Indebted Poor Country (HIPC) Initiative: Strengthening the Link between Debt Relief and Poverty Reduction*, joint World Bank/IMF paper, September 13, 1999, Washington, DC, 27.

30 Francisco Ferreira, Giovanna Prennushi, and Martin Ravaillon, "Protecting the Poor from Macroeconomic Shocks," Washington, DC, World Bank: 1999, 16.

31 Carol Graham, *Safety Nets, Politics, and the Poor: Transitions to Market Economies*, Washington, DC: The Brookings Institution, 1994, 5.

32 Nancy Alexander, "Remaking the World Bank & International Monetary Fund," In: *Hunger in a Global Economy: Hunger 1998*, Marc J. Cohen, ed., Bread for the World Institute: Silver Spring, MD, 1997, 75.

33 *Assessment of Paticipatory Approaches in Identification of World Bank Projects*, InterAction, March 1999, ix.

34 "Global Civil Society Endeavor to Assess the Impact and Shape the Future of Economic Reform Programs," Development GAP web site, www.igc.apc.org/dgap/saprin/profile.html.

35 *Ibid.*

36 "Comprehensive Development Framework Questions and Answers," at World Bank web site: www.worldbank.org/cdf-faq.htm.

37 Nancy Alexander, *News & Notices for World Bank Watchers*, Silver Spring, MD: Bread for the World Institute, March, 1999, 23.

38 James Wolfensohn, "Proposal for a Comprehensive Development Framework," at: www.worldbank.org.

39 See Nancy Alexander, *News & Notices for World Bank Watchers*, March, 1999, Bread for the World Institute: Silver Spring, Maryland, 24.

40 Marc J. Cohen, ed., *Hunger in a Global Economy: Hunger 1998*, Silver Spring, MD: Bread for the World Institute.

41 Bruce L. Gardner, "Agricultural Relief Legislation in 1998: The Bell Tolls for Reform," *Regulation*, Volume 22, No. 1, Washington, DC: Cato Institute, 1999, 33.

42 *The New York Times*, October 15, 1999.

43 *Ibid.*

44 "Within the U.N. system, the ILO has a unique tripartite structure with workers and employers participating as equal partners with governments in the work of its governing organs." ILO web site at: www.ilo.org.

45 "Third World Intellectuals and NGOs Statement Against Linkage," CUTS Centre for International Trade, Economics & Environment," September 1, 1999.

46 Julius K. Nyerere, "Are Universal Social Standards Possible?" address at the North-South Conference for Sustainable Development, 26 May 1998, 3, at: www.twnside.org.sg/souths/twn/title/juli1-cn.htm. Nyerere also stated: "When an economic union seeks to establish common standards among its members, its foundation treaty does not just require that each member state undertake to meet those standards. It also lays down other obligations on members which will enable the poorer members to do so. For example, the richer countries of the European Union have a legally binding obligation to pay to the European Commission certain stated amounts, or proportions which will be transferred to the less rich member states. *This is not regarded as charity*; it is *a legal obligation* attached to membership," 2.

47 "Environment and Trade," Background Paper for FAO/Netherlands Conference on MFCAL, 121, on FAO web site at: www.fao.org/mfcal/.

48 Gordon Conway, *The Doubly Green Revolution: Food for All in the 21st Century*, Ithaca, New York: Cornell University Press, 1997, 81.

49 "Traditional and informal knowledge developed and maintained by indigenous and local communities is a significant 'prior art' resource for innovation, particularly in pharmaceutical and other technologies based upon biological diversity and biological resources." Cited in: "CIEL Calls on U.S. Patent Office to Give More Protection to Indigenous Peoples' Knowledge of Biodiversity," August 2, 1999, Center for International Environmental Law.

50 *Global Development Finance 1999*, Washington: The World Bank, 1999, 24.

51 Dani Rodrik, *The New Global Economy and Developing Countries: Making Openness Work*, Washington, DC: Overseas Development Council, 1999, 148.

52 *Ibid.*

Chapter 4

[1] Ismail Serageldin, "Biotechnology and Food Security in the 21st Century," *Science*, Vol. 285, 16 July 1999, 387.

[2] Gaurav Datt and Martin Ravallion, "Farm Productivity and Rural Poverty in India," FCND Discussion Paper No. 42, Washington, DC: IFPRI, Food Consumption and Nutrition Division, March 1998, 31.

[3] ACC/SCN, *The Third Report on the World Nutrition Situation*, Geneva: ACC/SCN, December 1997, 84.

[4] Per Pinstrup-Andersen and Marc J. Cohen, "Aid to Developing Country Agriculture: Investing in Poverty Reduction and New Export Opportunities," *2020 Brief 56*, Washington, DC: IFPRI, October 1998.

[5] Per Pinstrup-Andersen, "Changing Approaches to Development Aid: The Effect on International Stability," *Global Governance*, 4(4), 1998, 387.

[6] ACC/SCN, *The Third Report on the World Nutrition Situation*, Geneva: ACC/SCN, December 1997, 88.

[7] Interview with Damoni Kitabire, Uganda Case Study, World Bank and World Trade Organization: Geneva, 1997, page 1, at: www.itd.org/issues/ugan7.htm.

[8] *Ibid.*

[9] David Beckmann and Arthur Simon, *Grace at the Table: Ending Hunger in God's World*, New York: Paulist Press, 1999, 122.

[10] Ebbe Schioler, *Good News from Africa: Farmers, Agricultural Research, and Food in the Pantry*, Washington, DC: IFPRI, 1998, 42-3.

[11] Francisco J. Pinchon and Jorge E. Uquillas, "Sustainable Agriculture Through Farmer Participation: Agricultural Research and Technology Development in Latin America's Risk-Prone Areas," In: *Mediating Sustainability: Growing Policy from the Grassroots*, Jutta Blauert and Simon Zadek, eds., West Hartford, CT: Kumarian Press, 1998, 21-54.

[12] Thomas Reardon, Christopher B. Barrett, Valerie Kelley, and Kimseyinga Savadogo, "Sustainable Versus Unsustainable Agricultural Intensification in Africa: Focus on Policy Reforms and Market Conditions," In: *Agricultural Intensification, Development and Environment*, David R. Lee and Christopher B. Barrett, eds., forthcoming.

[13] Lester B. Brown, "Feeding Nine Billion," In: *State of the World 1999*, New York: W. W. Norton & Company, 1999, 129.

[14] The Hunger Project, "Economic Empowerment of the African Woman Food Farmer," A Strategy Meeting of Women Activists in The Hunger Project-West Africa, 22-23 June 1999, Accra, Ghana, 7.

[15] Tom Rachman, "India Women Put a Pittance to Work," *Associated Press*, August 24, 1999.

[16] Binswanger et al., cited in Klaus Deininger, "Making Negotiated Land Reform Work: Initial Experience from Colombia, Brazil, and South Africa," Policy Research Working Paper No. 2040, Washington, DC: World Bank, 1999, 4.

[17] Klaus Deininger, *op. cit.*, 4.

[18] *Ibid.*, 5.

[19] "[L]and reform in *haciendas*, i.e. systems where tenants had a small house-plot for subsistence but worked the majority of the time on the landlord's home farm, has been very difficult, up to the point where the 'game of Latin American Land Reform' was declared to be lost (deJanvry and Sadoulet, 1989)", Klaus Deininger, *op.cit.*, 5.

[20] Siddarth Dube, "India's Tragic Destiny," *The Washington Post*, September 21, 1999, A-19.

[21] Bahman Mansuri, IFAD, "An Overview," paper presented at the "Conference on Hunger and Poverty – A Popular Coalition for Action," held in Brussels, 1995, 12.

[22] *Ibid.*

[23] Klaus Deininger, *op. cit.*, 3.

[24] National Forum for Land Reform and Rural Justice, letter to World Bank President and Board and Inspection Panel Chair, August 27, 1999.

[25] World Food Programme, "Policy Issues: Reaching Mothers and Children at Critical Times of Their Lives," Rome: WFP/EB.3/97/3-B, 26 August 1997.

[26] Inter-American Development Bank, *The Path Out of Poverty*, Washington, DC, April 1998, 18.

[27] Lisa Smith and Lawrence Haddad, "Explaining Child Malnutrition in Developing Countries: A Cross-Country Analysis," FCND Discussion Paper No. 60, Washington, DC: IFPRI, Food Consumption and Nutrition Division, April 1999, 59.

[28] Lester B. Brown, *op. cit.*, 130.

[29] Mary Ann Brocklesby and Jeremy Holland, "Participatory Poverty Assessments and Public Services: Key Messages from the Poor," Centre for Development Studies, University of Wales, Swansea, UK, September 1998, 10-11.

[30] Judy Mann, "Saving Young Lives with a 2-Cent Capsule," *Washington Post*, March 17, 1999, C-15.

[31] A. Hussain, "Preventing and Controlling Micronutrient Malnutrition through Food-Based Actions in South Asian Countries," *Food, Nutrition and Agriculture*, 22:63-5, Rome: FAO, 1998.

[32] Suttilak Smitasiri and Sakorn Dhanamitta, "Sustaining Behavior to Enhance Micronutrient Status: Community- and Women-Based Interventions in Thailand," Research Report Series 2, Washington, DC: International Center for Research on Women, 1999, 24-5.

[33] Marie T. Ruel, Carol E. Levin, Margaret Armar-Klemesu, Daniel Maxwell, and Saul S. Morris, "Good Care Practices Can Mitigate the Negative Effects of Poverty and Low Maternal Schooling on Children's Nutritional Status: Evidence from Accra," FCND Discussion Paper No. 62, Washington, DC: IFPRI, Food Consumption and Nutrition Division, April 1999, 25.

[34] Daniel Maxwell, Carol Levin, and Joanne Csete, "Does Urban Agriculture Help Prevent Malnutrition? Evidence from Kampala," FCND Discussion Paper No. 45, Washington, DC: IFPRI, Food Consumption and Nutrition Division, June 1998, 26-7.

[35] The Hunger Project, "Economic Empowerment of the African Woman Food Farmer," A Strategy Meeting of Women Activists in The Hunger Project-West Africa, 22-23 June 1999, Accra, Ghana, 3.

[36] *Ibid.*

[37] Jean Drèze and Amartya Sen, *Hunger and Public Action*, Oxford: Clarendon Press, 1989.

[38] Bob Currie, "Public Action and Its Limits: Re-examining the Politics of Hunger Alleviation in Eastern India," *Third World Quarterly*, 19(5), 1998, 888.

39 Nora McKeon, "Grassroots Development and Participation in Policy Negotiations: Bridging the Micro-Macro Gap in Senegal," Paper presented at the International Workshop on Grassroots Organizations, Decentralization and Rural Development: African Experiences in the 1990s, Turin, 4-5 September 1998.

40 "After the Election," *Washington Post*, September 1, 1999, A-22.

41 Per Pinstrup-Andersen, "Changing Approaches to Development Aid," 386.

42 *Ibid.*, 385.

43 Christopher L. Delgado, Jane Hopkins and Valerie A. Kelly, *Agricultural Growth Linkages in Sub-Saharan Africa*, Research Report 107, Washington, DC: IFPRI, 1998; Thomas Reardon et al., *op. cit.*

44 Per Pinstrup-Andersen, "Changing Approaches to Development Aid;" M. Rukini, M. J. Blackie and C. K. Eicher, "Crafting Smallholder-Driven Agricultural Research Systems in Southern Africa, *World Development*, 26(6):1073-1088, 1998.

45 Lawrence Haddad, ed., *Achieving Food Security in Southern Africa: New Challenges, New Opportunities*, Washington, DC: IFPRI, 1997; Per Pinstrup-Andersen, *op. cit.*

46 Princeton N. Lyman, "Facing a Global AIDS Crisis," *Washington Post*, August 11, 1999, A-19.

47 Lester R. Brown, *Who Will Feed China? Wake-Up Call for a Small Planet*, New York: W.W. Norton & Co., 1995; S. Rozelle and Mark Rosegrant, "China's Past, Present, and Future Food Economy: Can China Continue to Meet the Challenges?" *Food Policy*, 22(3):191-200.

48 Vaclav Smil, *China's Environmental Crisis: An Inquiry into the Limits of National Development*, Armonk, NY: M.E. Sharpe Press, 1993.

49 Jikan Huang, Scott Rozelle, and Mark W. Rosegrant, *China's Food Economy to the Twenty-First Century: Supply, Demand, and Trade*, Food, Agriculture, and the Environment Discussion Paper 19, Washington, DC: IFPRI, January 1997, 1-4.

50 Shenggen Fan and Marc J. Cohen, "Critical Choices for China's Agricultural Policy," *2020 Brief 60*, Washington, DC: IFPRI, May 1999, 2; Lester B. Brown, "Feeding Nine Billion," In: *State of the World 1999*, New York: W.W. Norton & Company, 1999.

51 ACC/SCN, *The Third Report on the World Nutrition Situation*, Geneva: ACC/SCN, December 1997, 87.

Chapter 5

1 Cited in: T.R. Reid, "Feeding the Planet," *National Geographic*, October 1998, 74.

2 Catholic Charities USA agencies reported an average increase in demand of 11 percent in 1996. Second Harvest reported that 21 million people turned to their food programs in 1997, a 17 percent increase over 1996. The U.S. Conference of Mayors reported that eight out of ten cities experienced increases in requests for food averaging 14 percent in 1998.

3 For an analysis of the USDA food security data from 1995 to 1998, see Chapter 2.

4 See "Table 1: Size of the Economy," in: World Bank, *World Development Report 1999/2000*, Washington, DC: World Bank, 1999, 230-1.

5 Ibid.

6 See "Half-Measures for Poor Nations," *New York Times*, June 9, 1999.

7 OECD, *OECD in Figures 1999*, Paris: OECD, 1999, 89.

8 Christopher Wren, "U.S. Told It Must Pay $550 Million or Risk Losing U.N. Vote," *New York Times*, October 6, 1999.

9 Estimated expenditures on lobbying for Fiscal Year 1998 include: $2,778,236 for Bread for the World, (*1998 Annual Report*, Silver Spring, MD: Bread for the World); $858,312 for Results (personal communication, Kim Posich, Managing Director); $135,615 for InterAction (*Annual Report 1998*, Washington, DC: InterAction); and $47,000 for America's Second Harvest (personal communication, Doug O'Brien, Director of Public Policy and Research). The denominational offices together probably devote the equivalent of six staff positions to international and domestic lobbying, or an estimated combined annual budget of $300,000.

10 Cited by David Beckmann and Arthur Simon, *Grace at the Table: Ending Hunger in God's World*, New York: Paulist and InterVarsity Press, 1999, 153.

11 Adrian Karatnycky, "Freedom in the Democratic Age," In: *Freedom in the World, 1997-1998*, Adrian Karatnycky, ed., New Brunswick, NJ: Transaction Publishers, 1998, 5.

12 National Academy of Sciences, National Research Council, *World Food and Nutrition Study: The Potential Contributions of Research*, Washington, DC: National Academy of Sciences, 1977; Office of the President, *Report of the Presidential Commission on World Hunger*, Washington, DC: Government Printing Office, 1980.

13 Henry A. Kissinger, "Address at the World Food Conference," 5-16 November 1974, Rome.

14 This section draws from the thinking about political strategy in *Grace at the Table: Ending Hunger in God's World*, which I co-authored with Arthur Simon. That book in turn, drew on *Transforming the Politics of Hunger: Hunger 1994*, Silver Spring, MD: Bread for the World Institute, 1993.

15 Figures from Doug O'Brien, Director of Public Policy and Research, Second Harvest, October 20, 1999.

16 The ICSI and AFL-CIO figures are both from Richard Appelbaum and Peter Drier, "The Campus Anti-Sweatshop Movement," *The American Prospect*, September-October 1999, 76.

Sponsors

Bread for the World Institute seeks to inform, educate, nurture and motivate concerned citizens for action on policies that affect hungry people. Based on policy analysis and consultation with poor people, it develops educational resources and activities, including its annual report on the state of world hunger, policy briefs and study guides, together with workshops, seminars, briefings and an anti-hunger leadership development program. Contributions to the Institute are tax deductible. It works closely with Bread for the World, a Christian citizens' movement of 44,000 members who advocate specific policy changes to help overcome hunger in the United States and overseas.

>1100 Wayne Avenue, Suite 1000
>Silver Spring, MD 20910 USA
>Phone: (301) 608-2400
>Fax: (301) 608-2401
>E-mail: institute@bread.org
>Web site: www.bread.org

Brot für die Welt is an association of German Protestant churches that seeks to overcome poverty and hunger in developing countries, as an expression of their Christian faith and convictions, by funding programs of relief and development. Founded in 1959, Brot has funded more than 18,000 programs in over 100 nations in Africa, Latin America and Asia. The emphasis of the programs that Brot funds has shifted from relief to development and empowerment. Brot's programs of education in Germany are intended to lead to changes – in understanding and lifestyle at the personal level, and to policy changes at the national, European Community and international levels.

>Stafflenbergstrasse 76; Postfach 10 11 42
>D-70010 Stuttgart, Germany
>Phone: (49-7) 11-2159-0
>Fax: (49-7) 11-2159-110
>E-mail: bfdwinformation@brot-fuer-die-welt.org

Catholic Relief Services-USCC (CRS) is the overseas relief and development agency of the U.S. Catholic community. Founded in 1943, CRS provides over $200 million in development and relief assistance in more than 80 nations around the world. Working in partnership with the Catholic Church and other local institutions in each country, CRS works to alleviate poverty, hunger and suffering, and supports peace-building and reconciliation initiatives. Assistance is given solely on the basis of need. Even while responding to emergencies, CRS supports over 2,000 development projects designed to build local self-sufficiency. CRS works in conjunction with Caritas Internationalis and CIDSE, worldwide associations of Catholic relief and development agencies.

Together, these groups build the capacity of local non-profit organizations to provide long-term solutions. In the United States, CRS seeks to educate and build awareness on issues of world poverty and hunger and serve as an advocate for public policy changes in the interest of the poor overseas.

>209 West Fayette Street
>Baltimore, MD 21201-3443 USA
>Phone: (410) 625-2220
>Fax: (410) 685-1635
>E-mail: webmaster@catholicrelief.org
>Web site: www.catholicrelief.org

Christian Children's Fund, recognized by *Consumers Digest* as one of the nation's most charitable charities, is a Richmond-based child development organization founded in 1938 to address the needs of children orphaned in the Sino-Japanese War. Regarded as one of the world's largest and most respected child development charities, Christian Children's Fund provides services to more than 2.5 million impoverished children regardless of race, religion, or gender. Christian Children's Fund works in 30 countries throughout Africa, Asia, Eastern and Central Europe, Latin America, the United States, and the Caribbean providing long-term, sustainable assistance to children in need.

>2821 Emerywood Parkway, P.O. Box 26484
>Richmond, VA 23261-6484 USA
>Phone: (804) 756-2700
>Fax: (804) 756-2718
>Web site: www.christianchildrensfund.org

Congregation of the Sisters of Charity of the Incarnate Word. In the early 1860s in Texas, threatening epidemics such as yellow fever, as well as the continuing horror of war, brought suffering and death throughout the state. Bishop Claude Dubuis was determined to find Sisters who would minister to the sick and dying as well as to children left orphaned by epidemics and war. In 1866, three sisters from Lyons, France, responding to the call, came to Galveston, Texas, and founded the Congregation of the Sisters of Charity of the Incarnate Word. Since then, the Sisters of Charity have expanded their ministries of prayer, healing and education to California, Louisiana, Utah, Guatemala, El Salvador, Ireland and Kenya. Sisters of Charity are committed to upholding the dignity of persons and to promoting justice and equality.

>6510 Lawndale Avenue
>Houston, TX 77023 USA
>Phone: (713) 928-6053
>Fax: (713) 928-8148

The **Evangelical Lutheran Church in America World Hunger Program** is a 25-year-old ministry that confronts hunger and poverty through emergency relief, long-term development, education, advocacy and stewardship of financial resources. Seventy-two percent of the program works internationally and 28 percent within the United States. Lutheran World Relief (New York City) and Lutheran World Federation (Geneva, Switzerland) are key implementing partners in international relief and development. Twelve percent is used for domestic relief and development, 10 percent for education and advocacy work in the United States and 6 percent for fundraising and administration.

> 8765 West Higgins Road
> Chicago, IL 60631-4190 USA
> Phone: (800) 638-3522, ext. 2709
> Fax: (773) 380-2707
> E-mail: jhalvors@elca.org

The **International Fund for Agricultural Development** (IFAD) is an international financial institution headquartered in Rome, Italy. Established in 1977 as a result of the 1974 World Food Conference, IFAD is a Specialized Agency of the United Nations with an exclusive mandate to provide the rural poor of the developing world with cost-effective ways of overcoming hunger, poverty and malnutrition. IFAD advocates a targeted, community-based approach to reducing rural poverty. The Fund's task is to help poor farmers raise their food production and improve their nutrition by designing and financing projects which increase their incomes. Since 1978, IFAD has mobilized $5.6 billion for 489 projects in 111 developing countries. The governance and funding of the institution are the result of a unique partnership among developed and developing countries. With the recent additions of South Africa and Croatia, IFAD now has 160 Member States.

> Via del Serafico, 107
> 00142 Rome, Italy
> Phone: (39-06) 5459-1
> Fax: (39-06) 5043-463

> 1775 K Street, NW, Suite 410
> Washington, DC 20006 USA
> Phone: (202) 331-9099
> Fax: (202) 331-9366

> E-mail: ifad@ifad.org
> Web site: www.ifad.org

LCMS World Relief (The Lutheran Church – Missouri Synod) provides relief and development funding for domestic and international projects. Based under the Synod's Department of Human Care Ministries, LCMS World Relief provides domestic grants for Lutheran congregations and social ministry organizations as well as other groups with Lutheran involvement which are engaged in ministries of human care. Domestic support is also provided to Lutheran Disaster Response and Lutheran Immigration and Refugee Service. International relief and development assistance is channeled through the Synod's mission stations and partner churches as well as Lutheran World Relief.

> 1333 So. Kirkwood Road
> St. Louis, MO 63122-7295 USA
> Phone: (800) 248-1930, ext. 1392
> Fax: (314) 965-0541
> E-mail: ic_schroepj@lcms.org

Lutheran World Relief (LWR) acts on behalf of U.S. Lutherans in response to natural disasters, humanitarian crises and chronic poverty in some 50 countries of Asia, Africa, Latin America and the Middle East. In partnership with local organizations, LWR supports over 150 community projects to improve food production, health care, environment and employment, with special emphasis on training and gender. LWR monitors legislation on foreign aid and development, and advocates for public policies which address the root causes of hunger and poverty. LWR values the God-given gifts that each person can bring to the task of promoting peace, justice and human dignity. LWR began its work in 1945.

> Lutheran World Relief
> 700 Light Street
> Baltimore, MD 21230-3850 USA
> Phone: (410) 230-2700
> Resources: (800) LWR-LWR2
> E-mail: lwr@lwr.org
> Web site: www.lwr.org

> LWR/CWS Office on Public Policy
> 122 C Street, NW, Suite 125
> Washington, DC 20001 USA
> Phone: (202) 783-6887
> Fax: (202) 783-5328
> E-mail: jbowman@igc.org

For 30 years, the **Presbyterian Hunger Program** has provided a channel for congregations to respond to hunger in the United States and around the world. With a commitment to the ecumenical sharing of human and financial resources, the program provides support for programs of direct food relief, sustainable development and public policy advocacy. A network of 100 Hunger Action Enablers leads the Presbyterian Church (USA) in the study of hunger issues, engagement with communities of need, advocacy for just public policies, and the movement toward simpler corporate and personal lifestyles.

> 100 Witherspoon Street
> Louisville, KY 40202-1396 USA
> Phone: (502) 569-5816
> Fax: (502) 569-8963
> Web site: www.pcusa.org/hunger

The **United Methodist Committee on Relief**

(UMCOR) was formed in 1940 in response to the suffering of people during World War II. It was a "voice of conscience" expressing the concern of the church for the disrupted and devastated lives churned out by the war. UMCOR has expanded its ministry into more than 70 countries to minister with compassion to "persons in need, through programs and services which provide immediate relief and long-term attention to the root causes of their need." Focusing on refugee, hunger and disaster ministries, the work of UMCOR, a program department of the General Board of Global Ministries of the United Methodist Church, is carried out through direct services and a worldwide network of national and international church agencies that cooperate in the task of alleviating human suffering.

> 475 Riverside Drive, Room 330
> New York, NY 10115 USA
> Phone: (212) 870-3816
> Hotline: (800) 841-1235
> Fax: (212) 870-3624
> E-mail: umcor@gbgm-umc.org

The **United Nations Development Programme** (UNDP) is the United Nations' largest provider of technical cooperation grants and the main coordinator of United Nations Development Assistance. It helps people in 174 countries and territories to help themselves, focusing on poverty eradication, environmental protection and regeneration, job creation and sustainable livelihoods, and the advancement of women. In support of these goals, UNDP frequently assists in promoting sound governance and market development and helps rebuild societies in the aftermath of war and humanitarian emergencies. UNDP's total income reached $2.53 billion in 1998, which combines voluntary contributions by governments to core and non-core resources as well as other funds. This includes contributions to such UNDP-administered special funds as the United Nations Capital Development Fund, United Nations Development Fund for Women, and United Nations Volunteers. UNDP also works in partnership with the World Bank and the United Nations Environment Programme to administer the Global Environment Facility.

> 1 United Nations Plaza
> New York, NY 10017 USA
> Phone: (212) 906-5000
> Fax: (212) 906-5001
> E-mail: HQ@undp.org
> Web site: www.undp.org

The **United Nations World Food Programme** (WFP) is the food aid arm of the United Nations system. Food aid is one of the many instruments that can help promote food security, which is defined as access of all people at all times to the food needed for an active and healthy life. The policies governing the use of World Food Programme food aid must be oriented toward the objective of eradicating hunger and poverty. The ultimate objective of food aid should be the elimination of the need for food aid.

> Via Cesare Giulio Viola, 68
> Parco dei Medici
> 00148 Rome, Italy
> Phone: (39-06) 6513-1
> Fax: (39-06) 6590-632/637
> Web site: www.wfp.org

Co-Sponsors

The **Academy for Educational Development** (AED), founded in 1961, is an independent, nonprofit organization committed to solving critical social problems in the U.S. and throughout the world through education, social marketing, research, training, policy analysis and innovative program design. AED is dedicated to improving people's lives by increasing knowledge and promoting democratic and humanitarian ideals. AED is registered with the U.S. Agency for International Development as a private voluntary organization. AED is exempt from federal income taxes under Section 501(c)(3) of the Internal Revenue Code. Contributions to AED are tax deductible.

> 1875 Connecticut Avenue, NW
> Washington, DC 20009-1202 USA
> Phone: (202) 884-8000
> Fax: (202) 884-8400
> E-mail: admin@aed.org
> Web site: www.aed.org

ACDI/VOCA is a U.S.-based private non-profit development organization that advances the pace of progress in emerging democracies and developing countries. Offering a comprehensive range of technical assistance services and strategies, ACDI/VOCA benefits small- and medium-scale enterprises – particularly agribusinesses, private and public associations, governmental agencies and others. ACDI/VOCA offers both long- and short-term assistance that focuses on economic growth at the grassroots level where long-lasting advancement begins and democratic traditions take hold. As appropriate, ACDI/VOCA provides a mix of volunteers and consultants, as well as methodologies honed through years of economic development success. This assistance is tailored to meet the unique needs of every ACDI/VOCA partner.

> 50 F Street, NW, Suite 1075
> Washington, DC 20001 USA
> Phone: (202) 383-4961
> Fax: (202) 783-7204
> Web site: www.acdivoca.org

Adventist Development and Relief Agency International (ADRA) is the worldwide agency of the Seventh-day Adventist church set up to alleviate poverty in developing countries and respond to disasters. ADRA works on behalf of the poor in more than 150 developing countries spanning Africa, Asia, the Middle East, and Central and South America, without regard to ethnic, political or religious association. ADRA's projects include working to improve the health of mothers and children, developing clean water resources, teaching agricultural techniques, building and supplying clinics, hospitals and schools training people in vocational skills, and feeding people in countries where hunger is a long-term problem. When disasters strike, ADRA sends emergency supplies and stays in the disaster area to help rebuild.

> 12501 Old Columbia Pike
> Silver Spring, MD 20904 USA
> Phone: (301) 680-6380
> Fax: (301) 680-6370
> Web site: www.adra.org

America's Second Harvest is the largest domestic charitable hunger-relief organization in the United States. Through a nationwide network of 189 food banks, America's Second Harvest distributes more than one billion pounds of donated food and grocery product annually to nearly 50,000 local charitable agencies. These food pantries, soup kitchens, women's shelters, Kid's Cafes and other feeding programs serve more than 26 million hungry Americans each year, including 8 million children and four million seniors.

> 116 South Michigan Avenue, Suite 4
> Chicago, IL 60603-6001 USA
> Phone: (312) 263-2303
> Fax: (312) 263-5626
> Web site: www.secondharvest.org

Baptist World Aid (BWAid) is a division of the Baptist World Alliance, a fellowship of almost 200 Baptist unions and conventions around the world, comprising a membership of over 42 million baptized believers. This represents a community of over 100 million Baptists ministering in more than 200 countries. For 80 years Baptists have been working in partnership to entrust, empower and enable the indigenous Baptist leadership to carry out programs of emergency relief, sustainable development and fellowship assistance.

> 6733 Curran Street
> McLean, VA 22101-6005 USA
> Phone: (703) 790-8980
> Fax: (703) 790-5719
> E-mail: bwaid@bwanet.org
> Web site: www.bwanet.org/bwaid

The **Board of World Mission of the Moravian Church** (BWM) represents the Moravian Church in America in overseas ministries. BWM nourishes formal mission partnerships with Moravian Churches in Alaska, the eastern Caribbean, Guyana, Honduras, Labrador, Nicaragua and Tanzania, and with the Evangelical Church of the Dominican Republic. BWM supports medical clinics in Honduras and Nicaragua and has a long tradition of supporting educational efforts of all kinds. In addition, as a missionary sending agency, BWM is involved in evangelistic witness among people who have had little opportunity to hear the gospel. Offices are in Bethlehem, Pennsylvania and Winston-Salem, North Carolina.

Reverend Hampton Morgan Jr., Executive Director
1021 Center Street
Bethlehem, PA 18018 USA
Phone: (610) 868-1732
Fax: (610) 866-9223
E-mail: bwm@mcnp.org

Call to Action is a Catholic organization of 20,000 lay people, religious, priests and bishops working together to foster peace, justice and love in our world, our church and ourselves in the spirit of the Second Vatican Council and the U.S. Catholic Bishops' Call to Action (1976). Programs include publications each month (*CTA News*, *ChurchWatch* and *Spirituality/Justice Reprint*); annual *We Are the Church* national conference, 40 local chapters, a *Church Renewal Directory* of 670 national and local faith groups committed to church and societal renewal; the Future of Priestly Ministry Dialogue Project and a speakers and Artists Referral Service.

4419 N. Kedzie
Chicago, IL 60625 USA
Phone: (773) 604-0400
Fax: (773) 604-4719
E-mail: cta@cta-usa.org
Web site: www.cta-usa.org

Canadian Foodgrains Bank is a specialized food programming agency established and operated by 13 church-related relief and development organizations. It collects substantial amounts of foodgrain donations directly from Canadian farmers using an extensive network of grain elevators. The Foodgrains Bank uses donated cash and grain matched by cost-sharing funds from CIDA to procure and ship food assistance to food-deficit countries, and to provide related services to partner agencies. Using food assistance to build and reconcile relationships with and within communities and countries such as Cuba, North Korea, Iran, Afghanistan, Rwanda and Guinea is a key interest. Other program involvements include monetization, food security reserves and household food security monitoring. Canadian Foodgrains Bank staff and partners also take a very active interest in food security policy issues. To support this policy dialogue, the Foodgrains Bank has a number of discussion papers related to the relationship between food security and peace, human rights, economic sanctions, gender, humanitarian action and international action.

Box 747, 400-280 Smith Street
Winnipeg, MB, Canada R3C 2L4
Phone: (204) 944-1993
Fax: (204) 943-2597

Catholic Charities USA is the nation's largest network of independent social service organizations. The 1,400 agencies and institutions work to reduce poverty, support families and empower communities. Catholic Charities organizations provide social services ranging from adoption and counseling to emergency food and housing. More than 12 million people of all religious, national, racial, social and economic backgrounds received services in 1996. Catholic Charities USA promotes public policies and strategies that address human needs and social injustices. The national office provides advocacy and management support for agencies. The Disaster Response Office organizes the Catholic community's response to U.S. disasters.

1731 King Street, Suite 200
Alexandria, VA 22314 USA
Phone: (703) 549-1390
Fax: (703) 549-1656
E-mail: info@catholiccharitiesusa.org
Web site: www.catholiccharitiesusa.org

The **Christian Reformed World Relief Committee** (CRWRC) is a ministry of the Christian Reformed Church in North America. CRWRC shows God's love to people in need through *development* - working with families and communities in food production, income earning, health education, literacy learning, spiritual and leadership skills – through relief – working with disaster survivors by providing food, medicines, crisis counseling, rebuilding and volunteer assistance – and through education – working with people to develop and act on their Christian perspective of poverty, hunger and justice. CRWRC works with communities in North America and in over 30 countries worldwide to create permanent, positive change in Christ's name.

CRWRC U.S.
2850 Kalamazoo Avenue, SE
Grand Rapids, MI 49560-0600 USA
Phone: (800) 552-7972
Fax: (616) 246-0806

CRWRC Canada
3475 Mainway
P.O. Box 5070 STN LCD1
Burlington, ON L7R 3Y8 Canada
Phone: (800) 730-3490
Fax: (905) 336-8344
E-mail for U.S. & Canada: CRWRC@crcna.org

Church World Service (CWS) is a global relief, development and refugee-assistance ministry of the 34 Protestant and Orthodox communions that work together through the National Council of the Churches of Christ in the U.S.A. Founded in 1946, CWS works in partnership with local church organizations in more than 70 countries worldwide, supporting sustainable self-help development of people that respects the environment, meets emergency needs, and addresses root causes of poverty and powerlessness. Within the United States, CWS resettles refugees, assists communities in responding to disasters, advocates for justice in U.S. policies which relate to global issues, provides educational resources, and offers opportunities for communities to join a people-to-people network of global and local caring through participation in a CROP WALK.

The Rev. Dr. Rodney Page, Executive Director
475 Riverside Drive, Suite 678
New York, NY 10115-0050 USA
Phone: (212) 870-2257 or (212) 870-2175
Fax: (212) 870-3523
Web site: www.ncccusa.org/cws

The **Compton Foundation** was founded in 1973 to address community, national and international concerns in the fields of Peace and World Order, Population and the Environment. Other concerns of the Foundation include Equal Educational Opportunity, Community Welfare and Social Justice, and Culture and the Arts. The Foundation is concerned first and foremost with the prevention of war and the amelioration of world conditions that tend to cause conflict. Primary among these conditions are the increasing pressures and destabilizing effects of excessive population growth, the alarming depletion of the earth's natural resources, the steady deterioration of the earth's environment and the tenuous status of human rights. The Foundation believes that prevention is a more effective strategy than remediation, that research and activism should inform each other and that both perspectives are needed for a productive public debate. In order to demonstrate what can be done to bring about the necessary societal transformations, the Foundation seeks to encourage positive models of change. It actively encourages collaboration between agencies, institutions, and/or foundations, and projects that connect theory, research and practice.

15040 Oriole Road
Saratoga, CA 95070 USA
Phone: (408) 354-3573

Congressional Hunger Center (CHC) was formed in 1993 by Democratic and Republican Members of Congress after the Select Committee on hunger was eliminated. Now in its seventh year, CHC is training over 100 leaders at the community, national, and international levels annually. *Beyond Food* team members work at the community level in the Mississippi Delta, rural Vermont, and in the urban centers of Milwaukee and Washington, DC, providing nutrition education, designing and planting community gardens, and strengthening the work of food banks. The *Mickey Leland Hunger Fellows* work six months at direct service sites across the nation, then return to Washington, DC where they help shape national food security policy at a broad spectrum of host sites. The *International Crisis Response Program* of the CHC trains existing leaders at U.N. and U.S. Disaster Response agencies, and nongovernmental humanitarian workers in coordination strategies during acute crises such as those in Rwanda, Bosnia, Sudan and North Korea. We are proud to be accomplishing our original mission: "To lead, speak, and act on behalf of the poor, the hungry, and the victims of humanitarian crises by developing leaders at the community, national, and international levels."

229½ Pennsylvania Avenue, SE
Washington, DC 20003 USA
Phone: (202) 547-7022
Fax: (202) 547-7575
E-mail: NOHUNGR@aol.com
Web site: www.hungercenter.org

Covenant World Relief is the relief and development arm of The Evangelical Covenant Church. Dr. Timothy Ek is Vice President of the Covenant and Director of Covenant World Relief. The Evangelical Covenant Church has its national offices in Chicago, IL. Covenant World Relief was formed in response to the Covenant's historic commitment to being actively involved in Christ's mission to respond to the spiritual and physical needs of others.

5101 North Francisco Avenue
Chicago, IL 60625-3611 USA
Phone: (773) 784-3000
Fax: (773) 784-4366
E-mail: 102167.1330@compuserve.com
Web site: www.covchurch.org

EuronAid is a European association of nongovernmental organizations (NGOs) which facilitates dialogue with the Commission of the European Union in the areas of food security and food aid. EuronAid cooperates with the Commission in programming and procuring food aid for the NGOs, then arranges and accounts for delivery to Third World NGOs for distribution. In recent years, triangular operations (purchases within Third World nations) have accounted for half of EuronAid's food aid, which meets mainly development purposes. EuronAid assimilates the experiences of NGOs involved in food aid and employs this knowledge in its dialogue with the Commission and the European Parliament to achieve improved management of food aid. EuronAid was created in 1980 by major European NGOs in cooperation with the Commission of the European Union. The association has at present 29 member agencies and services an additional 60 European and Southern NGOs on a regular basis.

P.O. Box 12
NL-2501 CA Den Haag
The Netherlands
Phone: (31-70) 330-57-57
Fax: (31-70) 362-17-39
E-mail: euronaid@euronaid.nl

Food for the Hungry International (FHI) is an organization of Christian motivation committed to working with poor people to overcome hunger and poverty through development and, where needed, as appropriate relief. Founded in 1971, FHI is incorporated in Switzerland and works in over 30 countries of Asia, Africa and Latin America. As its name implies, FHI focuses on poverty needs that relate to food and nutrition. Its primary emphasis is on long-term development among the extremely poor, recognizing their dignity, creativity and ability to solve their own problems. The international staff numbers more than 1,300 persons. Autonomous Food for the Hungry National Organizations (N.O.s) in many different countries such as Food for the Hungry (USA) contribute resources.

7807 East Greenway Road, Suite 3
Scottsdale, AZ 85260 USA
Phone: (480) 951-5090
Fax: (480) 951-9035
E-mail: general@fhi.net
Web site: www.fhi.net

Founded in 1946, **Freedom from Hunger** fights chronic hunger with two of the most powerful and flexible resources ever created: money and information. Operating in rural regions of 10 developing nations, our *Credit with Education* program builds on the success of village banking by integrating basic health, nutrition, family planning, and microenterprise management education into group meetings. Results from recent studies show beneficial impacts, not only on income and income-generating activities, but also on the health and nutrition of participants and their children. Freedom from Hunger's goal is to bring *Credit with Education* to 2.2 million women by the year 2005.

1644 DaVinci Court
Davis, CA 95617 USA
Phone: (800) 708-2555
Fax: (530) 758-6241
E-mail: info@freefromhunger.org

Heifer Project International. In response to God's love for all people, the mission of Heifer Project International is to alleviate hunger and poverty in all parts of the world. HPI does this by:
- Providing food-producing animals, training and related assistance to families and communities.
- Enabling those who receive animals to become givers by "passing on the gift" of training and offspring to others in need.
- Educating people about the root causes of hunger.
Heifer Project International is supported by contributions from churches, individuals, corporations and foundations.

1015 Louisiana Street
Little Rock, AR 72202 USA
Phone: (800) 422-0474
Fax: (501) 376-8906
Web site: www.heifer.org

MAZON: A Jewish Response to Hunger has granted more than $15 million since 1986 to nonprofit organizations confronting hunger in the United States and abroad. MAZON (the Hebrew word for "food") awards grants principally to programs working to prevent and alleviate hunger in the United States. Grantees include emergency and direct food assistance programs, food banks, multi-service organizations, anti-hunger advocacy/education and research projects, and international hunger-relief and agricultural development programs in Israel and impoverished countries. Although responsive to organizations serving impoverished Jews, in keeping with the best of Jewish tradition, MAZON responds to all who are in need.

> 12401 Wilshire Boulevard, Suite 303
> Los Angeles, CA 90025-1015 USA
> Phone: (310) 442-0020
> Fax: (310) 442-0030
> Web site: www.shamash.org/soc-action/mazon

Mennonite Central Committee (MCC), founded in 1920, is an agency of the Mennonite and Brethren in Christ churches in North America, and seeks to demonstrate God's love through committed women and men who work among people suffering from poverty, conflict, oppression and natural disaster. MCC serves as a channel for interchange between churches and community groups where it works around the world and North American churches. MCC strives for peace, justice and dignity of all people by sharing experiences, resources and faith. MCC's priorities include disaster relief and refugee assistance, rural and agricultural development, job creation, Ten Thousand Villages (formerly known as SELFHELP Crafts), health education and peace-building.

> 21 South 12th Street
> Akron, PA 17501-0500 USA
> Phone: (717) 859-1151
> Fax: (717) 859-2171
> E-mail: mailbox@mcc.org
> Web site: www.mcc.org

The mission of the **National Association of WIC Directors** (NAWD) is to provide leadership to the WIC community to promote quality nutrition services, serve all eligible women, infants and children and assure sound and responsive management of the Special Supplemental Nutrition Program for Women, Infants and Children (WIC). The purpose of the association is to link state WIC directors, local WIC directors, nutrition services coordinators and others in a national forum to act collectively on behalf of the program to include the following functions: A) To promote the improved health, well-being and nutritional status of women, infants and children; B) To provide a national resource network through which ideas, materials and procedures can be communicated to persons working in the WIC community; C) To promote good management practices and to assist WIC program directors at the state and local levels; D) To act as a resource at the request of governmental bodies and individual legislators regarding issues particular to the health and nutrition of women, infants and children and to assist WIC clients; and E) To do whatever is necessary to promote and sustain the WIC program.

> 2001 S Street, NW, Suite 580
> Washington, DC 20009-3355 USA
> Phone: (202) 232-5492
> Fax: (202) 387-5281
> Web site: www.wicdirectors.org

Nazarene Compassionate Ministries (NCM) is dedicated to facilitating the practices of Christian compassion by responding to pressing human needs an addressing the root cause of problems confronting the poor and powerless. NCM is the vehicle through which the Nazarene Church reaches out to needy people around the world. To accomplish its mission, NCM has a four-fold approach to ministering to those in need: child development, disaster response, development education and social transformation. In short, Nazarene Compassionate Ministries seeks to put "hands and feet" to Scriptural holiness and to transform darkness to light by providing a practical demonstration of the love of Jesus Christ for all mankind.

> 6401 The Paseo
> Kansas City, MO 64131 USA
> Phone: (816) 333-7000

Oxfam America is dedicated to creating lasting solutions to global poverty and hunger by working in partnership with grassroots organizations promoting sustainable development in Africa, Asia, the Caribbean and the Americas, including the United States. Our grant-making and advocacy work aims to challenge the structural barriers that foster conflict and human suffering and limit people from gaining the skills, resources, and power to become self-sufficient. Oxfam America envisions a world in which all people shall one day know freedom – freedom to achieve their fullest potential and to live secure from the dangers of hunger, deprivation and oppression – through the creation of a global movement for economic and social justice.

> 26 West Street
> Boston, MA 02111 USA
> Phone: (800) 77-OXFAM
> Fax: (617) 728-2594
> E-mail: oxfamusa@igc.apc.org
> Web site: www.oxfamamerica.org

Reformed Church World Service (RCWS) is the relief and development program for the Reformed Church in America. RCWS works through mission personnel and partners around the world to provide emergency relief to disaster victims, to offer rehabilitation for those who have lost their homes and jobs, to encourage development on long-term solutions to overcome hunger and poverty, and to seek justice on behalf of poor and disadvantaged people.

> 4500 60th Street SE
> Grand Rapids, MI 49512 USA
> Phone: (616) 698-7071
> Fax: (616) 698-6606

The mission of **RESULTS**, a 501(c)(4) organization, is to generate the political will to end hunger and the worst aspects of poverty. Throughout our history, RESULTS has advocated for effective poverty-fighting legislation. We have consistently placed microcredit for the poorest as one of our top legislative goals. We aim to make microenterprise services available to literally millions of poor and low-income families. In this past year, our legislative agenda included such topics as direct debt relief to Third World countries without structural adjustments, increased funding for tuberculosis eradication and the Child Survival Fund, as well as increased accessibility to Head Start and the Women, Infants and Children (WIC) programs.

Our lobbying efforts are complemented by the awareness raising activities of RESULTS Educational Fund, a 501(c)(3) organization. Founded in 1983, the Educational Fund raises awareness on the severity of hunger and poverty and the effective poverty-fighting strategies. Specifically, we organize and train citizen volunteers to educate the media and members of congress on poverty and its solutions. Their actions help bring these issues to the forefront of public concern, influence the national policy-making process and create the foundation for social change.

> 440 First Street, NW, Suite 400
> Washington, DC 20001 USA
> Phone: (202) 783-7100
> Fax: (202) 783-2818
> E-mail: results@action.org
> Web site: www.action.org

The **RLDS World Hunger Committee** was established in 1979 to engage the membership of the Reorganized Church of Jesus Christ of Latter Day Saints in a corporate response to the needs of hungry persons throughout the world. Included in the charge to the committee is a three-fold purpose: to provide assistance for those who are suffering from hunger, to advocate for the hungry, and to educate about the causes and alleviation of hunger in the world. The committee meets several times a year to consider applications for funding. The majority of the proposals considered by the committee originate with Outreach International and World Accord, both of which are recognized by the church as agencies engaged in comprehensive human development on a global scale. Projects that support food production or storage, economic development, the providing of potable water, nutrition or food preparation information, the providing of animals for transportation or cultivation are among those that receive favorable consideration by the committee.

> P.O. Box 1059
> Independence, MO 64051-0559 USA
> Phone: (816) 833-1000
> Fax: (816) 521-3096
> E-mail: ritasmck@rlds.org
> Web site: www.rlds.org

Save the Children Federation/U.S. works to make lasting, positive change in the lives of children in need in the United States and 40 countries around the world. International programs in health, education, economic opportunities and humanitarian response place children at the center of activities and focus on women as key decision-makers and participants. Key principles are child centeredness, women focus, participation and empowerment, sustainability, and maximizing impact. Programs in the United States emphasize youth and community service.

> 54 Wilton Road
> Westport, CT 06880 USA
> Phone: (203) 221-4000
> Fax: (203) 454-3914
> Web site: www.savethechildren.org

Share Our Strength (SOS) works to alleviate and prevent hunger and poverty in the United States and abroad. By supporting food assistance, treating malnutrition and other consequences of hunger, and promoting economic independence among people in need, Share Our Strength meets immediate demands for food while investing in long-term solutions to hunger and poverty. To meet its goals, SOS both mobilizes industries and individuals to contribute their talents to its anti-hunger efforts and creates community wealth to promote lasting change. Since 1984, Share Our Strength has distributed more than $45 million in grants to more than 1,000 anti-hunger, anti-poverty organizations worldwide. SOS's Operation Frontline is a food and nutrition education program that trains volunteer culinary professionals to teach six-week cooking, nutrition and food budgeting classes to low-income individuals in 90 communities nationwide. SOS's Taste of the Nation, presented by American Express and Calphalon, is the nation's largest culinary benefit to fight hunger, with 100 events each spring. SOS's Writers Harvest: The National Reading, is the nation's largest literary benefit. Every fall, thousands of writers read in bookstores and on college campuses to fight hunger and poverty. Corporate partnerships and publishing ventures also provide substantial support for SOS's anti-hunger, anti-poverty efforts.

> 1511 K Street, NW, Suite 940
> Washington, DC 20005 USA
> Phone: (202) 393-2925
> Fax: (202) 347-5868
> E-mail: info@strength.org
> Web site: www.strength.org

The Hunger Project is a strategic organization and global movement committed to the sustainable end of world hunger. In Africa, Asia and Latin America, it empowers local people to create lasting society-wide progress in health, education, nutrition and family incomes. It uses a two-prong strategy: mobilizing grass-roots self-reliant action, and mobilizing local leadership to clear away obstacles to enable grassroots action to succeed. The highest priority in all activity is the empowerment of women. Women bear responsibility for family health, education and nutrition – yet, by tradition, culture and law they are denied the means, information and freedom of action to fulfill their responsibility. The Hunger Project is committed to transforming this condition.

> 15 East 26th Street
> New York, NY 10010 USA
> Phone: (212) 251-9100
> Fax: (212) 532-9785
> E-mail: info@thp.org
> Web site: www.thp.org

United Church Board for World Ministries (UCBWM) is the instrumentality of the United Church of Christ for the planning and conduct of its program of global missions, development and emergency relief. The UCBWM's fundamental mission commitment is to share life in partnership with global church partners and ecumenical bodies. Through service, advocacy and mission program, the UCBWM sends as well as receives persons in mission; is committed to the healing of God's creation; engages in dialogue, witness and common cause with people of other faiths; and seeks a prophetic vision of a just and peaceful world order so that all might have access to wholeness of life.

> 475 Riverside Drive, Floor 16
> New York, NY 10115 USA
> Phone: (212) 870-2637
> Fax: (212) 932-1236
> E-mail: petrucel@ucc.org

U.S. Committee for UNICEF works for the survival, protection and development of children worldwide through education, advocacy and fund raising. UNICEF is currently in over 160 countries and territories providing needed assistance in the areas of health, nutrition, safe water and sanitation, girls' and women's issues, education, emergency relief, and child protection.

U.S. Committee for UNICEF
333 East 38th Street, 6th Floor
New York, NY 10016 USA
Phone: (212) 686-5522
Fax: (212) 779-1679
E-mail: information@unicefusa.org
Web site: www.unicefusa.org

World Concern is sharing Christ's love in word and deed with the poorest families worldwide through emergency relief, rehabilitation, and long-term development programs. Vulnerable children and families at risk are our highest priorities. Since 1955 World Concern has been living out the commitment to strengthen families by enabling them to have meaningful work and skills that allow them to be able to lead productive lives and feed their families. World Concern serves over four million of the world's poorest people in over 80 countries each year.

19303 Fremont Avenue, North
Seattle, WA 98133 USA
Phone: (800) 755-5022 or (206) 546-7201
Fax: (206) 546-7269
Web site: www.worldconcern.org

World Hope International, Inc. seeks to mobilize individuals and organizations to exercise their specific gifts and abilities (personally and fiscally) by working in active partnership with persons around the world for the purpose of relief, economic and social development. World Hope is currently active in 22 countries around the world as well as communities in North America.

116 E. Booneslick Road
P.O. Box 31
Warrenton, MO 63383 USA
Phone: (314) 456-4257
Fax: (314) 456-7817
E-mail: whi@worldhope.net
Web site: www.worldhope.net

World Relief is the disaster response, refugee assistance and community development arm of the National Association of Evangelicals. World Relief's mandate, as stated in its mission statement, is "to work with the church in alleviating human suffering worldwide in the name of Christ." Founded in 1944, World Relief helps U.S. churches help churches around the world help the poor in their communities.

P.O. Box WRC
Wheaton, IL 60189-8004 USA
Phone: (800) 535-LIFE
Fax: (630) 665-0129
E-mail: worldrelief@wr.org
Web site: www.worldrelief.org

World Vision is the largest privately-funded Christian humanitarian agency in the world. Founded in 1950 to assist Korean War orphans, the organization has become internationally recognized for its relief and development programs. In its 50-year history, World Vision has grown to include more than 4,000 projects in nearly 100 countries. Today, World Vision helps improve the lives of more than 70 million people in Africa, Asia, Latin America, Europe and North America. World Vision is committed to communities and the empowerment of individuals. World Vision staff work alongside people in local communities and organizations representing a variety of cultures and faiths in providing assistance to children and their families regardless of one's ethnicity, religion, politics, or economic status. Aid is based on the level of poverty and need. Staff members help deliver education, clean drinking water, nutritious food, basic health care and economic opportunities. World Vision also advocates for public policies that address root causes of hunger, poverty and injustice through public awareness and education.

P.O. Box 9716
Federal Way, WA 98063-9716 USA
Phone: (253) 815-2184
Fax: (253) 815-3445
E-mail: bpeterse@worldvision.org
Web site: www.worldvision.org

220 I Street, N.E.
Washington, DC 20002 USA
Phone: (202) 608-1837
Fax: (202) 547-4834
E-mail: sduss@worldvision.org
Web site: www.worldvision.org